Maricel Oró-Piqueras, Anita Wohlmann (eds.)
Serializing Age

Aging Studies | Volume 7

The series **Aging Studies** is edited by Heike Hartung, Ulla Kriebernegg and Roberta Maierhofer.

Maricel Oró-Piqueras, Anita Wohlmann (eds.)
Serializing Age
Aging and Old Age in TV Series

[transcript]

Printed with support from the DFG-funded research training group »Life Sciences – Life Writing« (2015/1) at Johannes Gutenberg University Mainz, the University of Graz, SIforAGE (7th Framework Programme) and Universitat de Lleida.

DFG Deutsche Forschungsgemeinschaft

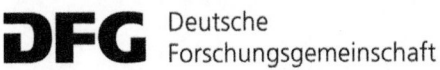
KARL-FRANZENS-UNIVERSITÄT GRAZ
UNIVERSITY OF GRAZ

SIforAGE

Universitat de Lleida

Bibliographic information published by the Deutsche Nationalbibliothek
The Deutsche Nationalbibliothek lists this publication in the Deutsche Nationalbibliografie; detailed bibliographic data are available in the Internet at http://dnb.d-nb.de

© 2016 transcript Verlag, Bielefeld

All rights reserved. No part of this book may be reprinted or reproduced or utilized in any form or by any electronic, mechanical, or other means, now known or hereafter invented, including photocopying and recording, or in any information storage or retrieval system, without permission in writing from the publisher.

Cover layout: Kordula Röckenhaus, Bielefeld
Cover illustration: Fotolia
Printed and bound in Great Britain by Marston Book Services Ltd, Oxfordshire
Print-ISBN 978-3-8376-3276-7
PDF-ISBN 978-3-8394-3276-1

Table of Contents

Acknowledgements | 7

Serial Narrative, Temporality and Aging: An Introduction | 9
Anita Wohlmann and Maricel Oró-Piqueras

BETWEEN SCREEN AND REALITY: NEGOTIATING THE EFFECTS OF OLD AGE AND AGING

"Time, Memory, and Aging on the Soaps" | 25
C. Lee Harrington

"Business as Usual: Retirement on *The Wire*" | 49
Neal King

"Heroine and/or Caricature? The Older Woman in *Desperate Housewives*" | 71
Ros Jennings and Maricel Oró-Piqueras

TEMPORALITY AND AGING: EXPERIMENTS WITH MAGIC, NARRATIVE AND GENRE

"'Vampires Don't Age, But Actors Sure Do': The Cult of Youth and the Paradox of Aging in *Buffy the Vampire Slayer*" | 91
Sally Chivers

"'In the Twilight of Their Lives? Magical Objects as Serial Devices and Catalysts of Aging in *The Twilight Zone*" | 109
Marta Miquel-Baldellou

"Wait For It...! Temporality, Maturing, and the Depiction of Life Concepts in *How I Met Your Mother*" | 137
Cecilia Colloseus

"Serial Cougars: Representations of a Non-Normative Lifestyle in a Sitcom, an Episodic Serial, and a Soap Opera" | 159
Anita Wohlmann and Julia Reichenpfader

SEX AND DESIRE THROUGH THE LENS OF TELEVISION TIME

"Still *Looking*. Temporality and Gay Aging in US Television" | 187
Dustin Bradley Goltz

"'You've Got Time': Ageing and Queer Temporality in *Orange is the New Black*" | 207
Eva Krainitzki

"'I'm Too Old to Pretend Anymore': Desire, Ageing and *Last Tango in Halifax*" | 233
Kristyn Gorton

"'Blanche and the Younger Man': Age Mimicry and the Ambivalence of Laughter in *The Golden Girls*" | 251
Thomas Küpper

EPILOG: THE SOCIAL AND CULTURAL RELEVANCE OF STUDYING AGE IN TELEVISION

"Aging beyond the Rhetoric of Aging" | 269
Mita Banerjee and Norbert W. Paul

Contributors | 275

Acknowledgments

We would like to extend our sincerest gratitude to the ongoing academic and generous financial support, which made this volume possible: the Center for Inter-American Studies (C.IAS) at the University of Graz (Austria); the European Network in Aging Studies (ENAS); the DFG-funded research training group "Life Sciences – Life Writing" (2015/1) at Johannes Gutenberg-Universität Mainz (Germany); the literature research Grup Dedal-Lit at Universitat de Lleida, (Spain) and the project SIforAGE (7th Framework Programme - EU/SiS 2012.1.2-1).

We would like to thank the general editors of the "Aging Studies" series, Roberta Maierhofer, Ulla Kriebernegg and Heike Hartung, for their immediate welcoming of our idea and for being so supportive when we asked for advice or guidance.

We are also greatly indebted to all the contributors of this volume who have made our work as editors an extraordinarily pleasurable and inspiring experience. Most of our authors were so generous to spend some of their precious time for an internal (blind) peer-review process, which we believe was very enriching for the quality of the chapters and for the cohesion of this interdisciplinary and methodologically diverse volume. It has been an honor to work with all of them.

Lastly, we want to express our warmest gratitude to Jule Mott, whose immensely accurate, swift and reliable work as a copy editor and proofreader has been invaluable to us.

Serial Narrative, Temporality and Aging: An Introduction

ANITA WOHLMANN AND MARICEL ORÓ-PIQUERAS

According to Melissa Ames, "never before has narrative time played such an important role in mainstream television" (9). Time travel, time retardation and time compression, disruptions of the chronological flow through flashbacks and flashforwards – these experimental uses of time have become key devices within contemporary television narratives (9). The following three examples of TV series exemplify this link between the narrative use of experimental time and serial formats. Simultaneously, they draw on themes that are commonly discussed in age studies. *24* (2001-2010), a fictional real-time TV series, sells the illusion to be a pure record of time passing, even though it is a show that is, of course, extensively edited. The TV series constructs narrative time through a sense of constant acceleration and complication of the narrative action. These temporal aesthetics of *24* are interwoven with the representation of its protagonist, Jack Bauer, who is a grandfather in the ninth and final season. On the one hand, *24* challenges stereotypical notions of what it means to be an aging man and a grandfather (Bauer's granddaughter stresses, for instance, that he does not look like a "grandpa", to which Bauer replies that he couldn't agree more with her). On the other hand, *24* substantiates and perpetuates stereotypes about male aging, such as mandatory resilience and a larger-than-life physical prowess. The second example, *Damages* (2007-2012) also experiments with narrative time, illustrating through its complex and multi-layered plot structure how temporality is intricately interwoven with knowledge production. In disrupting linearity and chronology through constant flashbacks and flashforwards, *Damages* implicitly critiques the idea of scientific, objective and chronological time (Pape 166). Within these narrative time experiments, *Damages* couches a conflictual intergenerational relationship of mentoring and rivalry between two female lawyers: Patty Hewes is the older star lawyer and Ellen Parsons embodies the younger mentee, who, throughout the five seasons of *Damages*, gradually emancipates from her mentor, leaving the older 'mother figure' behind. And, finally, in *Pushing Daisies* (2007-2009), the protagonist Ned is bestowed with the gift to reanimate the dead with his touch – a clue which reimagines the finality of death and offers a space to playfully engage with alternative temporalities, second chances and a lighthearted take on man's search for longevity and (im)mortality through each episode's fantastic and comic narrative.

Beyond such *narrative* temporal experiments, TV series have an idiosyncratic relation to time on a more *structural* level. William Uricchio analyzes television time through a focus on television as "a larger textual system" that is characterized by "heterochronia," which makes viewers "experience a distinctive kind of time" (27). According to Uricchio, television's time revolves around sequence (e.g., the sequence of the programming), interpenetration (e.g., the fragmentation of programs with advertisements) and repetition (e.g., headlines, advertisements, iconic footage) (32). In doing so, television disrupts time and vitiates sequence (32). Similarly, in their volume *Previously on...* (2010), Arno Meteling, Isabell Otto and Gabriele Schabacher argue that watching serial formats rhythmizes and structures our lives through an interplay of stasis and dynamics, continuity and interruption, repetition and variation (7). TV series thus have an immediate influence on how viewers experience time.

This effect is further heightened through the *genres* of television programming. The temporal experience of a sitcom, for example, which is commonly categorized as an episodic series, is different from watching a soap opera (serial) over years and even decades. While the episodic series stresses circularity, repetition and finitude, the serial is defined by linearity, open-endedness and a focus on change and process over time (e.g., Fiske 145, Mills 28). In the case of a soap opera, seriality implies an "infinitely extended middle" (Fiske 180), which entails a particular narrative structure (lacking closure, for example) and which implies, outside of the narrative, that the actors are aging with their audiences. Thus, the storylines on television and our own stories become intertwined in time throughout the episodes, seasons, years and sometimes decades through which we follow a program. This linearity and sequential programming has been potentially disrupted and fundamentally changed with the new TV consumption practices, which allow viewers to radically change, control and individually pace their modes of watching a program through convenience technologies (e.g., DVD, DVR), or online watching and streaming possibilities. The infamous 'binge watching' is only one possible consequence of experiencing a TV series. Melissa Ames has noted another effect in her volume *Time in Television Narrative* (2013): The advent of the new viewing practices have also allowed producers and writers of TV series to be more adventurous, experimental and complex in how they tell their stories (4) – exactly because viewers can rewatch an episode, rewind a scene or stop and resume the viewing of a series on their own terms.

With the emergence of Netflix, a video-on-demand provider that also started to produce original programming several years ago, TV critics are anticipating a new era of television. Todd VanDerWerff, for example, argues that Netflix is inventing a new art form, a kind of hybrid between TV series and film, in which stories can be told over a period of ten or twelve hours. Serial formats thus have extended temporal opportunities to develop their plots while the streaming options blur the episodic boundaries and enable a continuous, long-term engagement with characters. This viewing experience is different from the "slice" quality of TV episodes or the 90-minutes scripts of conventional Hollywood movies. In a sense, these developments in serial storytelling echo age scholars' calls for moving beyond the "slice-of-life approach" to aging in order to include more complex and expansive notions of what it means to live in time (e.g., Gullette 179).

These complex and multi-layered relations of TV series to temporality seem to offer alternatives to the chronological and linear notions of standardized time or 'clock' time. In this sense, Pamela Gravagne's concept of the magical quality of cinematic time seems to be pertinent to TV series. Gravagne explores Gilles Deleuze's concepts of the movement image (where time is "linear, orderly, knowable, and predictable" 50) and the time image (where time is "nonlinear and undecidable beforehand," where "the future remains open" 52), arguing that, according to Deleuze,

[t]ime . . . does not trap us but is more like a kind of magic that can free us to live, continually opening up possibilities for becoming by giving us chance after

chance to combine our past with our present in all sorts of new and unexpected ways. (57)

If it is true that TV series, due to their repetitive make-up, give us "chance after chance" to understand and experience the magic of time as something that continually opens up "possibilities of becoming," TV series emerge as a promising medium to study new, non-stereotypical, radical and inspirational representations of age and aging.

However, to our knowledge, the field of age studies does not seem to have explored this potential in TV series so far. While plenty of research has been conducted on the representation of age and aging in film, TV series, with their specific and peculiar relation to time, have not been studied in a comprehensive way – granted, of course, that there are analyses that focus on representations of age and aging in a specific TV series or contributions that examine both film and TV series side by side. A comprehensive volume, which combines the temporal specificities of TV series, television studies and age studies, is missing so far, and it is this lacuna that the present volume addresses.

The field, into which we are tapping, is a surprisingly rich field. Even though studies show that older people are still underrepresented in television compared to younger age groups (Harwood and Anderson), we found a number of intriguing examples of TV series which feature older protagonists. *The Golden Girls* (1985-1992), *Murder She Wrote* (1984-1996) or *Miss Marple* (1984-1992) focus on feisty older women who refuse to retire to a passive, detached and calm lifestyle. More recently, Netflix' *Grace and Frankie* (2015-present) as well as the British TV series *Vicious* (2013-present) and *Last Tango in Halifax* (2012-present) illustrate an interest in the lives of older characters. Similarly, soap operas, according to John Fiske, provide an open-ended, ever-evolving space for middle-aged and older female characters to explore economic power, desire and sexuality (183-4). The soap-opera's narrative aesthetics thus highlight process and continuity in representing femininity and aging (187). Besides these examples, there are numerous TV series featuring intriguing older figures as secondary characters, such as Mrs. McCluskey in *Desperate Housewives*, Lester Freamon in *The Wire* or the 'golden girls' in *Orange is the New Black* (for a closer analysis, please see the respective chapters in this volume).

In creating a link between television theory and concepts from age studies, we hope to tease out new approaches to understanding age and aging by emphasizing how the specific medium of TV series impacts and produces alternative concepts of time and time passing. For this reason, we asked our contributors to keep the following guiding questions in mind: How does a TV series, in contrast to a film, represent age and aging? Which elements of a TV series generate a different understanding of temporality compared to film? Which concepts from television studies and age studies can productively be brought into dialog to elicit an understanding of how TV series negotiate age and aging? Do TV genres, such as episodic series and episodic serials, produce different concepts of time and if so, how does this affect the representation of age?

Serializing Age: Aging and Old Age in TV Series aims at bringing together the fields of TV studies and age studies in order to consider the relationships between the undeniable impact of TV in our everyday lives as well as the exponential aging of worldwide population. Despite our contributors' heterogeneous points of departure, that range from literary and cultural studies, television studies to sociology and anthropology, their contributions share the conducting line of analyzing portrayals, representations and cultural beliefs related to old age and the aging process within TV series, specifically focusing on how the temporal construction of the narrative contributes to present alternative views of aging. As a complex experience, both at an individual and social level, the understanding of aging and the still limiting conceptions related to the aging body and old age require the consideration of an interdisciplinary and multidisciplinary perspective in order to thresh pervading stereotypes of the aging process and old age and reformulate them as a continuation of individual concerns and hopes, traumas and desires that a person has encountered in his or her youth and middle age.

Together with the questioning of established beliefs and structures that the postmodern era brought with it, there are two key concepts that have triggered the conception of this volume: a new way of producing and watching TV programs in which the disruption of linearity and chronology contributes to challenge established cultural and social parameters, as well as a more fluid conceptualization of the life course in which age stages become movable markers. In relation to the second concept, in 1991, sociologists Mike Hepworth and Mike Featherstone noted how "[t]heorists of the movement towards a postmodern society point to an emerging de-institutionalisation and a de-differentiation of the life course, with less emphasis than in the past being placed upon age-specific role transitions and scheduled identity development" (373). In this respect, Hepworth and Featherstone, among other age scholars, point to an economy based on services rather than physical work, the proliferation of an industry that relies on the obsession of taking care of external appearance in order to keep the external signs of ageing at bay and a globalized culture in which traditional values as well as family and social structures take as many shapes as citizens exist to account for the blurring of boundaries in age categories. Thus, given the extended format of TV series in time, both in relation to fictional time as well as broadcast time (even when binge watching), TV series become especially meaningful media in order to study and analyze how time is ordered and institutionalized and, with it, how age, aging and old age are negotiated in the contemporary Western world.

Within TV studies, the so-called post-network era television "has challenged its viewers like never before", as Todd M. Sodano puts it (2012: 29) and, with it, concepts of time, linearity and chronology have also been shaken. Post-network TV refers to the changes in the industry both in the production and consumption of TV series which, according to Ames (2012), have resulted in "increasingly complex television narratives and alternative viewing practices" (4). The fact that viewers can ignore the flow planned by broadcast TV and decide on when, how and the intensity with which they will watch a TV series has made storytelling more sophisticated through narrative and temporal experimentations that Ames define as "the temporal tease" (8). Whereas this temporal tease has been present in soap operas for some time due to their lengthy duration which was translated, for example, in the coming back of characters that had supposedly died or the portrayal of characters who seemed not to age, temporal alterations have increased in post-network TV. TV series such as *Lost* and *24* set the grounds for such experimentations followed by series such as *How I Met you Mother* and *Orange is the New Black* in which the constant and complex use of flashbacks portray past and present, and even future, as inescapably merging with each other, in the same way as time merges in our minds and memory. In this respect, temporal experimentation in TV series becomes a laboratory in which cultural constructions related to the aging process may be deconstructed and challenged in inventive and creative ways. As Anita Wohlmann (2014) argued in *Aged Young Adults*, "paying close attention to the ways in which people refer to temporality and timing is therefore crucial for understanding how these references can carry connotations that point to cultural meanings of age and aging" (50).

In *Figuring Age: Women, Bodies, Generations* (1999), Kathleen Woodward, drawing on Margaret Morganroth Gullette's research, highlights the need to differentiate between biological aging and cultural aging and "abandon the older models of age-appropriate behavior and experience" (xiv). In other words, our lives are measured according to what Jan Baars (2012) names "chronometric time" which usually differs from "human time" (143). On the contrary, as Baars argues, "there is no such clock inside human beings which determines for all time and all places how people age" (148). As a complex experience in human beings, which is very much related to social and cultural conceptions of time patterned by the rituals through which a person is supposed to go in each appropriate age stage, the temporal disruption of contemporary TV series contributes to present life as a flexible and fluid continuum, rather than well-established stages, in which decisions are taken according to circumstances rather than imposed chronometric time. In this respect, the postmodern conception of the life course to which Featherstone and Hepworth referred is translated into narrative and temporal experimentation to which the contemporary viewer has become an expert, as both Ames and Sodano point out.

The volume is divided into three sections which group the articles according to the narrative and temporal experimentation as well as the main topics tackled in the series analyzed in each chapter. The articles in section 1, "Between Screen and Reality: Negotiating the Effects of Old Age and Aging" establish connections between the fictional narratives of the series and experiences of aging and old age in real life. These connections either draw on how the actors' lives intersect with the characters' storylines or how some TV series aim at a realistic or sociological perspective on their characters' entanglement in the social world. In "Time, Memory, and Aging on the Soaps", C. Lee Harrington explores key issues of age and aging surrounding US daytime soap operas, focusing on temporal distortions such as rapid aging of infants and children or the elongation of young and mid-adulthood, a phenomenon which she names SORAS, in other words, "soap opera rapid aging syndrome." In addition, Harrington analyzes interviews with soap opera 'veterans' to illustrate how age and aging affects the self-image of the actors and how they deal with the challenges of working in a youth-oriented business. Whereas Harrington draws on a number of long-running American soap operas, from *Guiding Light* (1937-2009) to *General Hospital* (1963-2015), in order to support her arguments, Neal King focuses on the TV series *The Wire* (2002-2008) and the figure of Baltimore PD Detective Lester Freamon when facing retirement. In his contribution "Business as Usual: Retirement on *The Wire*," King analyzes how, by the end of the series, Detective Freamon is not completely retired, which is a narrative choice that conforms with other cop action movies in which the masculinity of the main characters is preserved by having them keep an active role in society, away from accusations of "idleness" or "unproductiveness." According to King, the innovative long-form narrative of *The Wire* focuses with an almost sociological interest on the minutiae of police work, representing it as tampered by politics and power hierarchies. Oddly, however, the series leaves aside the exploration of political, racial and particularly gendered inequality. In "Heroine or Caricature? The Older Woman in *Desperate Housewives*", Ros Jennings and Maricel Oró-Piqueras focus on the portrayal of Karen McCluskey in *Desperate Housewives* (2004-2012). Despite the fact that Karen McCluskey is presented as a secondary character in the first episodes, she becomes a central character as the series advances to the point of becoming the nexus among the four younger female protagonists of the series. Karen McCluskey moves from being portrayed as a stereotypical older woman, bad-humored and always nagging, to being presented under a more humane, though not less ambiguous lens as the series unfolds in time and space.

The four articles in section 2, "Temporality and Aging: Experiments with Magic, Narrative and Genre" share a playful tone provided by a conscious presentation of time as neither linear nor chronological. In "'Vampires don't age, but actors sure do:' Fantasies of Youth and the Paradox of the Aging Vampire in *Buffy the Vampire Slayer*", Sally Chivers analyzes the popular figure of the vampire as portrayed in Joss Whedon's television series *Buffy the Vampire Slayer* (1997-2003) and proves how its popularity reveals anxieties about population aging. At another level, directors have to deal with actors and actresses who play vampire roles for some years and whose bodies inescapably age. In "The Twilight of Their Lives? Magical Objects as Serial Devices and Catalysts of Aging in *The Twilight Zone*," Marta Miquel-Baldellou draws on conceptions of age, aging and the passing of time presented in the series through the use of tokens, domestic devices and technological apparatus that develop magical properties and metaphorical meanings to both highlight and subvert established cultural conceptions and expected roles in old age. Although *The Twilight Zone* (1959-1964) was composed of independent episodes with new characters, settings and plots, Miquel-Baldellou claims that seriality is achieved through the introduction of these magical and metaphorical devices that contribute to disrupt chronology and a fixed ideological frame as well as through recurrent thematic concerns within the TV drama. Cecilia Colloseus looks at how temporality and maturity are linked in *How I Met your Mother* (2005-2014) in "Flashbacks, Flashforwards and Life Plans in *How I Met Your Mother*." As Colloseus explains, in the series, the past of the story is the present of the audience, while the narrative is constructed by the main character who recollects, many times without exactitude, the past that he is retelling to his children. However, as Colloseus proves in her article, narrative experimentation is closer to giving a traditional message on expected social choices rather than the opposite. In the last contribution of this section, Anita Wohlmann and Julia Reichenpfader analyze the figure of the cougar in two American TV series, namely, *Damages* (2007-2012) and *Cougar Town* (2009-2015), and a German soap opera entitled *Verbotene Liebe* (1995-2015). In their article, Wohlmann and Reichenpfader explore the ways in which the different serialized formats curb or advance progressive representations of a figure "who is marked by non-normative notions of temporality" (182). The results of the analysis cautiously suggest that soap operas might be more open towards the representation of sexuality and desire in middle-age and old age compared to episodic series.

The articles in section 3, "Sex and Desire Through the Lens of Television Time," explore selected TV series through the lenses of gender and queer studies, linking them with temporal and narrative experimentation in order to discern whether and to what extent normative conceptions of gender and age are undermined or highlighted. In "Still Looking: Gay Aging and Future in Contemporary US Television," Dustin Goltz departs from an overview of gay men representations in TV series through the 80s and 90s, in which gay characters were mostly marginal and had no desirable future to look forward to. In contemporary American TV series, extended time and narrative innovation introduced by contemporary series present more comprehensive and nuanced representations of gay male characters within the life course. In analyzing two recent TV series that focus on older homosexual characters, *Vicious* (2012–present) and *Looking* (2014–present), Goltz explores the potential of contemporary TV series to complicate the earlier, youth-oriented representations. Eva Krainitzki's chapter entitled "'You've got time': Ageing and queer (spacio)temporality in *Orange is The New Black*" relates the narrative and temporal experimentation of a series produced and launched by streaming network company Netflix with the portrayal of non-normative representations of female aging by drawing on the concept of queer temporality and space introduced by Judith Halberstam. As the title of Regina Spektor's song already suggests, fluidity in the representations of sex and age identity is a key issue that Krainitzki analyzes and discusses in her article. In "*Last Tango in Halifax*: Desire and Ageing in Contemporary British Television", Kristyn Gorton explores how Sally Wainwright's TV series positions late-middle aged and older women's desire as a focus point in the narrative as opposed to previous representations of late-middle aged and older women in British television whose own desires were usually upstaged by their children's needs. On the contrary, in her article, Gorton highlights how the interrelationship between generations is strengthened when expressing and acknowledging each others' (sexual) desires. In the last chapter, "Assimilating to Aerobics Culture? Fitness and Age Mimicry in *The Golden Girls*", Thomas Küpper analyzes the interplay between the concepts of fitness and seductiveness in order to keep the signs of aging at bay, concepts which became popular in the 1980s with Jane Fonda. Drawing on Homi Bhaba's notion of mimicry, Küpper explores how Blanche Dubois' unsuccessful effort to imitate the behavior of a younger man in order to seduce him actually contributes to introduce mockery and humor in the representation of the apparently positive attributes of the younger man in the episode "Blanche and the Younger Man."

The last contribution, "Aging Beyond the Rhetoric of Aging," is a short essay by Mita Banerjee and Norbert Paul, which highlights the continuing relevance of investigating age and aging and, in doing so, expands the central concerns and concepts of this volume to the larger social significance of studying temporality, narrative and media. Banerjee and Paul link the central themes of this volume to the ways in which temporality, ability and corporeality are interwoven in the current cultural and biomedical rhetorics of aging.

This volume came together over the span of two years. In 2013, during the International Summer School Seggau in Austria, we discussed the first ideas and then quickly sent out a call for papers, which solicited contributions from age scholars who had been working in the areas of film and television before. In April 2014, we presented a panel on age and aging in TV series at the 8th International Conference on Cultural Gerontology and the 2nd Conference of the European Network in Aging Studies (ENAS) in Galway, Ireland. Neal King, Marta Miquel-Baldellou, Maricel Oró-Piqueras presented first drafts of their papers and Anita Wohlmann gave a general introduction into the overlapping interests of age, television and film studies. In autumn 2014, we had selected all our contributors and got started on putting the volume together. In May 2015, we presented another panel on age and aging in TV series during the inaugural conference of the North-American Network in Aging Studies (NANAS) in Oxford, Ohio. Eva Krainitzki presented her paper on *Orange is the New Black*, Roberta Maierhofer spoke about time travel in *Life on Mars* and *Ashes to Ashes* and Anita Wohlmann presented this volume's chapter on cougars. Over this short amount of time, we received much encouragement and support and felt that we were working on a project that was considered relevant by age scholars and television scholars alike. We hope that this volume will live up to their expectations.

WORKS CITED

Ames, Melissa. "Introduction. Television in the Twenty-First Century." *Time and Narrative. Exploring Temporality in 21st Century Programming*. Ed. Melissa Ames. Jackson: University Press of Mississippi, 2012. 3-24. Print.

Baars, Jan. "Critical Turns of Aging, Narrative and Time." *International Journal of Ageing and Later Life*. 7.2 (2012): 143-165. Print.

Bhabha, Homi. "Of Mimicry and Man: The Ambivalence of Colonial Discourse." *The Location of Culture*. London: Routledge, 1994. 85-92. Print.

Featherstone, M. and M. Hepworth. "The Mask of Ageing and the Postmodern Lifecourse." *The Body: Social Process and Cultural Theory*. Eds. Mike Featherstone, Mike Hepworth and Bryan S. Turner. London: Sage Publications, 1991. Print.

Fiske, John. *Television Culture*. London: Routledge, 2003. Print.

Gravagne, Pamela. "The Magic of Cinema: Time as Becoming in *Strangers in Good Company*." *International Journal in Ageing and Later Life* 8.1 (2013): 41-63. Print.

Gullette, Margaret Morganroth. *Aged by Culture*. Chicago: University of Chicago Press, 2004. Print.

Harwood, Jake and Karen Anderson. "The Presence and Portrayal of Social Groups on Prime-Time Television." *Communication Reports* 15.2 (Summer 2002): 81-97. Web. 13 June 2013.

Meteling, Arno, Isabell Otto and Gabriele Schabacher. "'Previously on...'". *'Previously On...': Zur Ästhetik der Zeitlichkeit neuerer TV-Serien*. Eds. Arno Meteling, Isabell Otto and Gabriele Schabacher. München: Fink, 2010. 7-16. Print.

Mills, Brett. *The Sitcom*. Edinburgh: Edinburgh University Press, 2009. Print.

Neale, Steve. *Genre and Hollywood*. London: Routledge, 2000. Print.

Pape, Toni. "Temporalities and Collision Course: Time, Knowledge, and Temporal Critique in *Damages*." *Time in Television Narrative: Exploring Temporality in Twenty-First-Century Programming*. Ed. Melissa Ames. Jackson: University Press of Mississippi, 2012. 165-177. Print.

Sodano, Todd M. "Television's Paradigm (Time)Shift. Production and Consumption Practices in the Post-Network Era." *Time and Narrative. Exploring Temporality in 21st Century Programming*. Ed. Melissa Ames. Jackson: University Press of Mississippi, 2012. 3-24. Print.

Uricchio, William. "TV as Time Machine: Television's Changing Heterochronic Regimes and the Production of History." *Relocating Television: Television in the Digital Context*. Ed. Jostein Gripsrud. London: Routledge, 2010. 27-40. Print.

VanDerWerff, Todd. "Netflix is Accidentally Inventing a New Art Form – Not Quite TV and Not Quite Film." *Vox*. Vox Media, 30 July 2015. Web. 31 July 2015.

Wohlmann, Anita. *Aged Young Adults: Age Readings of Contemporary American Novels and Films*. Bielefeld: Transcript, 2014. Print.

Woodward, Kathleen Ed. *Figuring Bodies. Women, Bodies, Generations*. Bloomington: Indiana University Press, 1999. Print.

TELEVISION

24. Creators Joel Surnow and Robert Cochran, Fox network (2001-2010).

Damages. Creators Todd A. Kessler, Glenn Kessler and Daniel Zelman, FX (2007-2009); DirecTV (2010-2012).

Desperate Housewives. Creator Marc Cherry, ABC (2004-2012).

Grace and Frankie. Creators Marta Kauffman and Howard J. Morris, Netflix (2015-present).

How I Met Your Mother. Creators Carter Bays and Craig Thomas, CBS (2005-2014).

Last Tango in Halifax. Creator Sally Wainwright, BBC One (2012-present).

Lost. Creators Jeffrey Lieber, J. J. Abrams and Damon Lindelof, ABC (2004-2010).

Miss Marple. Producer George Gallaccio, BBC One (1984-1992).

Murder She Wrote. Creators Peter S. Fischer, Richard Levinson and William Link, CBS (1984-1996).

Orange is the New Black. Creator Jenji Kohan, Netflix (2013-present).

Pushing Daisies. Creator Bryan Fuller, ABC (2007-2009).

The Golden Girls. Creator Susan Harris, NBC (1985-1992).

The Wire. Creator David Simon, HBO (2002-2008).

Vicious. Creators Mark Ravenhill and Gary Janetti, ITV (2013-present).

Between Screen and Reality: Negotiating
the Effects of Old Age and Aging

Time, Memory, and Aging on the Soaps[1]

C. LEE HARRINGTON

Introduction

Nearly 40 years ago, narrative scholar Dennis Porter articulated what has become the classic formulation of "soap opera time," the curious temporal elongations and truncations that mark the US daytime serial format. Whereas time *for* soap opera speaks to the circumstances under which soaps are viewed and is assumed to be a time for pleasure, fantasy, and leisure, time *of* soap opera is best understood through the distinct "compositional practices" of the genre, in particular its "life-imitating diachronic capaciousness" (783). Porter refers here to soaps' "implicit claim to portray a parallel life," depicting the trials and tribulations of a fictional community whose lives are separate from but temporally continuous with those of the viewers (783). In the world of soap operas, which "portray life in all its true banality" (Bordewich), a random Tuesday is a random Tuesday both on-

---

1 This chapter contains revised texts from two sources: (1) "Constructing the Older Audience: Age and Aging in Soaps" by C. Lee Harrington and Denise Brothers, which originally appeared in The Survival of Soap Opera: Transformations for a New Media Era edited by Sam Ford, Abigail De Kosnik, and C. Lee Harrington, published by University Press of Mississippi, Copyright © 2011 by University Press of Mississippi; (2) "A Life Course Built for Two: Acting, Aging, and Soap Operas" by C. Lee Harrington and Denise Brothers, which originally appeared in *Journal of Aging Studies* 24.1 (2010): 20-29. I thank University Press of Mississippi, Elsevier, and Denise Brothers for permission to reprint re-worked material from both sources.

and off-screen. More importantly, Porter refers to soaps' upending of the ultimate Aristotelian purpose of dramatic narratives: to end. Unlike many serial dramas that are designed to be close-ended, US soaps share with those of the UK and Australia (among others) an open-ended narrative structure or what Porter famously described as an "indefinitely expandable middle" (783). Traditionally offering "process without progression" and working toward "provisional denouements" rather than narrative closure, soap opera is "the drama of perepetia without anagnorisis" (784). The constant tension between these imperatives – to mimic the daily unspooling of human life but deny its inevitable finitude – results in a pattern of peculiar temporal distortions on the soaps: rapid aging (and occasional de-aging) of infants and children, elongation of young and mid-adulthood resulting in disquieting accumulation of significant life milestones, and the marginalization of old age and death-related issues and concerns. As such, temporality on US soap operas both mimics and warps that of real life.

This chapter builds on my prior research on aging, death, and media to explore four related issues: (a) images of (old) age on US daytime soap operas, including perspectives of long-term viewers and industry insiders; (b) aging as process in the soap genre, focusing on actor/character development and on- and off-screen aging; (c) the key role of memory in long-form and highly detailed storytelling; and (d) the life cycle of the soap genre itself, drawing on Igor Kopytoff's notion of the cultural biography of things. Here I explore how soap operas themselves are aging (dying) over time and how that informs our understandings of time, memory, and aging. My analysis is rooted in media and cultural studies with supplementary literatures such as gerontology and thanatology mobilized throughout.

Aging as Image: Representations

Mike Featherstone and Mike Hepworth point out that since "(e)very image of a human being is effectively an image of aging [. . .] the study of the history of images of aging is the study of the history of our ideas about aging" (137, 147). In an increasingly mediated and age-conscious society, televisual representations of age and aging matter in either perpetuating damaging stereotypes about older adults and the aging process or providing positive new role models for a 21st century vision of 'aging well' across the lifespan. Research on the TV portrayal of older adults dates back to the

1950s in North America, with the most prominent research stream focusing on the content of images. This body of literature finds (not surprisingly), that adults over 65 are one of the most under-represented age groups on US television, along with children under 10 (Harwood and Anderson). The few representations that do exist are troubling: older adults tend to occupy minor roles, are depicted as living alone, absent a love life, and/or lacking common sense, and are generally relegated to playing comedic, foolish, or eccentric characters. Perhaps most troubling, these findings echo comparable findings of the 1970s, indicating no discernible improvement on TV representations of late(r) life despite significant real-world demographic changes (Healey and Ross). More recent research has found that scripted primetime programs depict different stages of adulthood differently, with characters in their 20s occupying extended adolescence (more leisure time and sexual activity than other adult age groups) and characters in their 60s and older experiencing noticeably less leisure time or occupational power (Lauren, Dozier and Reyes). In the context of US daytime soaps, while 13% of soap characters are in the 51-to-64 demographic, generally matching that of the US population, the 65-and-older demographic is noticeably absent at just 3% of the soap opera landscape (Cassata and Irwin 227). Older soap characters tend to be portrayed positively but are rarely central figures, acting instead as occasional 'wise mentors' for younger characters with drama-filled lives. Soap veteran Don Hastings, who acted for nearly 50 years on *As the World Turns* (CBS), remarked near the end of the show's storied run:

Those of us who have been there for many, many years are not used as much as we used to be. The show had different age groups [in earlier eras], you always had all of the different age groups reacting [and] you had different points of view. [Now the writers] go from one story involving the young people to another story, and [older characters] are really kind of in the background now to give the show some texture (Harrington and Brothers *A Life Course Built for Two* 27).

This pattern of marginalization accompanies a near-absence of soap narratives addressing real-world late(r)-life issues such as retirement, widowhood, chronic illness, or lonelihood (Cassata and Irwin 218), a topic to which I return below.

In no small part, the continued under-representation of older adults on television reflects market considerations. One of the challenges facing the TV industry is that as the US population ages so too do media audiences, and increasingly out of the targeted demographic of 18-to-49-year-olds. The number of viewers 55 and older is increasing twice as fast as the general TV audience (Ibarra) and the median age of primetime network viewers reached 40 or older for the first time in 2007 (Levin). This shift is occurring in daytime as well; for example, on the top-rated soap opera *The Young & the Restless* (CBS), median viewer age is close to 60 years old (Lidz). Since the industry's ideal viewer is a child introduced to soaps by a parent or grandparent who continues to engage with the genre as s/he matures, this trend toward older audiences is troubling. How might it shape on-screen images of age and aging? In short, the TV industry assumes that viewers want to see characters of their own age bracket on-screen (despite an absence of any publicized industry data to that effect), which has left them chasing the youth demographic in a quest to deliver the 'right' kind of viewers to corporate sponsors. In his analysis of the 'dark side' of target marketing, Joseph Turow points out that as media firms launch strategies to attract certain segments of consumers they simultaneously launch different strategies to drive other consumers away. US daytime soaps began deliberately courting the youth market in the 1980s with teenage-lovers-on-the-run storylines dominating summer holidays (to attract teens during their school breaks), sending mid-to-old-age actors on unwelcomed hiatus for weeks on end. This pattern persisted for decades though there have been promising recent shifts in the four remaining broadcast soaps. *General Hospital* (ABC), for example, began celebrating its 50th year in 2013 by bringing back numerous fan favorite characters from the 1980s and 1990s, played by the same (now-older) actors who anchored core narratives that resurrected story elements from decades past. Moreover, the TV industry as a whole is witnessing a shift (back) to more widespread representation of '"young-old" adults on-screen, a shift heralded by gradual recognition of the buying power of 55-to-64-year-olds compared to that of younger generations (O'Connell). However, older adults (65+) remain marginalized in both daytime and primetime.

How do industry insiders and long-term viewers make sense of how the genre represents adulthood and old age? In part they reject the notion that only youthful on-screen images will attract a youthful audience. Remarks Michael Logan, veteran soap opera critic for *TV Guide*:

It's such a weird thing to always think that young people don't care about where they're headed, you know, what's life going to be like for me? [. . .] [Viewers] want to see [older characters] living full, amazing lives, [a] validation that being older is fascinating (Harrington and Brothers *Constructing the Older Audience* 308).

Soap professionals agree that narratives focused on later life concerns hold value in the world of daytime soaps, both in their melodramatic potential and in their reflection of the realities of older adults' lives. Muses Mimi Torchin, founding editor of the soap magazine *Soap Opera Weekly*:

Most of us who hit fifties and sixties, you start to [gain weight]. I think it would be something millions of women, especially in the Baby Boomer generation, could relate to [. . .] Maybe the sex drive [decline] that happens to both older women and older men [. . .] Maybe talk about having to wear glasses [. . .] Just facing the fact that you aren't what you once were, and how do you deal with that? [. . .] I think it would be very interesting [. . .] Soaps are very good for giving people life lessons (Harrington and Brothers *Constructing the Older Audience* 305).

Actress Jacklyn Zeman, who has portrayed Bobbie Spencer on-and-off for decades on *General Hospital*, agrees with Torchin's suggestions and points out that "soap operas are about life." The industry can't say "we're only going to show what happens [. . .] from 15 to 30," she continues, arguing that "we need to respect and honor [aging] and bring [viewers] something that is a true picture" (original data collected by Harrington and Brothers). Acknowledging the challenges of doing so from an industry perspective, *The Bold & the Beautiful*'s (CBS) headwriter, Kay Alden, explains:

Here is where one runs into the inevitable "business versus art" [question]. I think it's hard to figure out how to appeal to that [18-to-49] age group by telling stories that focus so much on the other end of life [. . .] There are wonderful, moving tales to be told. They are difficult to tell in daytime [because] you're asking people to tune in [every day] and some of these stories are just too painful (Harrington and Brothers *A Life Course Built for Two* 26-27).

While older viewers say they would welcome storylines featuring age-related issues such as retirement, grand-parenting, and romance, they disagree on how explicit they want the latter to be. One 52-year-old viewer says, "I'm not looking to see explicit love scenes of older actors [. . .] but I would like to see them in relationships, both romantic and platonic," whereas another (age 56) reports wanting to see a "full-blown love story with all the possible complications," and yet another (age 50) recalls a favorite *As the World Turns* (CBS) storyline which "proved that life, love and happiness do not end at age forty" (Harrington and Brothers *Constructing the Older Audience* 310). Most interestingly, and in contrast to Kay Alden's comments above, it is younger viewers (in the target demographic of 18-to-49) who report wanting to see narratives of aging that might be considered stereotypical, such as dealing with Alzheimer's, menopause, or caregiving. Older viewers, who see "all that I want in real life" of such challenges, report "absolutely detesting storylines of this type" (Harrington and Brothers *Constructing the Older Audience* 312). In short, there is clearly room in the US soap opera landscape for more diverse imagery regarding late(r) life, though the navigation may be tricky for scriptwriters.

Aging as Process: Temporalities

Central to the pleasures of soap opera is the temporal congruity of the aging of characters and viewers. Soaps remain unique in the entertainment world in their unfolding rhythms that mimic those of real life, as if the fictional communities of Salem or Genoa City (the settings for *Days of Our Lives* [NBC] and *The Young & the Restless* [CBS], respectively) were only a short car ride away but mysteriously inaccessible via that form of transport. The immediacy and intimacy that television itself offered as a new medium in the 1950s is exaggerated on soap opera, with its characters and their domestic and relational concerns unfolding five days per week, 52 weeks per year. Viewers grow up with the narratives, understanding their own maturation process through its correspondence (or lack thereof) with fictional others growing up in the same temporal frame:

Soaps accompanied my real life as a stay at home mother, chronicled my years as a working adult, kept me company when I was alone, gave me something to bond with my mother, sisters, daughters, and daughter-in-laws over (50-year-old soap viewer quoted in Harrington and Bielby).

Psychologists coined the phrase *autobiographical reasoning* to refer to a cognitive strategy that people use to create a sense of unity in their lives, by integrating life events with changing self-perceptions as they age. Autobiographical reasoning can be described as "the dynamic process of thinking about the past to make links to the self" (McLean, Pasupathi, and Pals, 263) or helping people explain how they came to be who they are (Pasupathi and Mansour, 798). For long-term soap opera fans, the fictional text, their own sense of self, and real-world family dynamics are inextricably bound together in the meaning-making process of growing up and growing old(er) (Harrington and Bielby; Scodari).

My primary interest here is less in the temporal congruity of *viewers'* experiences than it is that of *actors'*, who may spend decades living a dual life both on- and off-screen (Harrington and Brothers *A Life Course Built for Two*). While many actors see soaps as a stepping-stone to primetime or movies, others make daytime their home, entering roles in their 20s that they continue to play in their 40s and 50s. The longest running actor/character combination in the history of television was that of Helen Wagner/Nancy Hughes on *As the World Turns* (CBS). Ms. Wagner assumed the role of Nancy when the program launched in 1956 and played the character for the next 54 years until her (real-life) death in 2010. Both ends of the life-span unfold in real-time on the soaps – witness Kimberly McCullough, who adopted the role of Robin Scorpio (*General Hospital* [ABC]) at age 7 and continues on-and-off in her mid-30s, or Anna Lee who played matriarch Lila Quartermaine (*General Hospital* [ABC]) from the ages of 60 to 91. More typical, however, are the decades spent by actor/character combinations in adolescence and adulthood, given soaps' narrative focus on romance and domesticity. Indeed, one of the temporal distortions characteristic of US soap opera is termed SORAS or "soap opera rapid aging syndrome," an effort to "overnight express" infants into childhood and then adolescence so that looking-for-love storylines are reasonable and palatable. Viewers generally shrug and accept these temporal leaps, but not always:

On *The Bold and the Beautiful*, when Bridget was born in 1992 [. . .], her mother, Brooke, didn't know if Bridget's biological father was Eric or Eric's (later determined to be non-biological) son, Ridge. A fraudulent paternity test named Ridge [the father] and for four years, he raised Bridget. In 1996, a school-age Bridget was devastated to learn that her real father was, in fact, Eric. The trauma must have pushed her into accelerated puberty, because by 1997, she was a teen, and by 2000 she was an adult. It was Adult Bridget who began the brief flirtation with Ridge that had viewers shrieking in horror [. . .] [She] used to think of him as her dad! (Adams).

On rare occasions SORAS operates in reverse, keeping actor/character combinations in vampire-like limbo:

[On *Guiding Light* (CBS)] Harley gave birth to a daughter, Daisy, in 1987 and gave her up for adoption. When Daisy, now called Susan, came looking for her bio-mom in 1998, she was played by 13-year-old Brittany Snow [. . .] Then, in 2007, after a six-year absence, Susan, now once again called Daisy, returned to town, played by Bonnie Dennison, an actress three years younger than Snow – making the character a teenager again . . . er, still (Adams).

While all SORAS-ing and de-SORAS-ing is driven by narrative demands, it can prove detrimental to viewer pleasure if core story elements (such as kinship ties, as in the first quote) are altered as a result.

But what of actors' experiences in these long-running actor/character combinations? Given the requirement faced by writers to fill 130-260 hours of airtime each year, soap characters necessarily experience more dramatic life events than real-life persons, both familiar (weddings, divorces, health crises) and unfamiliar (kidnappings, Mob encounters, jewelry heists), and some actors feel little connection between their on- and off-screen 'lives'. Explains Robert Newman, who spent 20+ years playing Josh Lewis on *Guiding Light* (CBS):

Josh is a guy who's been through nine weddings [. . .] I really can't relate to that [. . .] Josh and Reva have been married to each other and divorced from each other three times now. I don't know anybody who's experienced that [. . .] Josh has had three wives come back from the dead. I've never experienced that either and I don't know anybody who has (Harrington and Brothers *A Life Course Built for Two* 23).

On- and off-screen synchrony does sometimes occur, however, and is reported with glee by the daytime press. At times the fictional informs the real, as when an actress learns what kind of dress she *doesn't* want for her own wedding after getting married on-screen (*Soap Opera Digest*, March 6, 2007), or when an actress ponders if a real-life pregnancy might help her play her role:

I talked to the producers about trying to get pregnant to tie it in to [my character's] storyline but everyone pretty much said, 'That's a bad idea and inevitably you won't time it right.' They told me to live my life and do what I had to do, but timing it to the story would not be a good idea (*Soap Opera Digest*, February 27, 2007).

In other cases, real-world events lead to on-screen re-enactments, as when an off-screen diagnosis of oral cancer results in the same scripted ailment for one's character (*Soap Opera Digest*, January 29, 2008) or when an actress' real-life surgical procedure (face-lift) is filmed by the soap's executive producer and the bandages removed on-screen, such that the character, the actress playing her, and the viewing audience first witness the results at the same time. In other words, actress Jeanne Cooper (*The Young & the Restless* [CBS]) saw the results of her own face-lift *as her character* (*Soap Opera Digest*, January 4, 2000).

More reflective of actors' experiences, however, are not so much specific *moments* of synchrony/asynchrony but rather the diffuse unfolding of dual narratives (one real, one fictional) across time. Some actors see their characters as pals or buddies ("It's like he's this really good friend of mine"; John McCook, 20+ years on *The Bold & the Beautiful* [CBS]), others as family members ("I feel like a sister to her"; Jacklyn Zeman, 30+ years on *General Hospital* [ABC]), and some describe a closer integration between self and character:

As I took on her skin more – I mean, through 25 years you sort of go into one. [N]ot that I come home and that I'm [my character] Esther but I definitely know how she thinks, how she feels, how she breathes, you know, everything about her. After 25 years [. . .] she doesn't surprise me (Kate Linder, 25+ years on *The Young & the Restless* [CBS]; Harrington and Brothers *A Life Course Built for Two* 25).

Concurs veteran actress Linda Dano:

[My character Felicia] and I somehow down the road, I don't know when it happened, became one person. So when anything happened to Felicia [. . .] it's almost like it was happening to me [. . .] [What] was healthy for me, and I think has to happen, is that when I stepped out the door I was Linda again (15+ years on *Another World* [NBC]; Harrington and Brothers *A Life Course Built for Two* 25).

Jacklyn Zeman (*General Hospital* [ABC]) says her character has given her a life lesson in empathy and an unexpected opportunity to live two lives at once:

[P]laying Bobbie has opened my mind to [. . .] a different way of thinking about people and circumstances and relationships that might not be Jackie's way of thinking, my way of thinking, but it's certainly valid [. . .] Two people can be in exactly the same moment at exactly the same time and yet have a completely different take on what actually happened [and] playing Bobbie has made me so aware of that [. . .] I feel like we've gone through life and we've gone through a lot of stuff together [. . .] My experiences as Bobbie are just as important to me as my experiences as Jackie (Harrington and Brothers *A Life Course Built for Two* 24).

Finally, and in reference to the prior section, soap actors are highly conscious of the fact that these dual narratives are unfolding across time and *on-screen*:

You go through life as this character, as this personality, as you're aging. I aged twenty some-odd years in front of millions of people who were aging with me [. . .] I think I got out [of soaps] just in time. [If] I'm at the gym now and look up at the TV at different friends of mine [. . .] everybody's looking pretty rough. I mean, we're all fighting a good fight but time has really had an impact [. . .] It's a very vulnerable and unique position to be in [because] you're putting it right [out] there from day-to-day. Week-to-week. Month-to-month. Year-to-year (Stephen Schnetzer, 25+ years playing Cass Winthrop on CBS' *Another World, As the World Turns*, and *Guiding Light*; Harrington and Brothers *A Life Course Built for Two* 26).

Actors' ambivalence about the physical realities of age and aging (as captured in the above quote) thus mimic those of soap viewers, but are distorted and magnified by their publicity. Overall, actors report both personally benefiting from their long-term portrayal of soap characters (such as the lesson in empathy reported by Jacklyn Zeman) and finding their character's lives increasingly distant from their own (as suggested by Robert Newman).

Audience, Industry, and Memory

Clearly, the "indefinitely expandable middle" (Porter 783) of daytime soaps generates pressure on writers to fill that middle with complex character development and plot twists, resulting in an accumulation of life experiences and relationship networks so intricate that even veteran actors are challenged to recall their own characters' life stories. Revealing of viewers' similar conundrum, many of the question/answer columns in each week's *Soap Opera Digest* revolve around questions of backstory. Here's a fan query published in one recent column:

I need my memory refreshed. On Y&R [*The Young and the Restless*] years ago, when Kevin Fisher was first introduced, he set Gina's restaurant on fire and trapped Colleen. I believe that Colleen eventually figured out he was the one responsible and they developed a friendship before her death but does anyone else know the truth about Kevin's crimes? Did he ever serve any time for this? [And did Kevin] have anything to do with the attempt to electrocute Britany? I believe Bobby's mobster enemies were responsible but I can't remember (*Soap Opera Digest*, 90).

Scholar Mimi White argues that US soaps have a peculiar historiography in that "there is no single coherent linearity or teleology that organizes their historical trajectory" (348). The genre projects a sense of longevity and continuity at the same time as all narrative and character developments are inherently unstable: spouses return from the dead, heroes become villains and shift back into heroes, never-before-heard-of-children suddenly appear on the doorstep, and former siblings become lovers and then distant rivals. While even long-term viewers cannot remember every narrative detail as the query above attests, they hold a "vast wealth of information about character relations and past events in their heads" (338) and this knowledge is one of the key rewards of committing years of leisure time to a television show. But at the same time, this knowledge is tantamount to "memory without nostalgia" (350) in that every memory is potentially reversible or delete-able – even death. As journalist Larissa MacFarquhar writes (with tongue firmly in cheek), on soap opera there is:

> dead, there's definitely dead, and then, rarely, there's dead-dead-dead-dead, an exotic state that must be indicated by extremely violent means such as the shooting of many bullets at close range into a corpse already in the casket, or an on-camera suttee (71).

Soap operas are marked simultaneously by "continuity, longevity, memory, discontinuity, redundancy and forgetfulness" (White 340), with the only narrative certainty being that "things change, albeit slowly" (337).

My interest in this section is primarily how the industry itself manages this contradictory historiography, and how the broader legacy of soap operas or their place in entertainment history is being preserved. One of the industry casualties of the recession-related budget cuts was the loss of dedicated continuity experts on staff at the networks, employees whose sole job was to ensure that both 'long history' (are two characters related by either blood or family ties?) and 'short history' (is an actress wearing the same shade of lipstick in two subsequent scenes?) are preserved as necessary. However, continuity checks are built into every soap production system with script continuity the "first line of defense against unstable meaning [or] holes in the fictional world" (Levine 74). Scriptwriters are given scene-by-scene summaries of each episode's happenings, writers' meetings and producers' notes function to "hammer out questions about character motivation and plot convolutions," and scenes are traded internally by writers to ensure consistent voicing of distinctive actors/characters (74). Despite these efforts continuity slips are inevitable, requiring implicit leaps of logic to keep plotlines coherent. Explains *General Hospital* scriptwriter Elizabeth Korte in reference to an error made when a character said she was leaving for Paris the next day but actually left that same night:

> There's this thing called justifying where it's like, maybe we can believe that it was so traumatic that she broke up with [her boyfriend] that she left earlier. Or we do this; this is our favorite thing that we do. It's the yellow sticky. This is a willing suspension of disbelief ticket and sometimes when I'm just asking people to believe,

I'm like, take a yellow sticky. It's like, that's what you get, we're doing it, it's gotta be that way (quoted in Levine 74).

An alternative to the yellow sticky and used for more significant discontinuities is the practice of retroactive continuity or retconning – the deliberate alteration of previously established storyworld facts to accommodate current plot or character demands. Retconning is practiced in many serialized entertainment forms including soap operas, comics, movie franchises, and video games. Perhaps the most famous retcon in US soap history is the 1979 "Luke raped Laura" plot twist on *General Hospital*, in which a clear instance of sexual assault was retrospectively treated as a seduction of the female character given the unexpected popularity of the actor playing Luke (who was originally hired for a short-term role only), the network's newfound desire to keep him on-contract, and the gradual establishment of Luke-and-Laura (hyphenation required) as one of the legendary soap supercouples of all time. This seduction (re)-interpretation persisted for two decades until what might be termed a ret-retcon episode that featured Luke (played by the same actor) acknowledging to his son – whose own wife was just assaulted – that the incident with his son's mother was, in fact, rape. This re-ordered the fictional community's internal history as portrayed on-screen and the revelation (read: acknowledgement) reverberated for years on the show. Retconning is frequently used to align a soap's current plot or character shifts with an inconvenient or disagreeable narrative record.

There are two larger points to be made about these temporal devices used by soaps. The first – and I thank a reviewer for this insight – is that the genre offers a disruptive (if not subversive) challenge to the normative understanding of time and its passage as linear, causal, and progressive. The genre routinely distorts these expectations and requires its viewers to be flexible and open to alternate temporal structures, and thus by implication, alternate realities of age and aging. Feminist analyses of open-ended serials in the 1980s emphasized this issue strongly, arguing that soaps were a counter-hegemonic narrative format in celebrating the central element of "feminine" existence: waiting (deferred gratification). Since soap operas do not end, the hermeneutic code is broken – "truth for women is seen to lie 'not at the end of expectation,' but *in* expectation, not in the 'return to order,' but in (familial) disorder" (Modleski 88). The temporal structure of soap opera, including processes such as ret-conning/ret-retconning and

SORASing/de-SORASing, was thus argued to mimic the temporal rhythms of (female) viewers' lives – indeed, of the (Western) adult female experience.

My second larger point about these temporal devices is somewhat of a departure and speaks more to my scholarly location in sociology. I have been repeatedly surprised by how dismissive the gerontological and geriatric literatures (rooted in social sciences and neurosciences) are about the role of television – specifically soap operas – in older adult lives. TV is seen as a capitulation to the vagaries of aging, less an agentic leisure choice than a signal of cognitive inactivity if not actual impairment (for examples, see Lindstrom and colleagues or Fogel and Carlson). While older adults are advised by both physicians and advocacy agencies to 'keep the mind sharp' by doing crossword puzzles or Sudoku, the idea that *watching soap opera* might aid in mental agility would be considered laughable. In an empirical study I have yet to design or implement (but somebody should), I would hypothesize that the cognitive acuity required to manage soaps' unique historiography (White) over a decades-long viewing experience engages the very neural pathways needed to "age well" in that domain.

Challenges of history and memory faced by individual soaps (and individual viewers) are magnified when considering the industry as a whole. As Mary Jeanne Wilson points out, US soap operas present specific challenges in trying to access past programming since episodes are typically broadcast only once and the "endless middle" format renders boxed DVD sets marginal (140).[2] While soap operas have a prominent place in television history, they are poorly preserved in institutional archives. These archives were established in the 1960s and 1970s to help certify television's emergent status as an art form, but to that end they sought "quality programming" for their holdings (which by definition omitted soap opera; 141). In her analysis of the holdings at three major US archives,[3] Wilson points to tension

---

2   In exceptions to this claim, the dedicated cable channel SoapNet (2000-2013) ran same-day repeats of many US soap operas and networks release the occasional DVD of a milestone anniversary episode or a beloved character's biography.

3   These include Film and Television Archive at the University of California-Los Angeles, the Paley Center for Media, and the Library of Congress Motion Picture, Broadcasting & Recorded Sound division.

between the genre's open-ended format and the financial and spatial constraints of archives, resulting in a chaotic if not incomprehensible selection of programs. For example, UCLA's archives include 2,000 episodes of *General Hospital*, which has broadcast 13,000+ episodes since its debut in 1963, but only 91 episodes of *Guiding Light* (CBS), the longest-running program in radio/television history which aired 18,000+ episodes before its cancellation in 2009. The archive has only 10 episodes of *Generations* (NBC), a short-lived program (1989-1991) that nevertheless is crucial to US soap history in its featuring both a Black and a White core family. Virtually none of the early serials have survived, their kinescopes jettisoned long ago as a cost-cutting measure (150). Overall, UCLA's collection "pays little attention to the strong importance in continuity across episodes in soap opera storytelling" (145), which is detrimental to scholars but even more damaging to the future of the soap opera form:

With no way to view the evolution of a soap over time, much of the discussion about soap opera conventions and the so-called formulaic nature of the genre lack historical evidence to properly support these claims [. . .] What does it mean for soaps' future if we cannot reassemble its past? (151, 150)

While Wilson concludes on an encouraging note, pointing to fan archival practices as an emergent form of preserving soap history, she also acknowledges that copyright infringement risks and lack of comparable security/preservation measures mean that fan archives cannot (yet?) replace public, institutional archives. I type this in the context of the launch of TiVo Mega, a DVR that can hold *26,000 hours* of standard-definition TV programming (Couch). If we were also in an era of the launch of new daytime soap operas, the concern with archival practices would be tempered for future programming. As it is, the memories and histories of the soap opera form remain fragile indeed.

The Life Cycle of Soaps

In this final section I take a more meta-level approach in considering the life cycle or biography of the US soap opera form. Daytime soap operas anchored radio and TV broadcast schedules throughout most of the 20th century and came to be seen, by many, as a permanent fixture of the US television landscape. The genre reached its peak number (n=18) of soaps aired in 1969, and in each year of the next two decades at least a dozen soaps (usually more) were available to viewers. The late 1990s ushered in a wave of network cancellations and as of this writing, only four soaps remain on the air. The general consensus among viewers, journalists, and entertainment scholars is that a combined range of factors ushered in the decline of the genre, including labor market expansion to include greater numbers of female workers, internal competition in the daytime industry, emergent entertainment options including cable and internet, the global recession which impacted production budgets and storytelling quality, and gradually shifting viewer tastes (Ford, DeKosnik, and Harrington 2010). While the four remaining soaps are doing well in the ratings and serialized narratives are popular in both domestic and global markets (witness the recent return of the primetime TV mini-series, for example), the 'death' of the US daytime soap genre appears to many a *fait accompli*: the inevitable destiny of this long-standing cultural form.

In his discussion of processes of commoditization, Kopytoff points out that objects can have multiple biographies – economic, physical, and sociocultural – and encourages us in exploring the life story of a cultural object to ask questions similar to those we would pose about humans: "What has been its career so far, and what do people consider to be an ideal career for such things?" "What are the recognized 'ages' or periods in the thing's 'life,' and what are the cultural markers for them?" "How does the thing's use change with its age, and what happens to it when it reaches the end of its usefulness?" (66, 67). Recent press coverage on soaps' decline includes a repeated refrain that the genre belongs to a bygone era – when the audience was full-time homemakers, when time-shifting technologies were non-existent, and when attention spans for a daily hour-long fictional narrative were not challenged by YouTube and TEDTalks and 6-second vines. Declaring that soaps' "time has come," many critics (and viewers alike) have dried their tears, bid a fond farewell, and re-positioned the genre firmly in broadcasting history:

No young viewer will *ever* be convinced that a soap opera that was around in grandma's age could ever be cool... they need shows for their own generation. For the mature or maturing soap opera viewer, I think this requires acceptance. Like Elvis, the Beatles [and] *All in the Family*...all had their place in history...so too perhaps the soaps need to be relegated to the past. They served a function and great value, and their impacts will linger, but maybe "worlds without end" is too much to expect in a society undergoing such rapid social and technological change.[4]

The infantilization thesis of aging – although thoroughly rebuked by contemporary gerontologists – provides an interesting conceptual framework through which to think through soap opera's later years. In short, this thesis suggests that aging is essentially cyclical, returning older adults to an infantile state (or second childhood) marked by dependency, diminished responsibilities and capacities, and child-like personalities and preferences. Rejected as inaccurate and ageist by experts in age and aging, the thesis lives on in the popular imagination, a frequent trope in greeting cards, movie roles, TV advertisements, and comic strips. In their critique of the thesis, Arnold Arluke and Jack Levin point to six different ways that second childhood is portrayed in popular culture, including old people given the dress of children, children and old people paired with each other, and role reversal of old people and their offspring such that the elderly become the children of their own children (22). The Sunday newspaper I received two days ago includes an 8-panel comic strip featuring a heterosexual middle-aged couple negotiating complex car pool arrangements for the husband's elderly mother and her friends. The strip ends with the wife remarking, "Have we been here before?" and the husband replying, "It does seem vaguely familiar" (Dunagin and Summers). While Arluke and Levin emphasize the negative consequences of such (mis)-representations, including the disempowerment of adults who might otherwise work for social and political change (24), the second childhood thesis remains firmly entrenched in popular media forms.

What does this have to do with US daytime soap operas? There has been an interesting return in televised soaps to the theatrical days of the genre's storied past, when 15-minute radio serials unfolded live on-air[5] and any mistakes – by narrator, actor, or on-set musician – had to be absorbed

---

4   Viewer data collected by the author for separate project. The comments were made by a 42-year-old male who has been watching soap operas since he was 8 years old. Emphasis and ellipses in the original.

5   Painted Dreams, created by the legendary Irna Phillips and debuting in 1930, is considered the first radio soap in the US.

improvisationally or simply ignored. In part this has been a purposeful ratings gambit within the industry, most notably via *One Life to Live*'s (ABC) highly publicized full-length live-on-air episode toward the end of the series' run (1968-2012) or even Executive Producer Christopher Goutman's confession that he briefly considered ("for about three seconds") bringing back the live format as a final send-off to *As The World Turns* (CBS) (1956-2010; McClure). More pointedly, however, is the unwelcomed return to near-improvisation forced by budget cuts. Lavish studio sets, leisurely rehearsal periods, and opportunities for multiple takes were routine in soaps' golden era of the 1980s but gave way by the 2000s to a rapid-fire production schedule resulting in comical on-screen errors – a front door refusing to open, a cellphone answered before it rings, an actor seen crouching at the top of a staircase that plainly leads nowhere, and so on. At the 2010 meetings of the Society for Cinema and Media Studies, a session attended by soap stars Tristan Rogers and Lisa LoCicero broke out in laughter when LoCicero exclaimed that the budget is so tight that unless an actor "pees on the carpet" during a scene (a reference perhaps unwittingly invoking infantilization), the days of re-takes are over. Actor Shemar Moore recently confirmed this, saying that after 10 years performing in primetime his brief return to daytime (on CBS' *The Young and the Restless*) was a shock:

> They go way faster! We used to ask for second, third and fourth tries and there is none of that [now]. That's a lot of pressure [. . .] I'm going to love going back to [my primetime show] *Criminal Minds* tomorrow with my seven pages and six lines that I get to do 48 times each (Stacy 32).

In another example, CBS' *Guiding Light*, the longest-running broadcast narrative in entertainment history (1937-2009), underwent radical changes in its production model in 2008-2009 in an unsuccessful effort to slash costs and thus save the show. There was no opportunity to test the new model prior to implementation, so glitches such as the sound of rain muffling actors' lines during outdoor shoots had to be resolved in real time and on-air (Erwin 183), much as early radio serials absorbed an actor's sneeze or the unexpected scrape of a microphone stand on the studio floor. Moreover, the new production model entailed a much smaller cast and vignette storytelling – short scenes with only one or two characters more reminiscent of the kitchen-table-slice-of-life approach taken by early radio soaps than the long-range story arcs associated with modern, established TV soap operas (182). Both actors and viewers reacted negatively to the new model – soap star Maureen Garrett said, "If this is what has to be done to save the [soap opera] form, I think there's room for debate about trying to preserve the process, too" (Erwin 185) – and it proved unable to save the show from cancellation.

However, an alternate reading of the infantilization thesis implies that an object's end-of-life return to its roots is marked not by dependency and vulnerability but rather coherence and closure: a "good death" if you will (Harrington, Shneidman). Thanatological literature suggests that a good human death is one that is both expected and prepared for, and the same might be argued for good object death – though in the case of television that remains an uncertainty afforded only primetime hits that can pre-negotiate their own end-date (e.g., *Lost* or *Breaking Bad*) and the world of daytime soap operas, whose creative teams are given months to pay homage to their fictional community and its residents. Jean Passanante, head-writer of *As the World Turns* (CBS) at the end of its 54-year run, emphasized continuity and cyclicality in reassuring viewers in advance of the on-screen ending: "We don't burn the house down or anything! What we wanted to suggest is that there's a place for these characters in our imagination, always [. . .] Birth, death, love and marriage – all those things are reflected in the last episode" (McClure). The genre's recent return to its theatrical roots might thus be read either negatively (as infantilization) or positively (as coherence).

Conclusion

To return to Dennis Porter's notion of soap opera time, this chapter has highlighted both the opportunities and challenges associated with the "diachronic capaciousness" (783) of US daytime soaps. Opportunities include the richness of the daily scripted format combined with the loyalty of both viewers and actors to the genre, allowing for a consideration of the unfolding of one's own life course in context of fictional ones unfolding in the same temporal framework. Viewers have a genuine sense of growing up with their favorite characters and communities, and actors report the unexpected pleasures of living dual lives, learning from their character's maturation in ways that inform and transform their own. From an industry perspective, soaps offer a unique ability for writers to mine their show's own history, drawing threads through decades-old events into story reverberations unfolding in the present; flashbacks on open-ended soaps are the best the world of TV entertainment has to offer in terms of representational memory, with original footage from the 1960s, 70s, 80s and 90s and (often) the same actors appearing on-screen in both past and the present. The rewards of long-term viewership are, to this soap fan at least, unparalleled.

Soaps' temporalities present challenges as well, from the marginalized status of aging out of soaps' target demographic experienced by both longtime viewers and veteran actors, to the dearth of on-screen representations of the realities of age and aging, to the discomfort actors experience in seeing themselves and their colleagues grow older in character, in real time, and in high definition, to the erratic preservation of the genre in professional archives, and to the questionable return to theatrical roots characteristic of the genre in recent years. US soaps were designed to tell stories *about* a multi-generational fictional community *to* a multi-generational real-life community of viewers, inviting women, men (hopefully), and children (ideally) to live with and through "the stories" in powerfully intimate ways. At their best, soap operas are akin to juicy novels that never end, and while their recent decline on US network television has been noteworthy they remain a model form of serialized storytelling.

WORKS CITED

Adams, Alina. "Sex and SORAS (Soap Opera Rapid Aging Syndrome)." *Entertainment Weekly Online*. Entertainment Weekly Inc., 5 Aug. 2014. Web. 12 Sept. 2014.

Arluke, Arnold, and Jack Levin. "Second Childhood." *Public Communication Review* 1.2 (1982): 21-25. Print.

Bordewich, Fergus M. "Why Are College Kids in a Lather Over TV Soap Operas?" *New York Times* 20 Oct. 1974: 157. Print.

Cassata, Mary, and Barbara Irwin. "Young by Day: The Older Person on Daytime Serial Drama." *Cross-Cultural Communication and Aging in the United States*. Ed. Hana S. Noor Al-deen. Mahwah, NJ: Lawrence Erlbaum Associates, 1997. 215-230. Print.

Couch, Aaron. "TiVo to Unveil DVR with 26,000 Hours of Storage Space." *The Hollywood Reporter*. The Hollywood Reporter, 8 Sept. 2014. Web. 9 Sept. 2014.

Dunagin, Ralph, and Dana Summers. "The Middletons." *Cincinnati Enquirer* 31 Aug 2014: Fun (comics insert), no page. Print.

Erwin, Patrick. "Guiding Light: Relevance and Renewal in a Changing Genre." *The Survival of Soap Opera: Strategies for a New Media Era*. Eds. Sam Ford, Abigail DeKosnik, and C. Lee Harrington. Jackson: University Press of Mississippi, 2010. 180-186. Print.

Featherstone, Mike, and Mike Hepworth. "Images of Aging: Cultural Representations of Later Life." *The Cultural Context of Aging* (3rd edition). Ed. Jay Sokolovsky. Westport: Praeger, 2009. 134-144. Print.

Fogel, Joshua and Michelle C. Carlson. "Soap Operas and Talk Shows on Television are Associated with Poorer Cognition in Older Women." *Southern Medical Journal* 99.3 (2006): 226-233. Print.

Ford, Sam, Abigail DeKosnik, and C. Lee Harrington (Eds.). *The Survival of Soap Opera: Strategies for a New Media Era*. Jackson: University Press of Mississippi, 2010. Print.

Harrington, C. Lee. "The *Ars Moriendi* of US Serial Television: Towards a Good Textual Death." *International Journal of Cultural Studies* 16.6 (2012): 579-595. Print.

Harrington, C. Lee, and Denise D. Bielby. "Autobiographical Reasoning in Long-Term Fandom." *Transformative Works and Cultures* 5 (2010). Web.

Harrington, C. Lee, and Denise Brothers. "A Life Course Built for Two: Acting, Aging, and Soap Operas." *Journal of Aging Studies* 24.1 (2010): 20-29. Print.

Harrington, C. Lee, and Denise Brothers. "Constructing the Older Audience: Age and Aging in Soaps." *The Survival of Soap Opera: Strategies for a New Media Era*. Eds. Sam Ford, Abigail DeKosnik, and C. Lee Harrington. Jackson: University Press of Mississippi, 2010. 300-314. Print.

Harwood, Jake, and Karen Anderson. "The Presence and Portrayal of Social Groups on Prime-Time Television." *Communication Reports* 15.2 (2002): 81-97. Print.

Healey, Tim, and Karen Ross. "Growing Old Invisibly: Older Viewers Talk Television." *Media, Culture & Society* 24 (2002): 105-120. Print.

Ibarra, Sergio. "Nielsen: Older Audiences Getting Bigger." *TVBizWire*. Dexter Canfield Media Inc, 29 Aug. 2008. Web. 22 July 2009.

Kessler, Eva-Marie, Katrin Rakoczy, and Ursula M. Staudinger. "The Portrayal of Older People in Prime Time Television Series: The Match with Gerontological Evidence." *Ageing & Society* 24 (2004): 531-552. Print.

Kopytoff, Igor. "The Cultural Biography of Things: Commoditization as Process." *The Social Life of Things*. Ed. Arjun Appadurai. Cambridge: Cambridge University Press, 1986. 64-91. Print.

Lauren, Martha M., David M. Dozier, and Barbara Reyes. "From Adultescents to Zoomers: An Examination of Age and Gender in Prime-Time Television." *Communication Quarterly* 55.3 (2007): 343-357. Print.

Levin, Gary. "Network Audiences Showing Their Age." *USA Today*. USA TODAY, 19 June 2009. Web. 23 July 2009.

Levine, Elana. "Toward a Paradigm for Media Production Research: Behind the Scenes at General Hospital." *Critical Studies in Media Communication* 18.1 (2001): 66-82. Print.

Lidz, Frank. "Slippery Soaps." *Portfolio*. American City Business Journals, 29 Jan. 2009. Web. 23 July 2009.

Lindstrom, Heather A., Thomas Fritsch, Grace Petot, Kathleen A. Syth, Chien H. Chen, and Sara M. Debanne. "The Relations Between Television Viewing in Midlife and the Development of Alzheimer's Disease in a Case-Control Study." *Brain and Cognition* 58 (2005): 157-165. Print.

MacFarquhar, Larissa. "Oakdale Days." *The New Yorker* 15 April 2002: 64-71. Print.

McClure, Danielle. "That's a Wrap." *Soap Opera Digest* 9 Sept. 2010: 76-79. Print.

McLean, Kate C., Monisha Pasupathi, and Jennifer L. Pals. "Selves Creating Stories Creating Selves: A Process Model of Self-Development." *Personality and Social Psychology Review* 11.3 (2007): 262–78. Print.

McClure, Danielle. "Last Merry-Go-Round." *Soap Opera Digest* 21 Sept. 2010: 44-47. Print.

Modleski, Tania. *Loving With a Vengeance: Mass-Produced Fantasies for Women*. Hamden, Connecticut: Archon Books, 2010. Print.

O'Connell, Michael. "'Alpha Boomer': TV Networks' Attempt Rebrand of Older Viewers." *The Hollywood Reporter*. The Hollywood Reporter, 9 Sept. 2012. Web. 9 Sept. 2012.

Pasupathi, Monisha, and Emma Mansour. "Adult age differences in autobiographical reasoning in narratives." *Developmental Psychology* 42.5 (2006): 798-808. Print.

Porter, Dennis. "Soap Time: Thoughts on a Commodity Art Form." *College English* 38.8 (1977): 782-788. Print.

Scodari, Christine. *Serial Monogamy: Soap Opera, Lifespan, and the Gendered Politics of Fantasy*. Cresskill, New Jersey: Hampton Press, 2004. Print.

Shneidman, Edwin S. "Criteria for a Good Death." *Suicide and Life-Threatening Behavior* 37.3 (2007): 245-247. Print.

Soap Opera Digest. "Ask Us: We've Got the Answers." 8 Sept. 2014: 88-91. Print.

Soap Opera Digest. "Art Imitates Life for ATWT's Pinter." 29 Jan. 2008: 12. Print.

Soap Opera Digest. "My Two Dads." 6 March 2007: 63. Print.

Soap Opera Digest. "Baby (Not) On Board." 27 Feb. 2007: 63. Print.

Soap Opera Digest. "Millennium Moments." 4 Jan. 2000: 52-55. Print.

Stacy, Tom. "Moore Encore." *Soap Opera Digest* 8 Sept. 2014: 30-32. Print.

Turow, Joseph. *Breaking Up America: Advertisers and the New Media World*. Chicago and London: University of Chicago Press, 1997. Print.

White, Mimi. "Women, Memory and Serial Melodrama." *Screen* 35.4 (1994): 336-353. Print.

Wilson, Mary Jeanne. "Preserving Soap History: What Will It Mean for the Future of Soaps?" *The Survival of Soap Opera: Strategies for a New Media Era*. Eds. Sam Ford, Abigail DeKosnik, and C. Lee Harrington. Jackson: University Press of Mississippi, 2010. 140-153. Print.

TELEVISION AND FILM

Another World. Creators Irna Phillips and William J. Bell, NBC (1964-1999).

As the World Turns. Creator Irna Phillips, CBS (1956-2010).

The Bold and the Beautiful. Creators William J. Bell and Lee Phillip Bell, CBS, (1987-present).
Breaking Bad. Creator Vince Gilligan, AMC (2008-2013).
Days of Our Lives. Creators Ted Corday and Betty Corday, NBC (1965-present).
General Hospital. Creators Frank and Doris Hursley, ABC (1963-present); SOAPnet (2000-2013).
Guiding Light. Creator Irna Phillips, NBC Radio (1937-1947); CBS Radio (1947-1952); CBS Television (1952-2009).
Lost. Creators Jeffrey Lieber, J. J. Abrams and Damon Lindelof, ABC (2004-2010).
One Life to Live. Creator Agnes Nixon, ABC (1968-2012); The Online Network (TOLN) (2013).
The Young & the Restless. Creators William J. Bell and Lee Phillip Bell, CBS (1973-2013); TVGN/Pop (2013-present).

Business as Usual

Retirement on *The Wire*

NEAL KING

The retirement of Detective Lester Freamon from the Baltimore Police Department, at the end of five seasons of the U.S. cable television serial *The Wire*, differs from that of his contemporaries in cinema, in ways that owe to the organization of the prime-time serial (PTS). This show and others like it (e.g., *Homicide: Life on the Street*, *The Shield*, *Southland*) have returned cop-focused storytelling to the degree of cynicism not seen on cinema screens since the early 1970s. In those early days of the cop action genre, fatalism ran deep as cops found that organizations constrained them from doing their jobs as they saw fit. Many at least considered quitting in disgust, shot criminals in cold blood without authorization, killed their manipulative bosses, or died in the line of duty, in such films as *Dirty Harry*, *Magnum Force*, *The French Connection*, *Badge 373*, *The New Centurions*, *Electra Glide in Blue*, and *Busting*. The recent return to this level of cynicism about police work, after decades, owes not to some shift in zeitgeist. It results instead from the development, in television production, of stories so long (dozens of hours) that scripts can detail the operation of bureaucracy rather than just the progress of an individual hero.

However, this attention to the constraining force of social structure does not extend to the gender and age relations that also shape Detective Freamon's retirement. In that portrayal, relations of inequality go unremarked. I demonstrate this by reviewing first the innovation of long form storytelling in television production, then how *The Wire* uses that tool to focus on organizational policy, and finally what relations of inequality go unexamined in its depiction of a hero's retirement. I conclude by suggesting that the paradox of a television series that makes a star out of an unassuming, publicity shy detective may have motivated that ignorance of age and gender privilege.

A Complex Story

The Wire results from a series of shifts in television production that freed screenwriters from the constraints of the stand-alone episode. First, Mittell notes that new means of playing back television shows proliferated over the last few decades, making it more likely that viewers could watch enough serial episodes, in sequence, to find the larger story satisfying and return for more (31). Time-shifting thus freed storytellers from the old stand-alone episode format that dominated broadcast-only television for decades before (Mittell, Ndalianis).

Cable television producers such as Home Box Office (HBO) and Showtime were willing to pay for the production of such serials for several years at a time because their business models focused on luring subscribers to their channels with prestigious shows. Serials could generate prestige that drew subscribers if they were suitably complex and intriguing, because those could inspire cultish following and much public conversation. And television was better positioned than cinema to do this:

> While innovative film narration has emerged as a "boutique" form over the past years in the guise of puzzle films like *Memento* and *Adaptation*, the norms of Hollywood still favor spectacle and formulas suitable for a peak opening weekend; comparatively, many narratively complex programs are among the medium's biggest hits. ... [and] appeal to a boutique audience of more upscale educated viewers who typically avoid television. (Mittell 31)

The attachment of viewers to a PTS, such that they return reliably, discuss it with friends, and even 'binge-watch' in several-episode doses, owes in part to the tendency of a many-hour long series to inspire interest in recurring characters (Newman 16). With serial plotting clarified by redundant verbal reminders of progress, articulated sometimes in voiceovers but mainly in exchanges between characters, series indulge their fans in many hours of conversation among characters about the events of the show, including their emotional responses, ones often shared by the viewers (18). The result is a particularly strong suture, generative of a cultish devotion to a show.

Finally, the proliferation of lateral media such as consumer-authored websites allows fans to elaborate their enthusiasm by sharing thoughts with each other, to build a 'collective intelligence' great enough to track complex narratives and sustained shared focus and pleasure (Mittell 31). They can remind each other of plot points easily forgotten or missed, keep each other up with the stories, and affirm each other's zeal. As Altman describes the consumption of film genres per se,

> knowledge that others found pleasure in the same genre even made it possible for genres to stand in for an absent community. With the growth of cinema culture, favoured not only by commercial interest but also by the need to constitute constellated communities in response to a loss of presence, genres concretized cinema's promise of community. Journalistic critics offered imaginary discussion partners, fan magazines established an instant peer group; film-related paraphernalia offered interpenetration between the film world and the daily world. (187)

This level of engagement, when extended over months and even years, can make a character familiar, his actions important to a fan. "The more interesting television characters grow and change over time, creating layers of depth in their metamorphoses" (Porter, Larson, Harthcock, Nellis 23). Indeed, most television shows have followed the Hollywood storytelling path toward novelistic focus on characters with rich inner lives implied, goals explicated, journeys followed. "Characters act as if they have been going about their daily activities from one prime-time evening's program to the following week's episode. And writers often encourage the notion that the characters lead off-screen lives." Exposed to such storytelling week after week, season after season, audiences may grow especially close to characters, a relationship to character that is "a defining quality of television narratives" (Porter, et al. 24).

The formulaic Hollywood feature-film script is limited by its brevity to presenting one, two, or sometimes a handful of protagonists whose attempts to achieve goals organize the story (Thompson 1999). The PTS, by developing the character from episode to episode, can combine the novelistic/theatrical approach of the Hollywood film, in which the character undergoes changes within a 1-3 hour period, and expand that into a multi-year experience.

Characterization in the PTS is more likely to have a certain kind of depth as the audience knows more about the characters' inner lives in serials than in many episodic shows. Especially in comparison to the episodic drama represented by the recent crop of procedurals in the mold of *Law & Order*, the PTS is a character-driven form, and this is one thing that makes it more easily figured as "quality TV" in popular and critical discourse. (Porter, et al. 24)

However, this is not the only path that the creators of *The Wire* followed. Serial narrative can use its length to field a much larger set of protagonists than can the two-hour feature film. By doing this, it can expand its focus to whole organizations and communities rather than individuals, couples, and very small groups.

Consider the pitch made by producer/writer David Simon, to the cable channel that produced the show. In his invidious comparison to more episodic shows, Simon promised to

create a cop show that seizes the highest qualitative ground through realism, good writing, and a more honest and more brutal assessment of police, police work, and the drug culture ... stepping up to the network ideal, pronouncing it a cheap lie, and offering instead a view of the world that is every bit as provocative as *The Sopranos* or *The Corner*. But because that world of cops and robbers is so central to the American TV experience, *The Wire* would stand as even more of a threat to the established order. (*The Wire*)

The order that Simon proposed to threaten was one that focused, as most television narratives do, on a few protagonists, as though crime issued from the proclivities of such individuals, as though public policy made little difference. Simon proposed instead to depict how urban organizations, especially bureaucratic ones, force employees to answer to long chains of command, some of which have only the most political of goals (e.g., win election to civic office, or gain promotion by supporting someone who does); that those political goals are most easily met by false shows of success in crime-prevention (e.g., by providing false statistical evidence of drops in rates of crime); and that those hoping to curry favor with rising politicians will aid them by producing those false results. He would show how this organization fosters political career-making and not only impedes law enforcement but actually allows destructive crime to go unchecked. That is, the mass homicide that plagues the poor, Black communities of Baltimore goes unpunished, uninvestigated, because careerist manipulators pull support from police work where it is needed most. This bureaucratic chicanery thus maintains racial and class oppression in the city. Where shows such as *CSI* and *NYPD Blue* depict protagonists vanquishing clearly demarcated foes, as though through sheer force of will or as if no impediments could block them, Simon would show that the mundane operation of bureaucratic corporations, city halls, public schools, newspapers, governors' offices, and police departments force cops and civilians to make choices that they otherwise would not, making criminals of most. In this vision, urban systems both defeat even the strongest of heroes, and perpetuate racism and poverty of the U.S. city.

This represents a break from Hollywood screenwriting formula, in which relations of race and class are subject to heroic intervention, and in which heroes who fail do so when beaten only by rival characters or overwhelmed by nature or fate. On *The Wire*, audiences watch not how individual characters meet goals against opposition, but instead how bureaucracies limit challenges to their authority, usually by defeating the protagonists in whose goals we become invested in our audience sympathy. On this show, organizations defeat the mavericks who break their rules in pursuit of noble goals, and reward those who appear to follow them for the sake of personal advancement. This, between promotion-hungry grooming of bureaucratic careers and the rule-breaking innovation that could solve or prevent crimes ("real police" work, in the parlance of the show), is the principal moral opposition of this series (Linkon, Russo, and Russo). And *The Wire* consistently links that struggle to the ingrained, racial poverty that fosters crime and hampers lives.

Taking advantage of five years of running time (nearly sixty hours, about thirty times the length of the average feature film produced in Hollywood), the series makes much of the endurance of institutional routine. It links successes and failures to the promotion of personnel within organizations, which they achieve by manipulating bureaucracies in ways that tend to disrupt heroes' investigations. Those who manipulate systems to appear as if they are meeting organizational goals (i.e., by 'juking' crime statistics to make it seem as if crime rates are lower than they are), profit by doing so. Those who refuse or even just inadvertently hinder such machinations lose their organizational support, which tends to curtail their investigative police work and so allows destructive crime (usually, homicide) to go unchecked. The show teaches this lesson dozens of times over five years by taking the time necessary to set up the investigations, show how racial inequalities are affected by the crime, demonstrate heroes' early successes and potential for more, and then depict the interference of bureaucrats as they climb their promotional ladders. The point is at all times to link long-term realization of goals to bureaucratic machination rather than to real police work, and to suggest that the machinations sustain inequality. This is the harsh lesson that Simon sought the time to teach.

However, this is not to say that the show focuses on all social relations. I turn next to those that go largely unremarked, before I turn to the depiction of a main character's gendered retirement.

Age and Gender

Relations of inequality that go largely unexamined in this show include gender and age. As a result, masculinity and middle age look much as they do in other depictions of cop work.

Masculinity is a form of *culture*, the activities by which groups distinguish among them, everything that some do differently than others do. Masculinity is what groups do to distinguish men from others and claim privileges that others cannot as easily claim for themselves. Those activities vary with time and place but have included the association with men of breadwinning labor defined as 'skilled' (in contrast to the less skilled and less valued work that women and children do); unpaid ways of playing and staying hard, through athletic recreation and sexual intercourse that bolsters their claim to be uniquely qualified to do the skilled work; and avoidance of formal dependency and most open expressions of grief, fear, or concern for others' needs, which characterize many forms of femininity. By celebrating such behavior even when they do not act in those ways, men maintain claims to women's unpaid support, and to the most highly rewarded jobs and positions of authority (King and Calasanti).

Relations of age likewise distinguish groups in terms of their claims on formal and informal support. Like masculinity, middle age is a form of culture, distinguishing some people from younger and older ones (Pietilä, Ojala, King, Calasanti). Ideals of middle age pose such people as especially fit for paid labor (in contrast to the retirement of older people and the less well paid labor of their less experienced juniors), decreasingly hard forms of work and play (in contrast to the exertions of youth and the relative passivity of old age), and a relative lack of formal and informal dependency. Celebrating such, middle aged people stake their claims to high rates of pay and celebration as productive citizens, as well as the unpaid support that they may request of retired kin.

Organizational policies that maintain these claims of the middle aged to the most rewarding work include those of "early exit", "age management", "redundancy" aimed at shuttling old people off their jobs (Chudacoff; Brooke and Taylor; Duncan). Laws notes that "exit from the labor force ... has played an important ideological role in defining old age" (114-15). In this cultural context, popular depictions of retirement may play small roles in shaping debate over controversial policies.

These age and sex specific ideals of labor, recreation, and dependency change with time and place, such that middle-aged men are more emotionally demonstrative, technically proficient, somber, etc., in some times and places than in others. What remains constant is the privilege granted to mid-adulthood and manhood. In the U.S. context, these relations of gender and age advantage middle-aged men as the highest status workers, the experienced and skilled breadwinners whose work keeps our cities in motion, whose guidance helps others find their places, who appear not to depend upon anyone.

Such advantages result from many organized group activities, including the policies of many bureaucracies. And a PTS could investigate those if it was so inclined. For instance, women do much unpaid support work in homes, which goes unrecognized by most groups as anything other than expression of familial love. The lack of public recognition of this labor allows men to appear to be either self-sustaining, inherently lovable, or both. I show next how *The Wire* depends upon this organization of labor and love without adding that to its analysis of urban life.

Freamon Stands Down

As one might expect in the cultural context of the age and gender relations outlined above, *The Wire* establishes Freamon as a man who takes pride in being highly skilled, experienced and knowledgeable, "real" or "natural police," and has no obvious wish to slow down, much less retire. He is romantically paired with a much younger woman; and he retires only when made to do so by the grinding force of bureaucracy on real police work.

Simon's pitch-script for the first episode describes the character to the potential funding agency at HBO:

Black detective, pawn-shop unit, 50-55. Is seemingly an empty suit gliding toward his pension, working in a paper unit with stacks of 3 x 5 cards. He's dumped on [the newly forming wiretap squad] when they ask for additional manpower and they regard him as fairly useless until he gradually and gently begins to show them that he is an extremely adept cop who has, for political reasons, been dumped into hibernation by the department – for once having attempted to do police work ... Lester is quiet, taciturn and oddly gracious in his actions. He says as little as possible, but always produces. He is widowed, with a quiet eye for whatever women stray near. (*The Wire*)

We first see Freamon stuck in a lonely office (the "paper unit" mentioned in the pitch above), passing the time by working another trade, the production of dollhouse furniture. Like all that he does, Freamon's craft requires patience, attention to detail, and indifference to what his colleagues might think. And like his investigative work, it yields great rewards if allowed to do so by the bureaucracy within which he toils. As fellow cops on the squad come to know Freamon, a more knowledgeable colleague notes that "he makes more money off of that [dollhouse] shit than you do off of this [police] job. Don't let Lester fool you ... he's natural police; he used to be homicide" ("Old Cases", 1.4).

Indeed, later in the same episode, Freamon confirms his status as "real police" by answering a colleague's questions, about how his banishment to the paper unit resulted from having offended a superior:

So, why'd they let you out of the box? Why now?
I guess they just forgot about me.

Shit, Lester. You back from the dead. You rolled away the stone. Bunk Moreland says you're natural police. One of the few.
Yeah, I've had my moments.

Though able to use a weapon and arrest a violent offender, Freamon does not focus on combat but prefers routine fact-checking and discovery, usually through the inspection of media (archived paperwork, recorded conversations) at a desk. As he explains to young colleagues, "this is the job" ("The Wire", 1.6). So long as he does this in service of the aggressive investigation of destructive crime, directed toward successful prosecution of threats to the safety of impoverished groups, he finds this to be a dignified pursuit, "natural police" work.

He illustrates the show's principal opposition by choosing "real police" work over bureaucratic advancement. His dialogue includes observations that may as well come directly from the writer about the relations of capital and destructive crime; noticing investments by drug dealers in legitimate business and politicians, he notes that, "more than the drugs, it's the money that matters" ("Game Day", 1.9).

Figure 1: Freamon mentors junior cops in tedious record-keeping done in a basement of a bureaucracy that does not care: "This is the job."

Source: DVD frame grab

Freamon increases surveillance of the drug dealers during the first season by wiring a sex worker in the club that they use as a base of operations. He flirts with the worker, as he puts her in danger, and before long appears to have begun an intimate relationship. The actress playing the character is sixteen years younger than Clarke Peters who plays Freamon; and the relationship appears at least to verge on being an intergenerational one.

The show pays little other attention to Freamon's private life and backstory, though it mentions military training and thus implies service during the Vietnam conflict. And the former sex worker Shardene recedes to the background of the show, appearing thereafter only as Freamon's girlfriend. She shows up once during the second season, to testify to Freamon's character. She reports going to "Nursing school right now ... Lester's been pushing me, you know? He does it, kind of without you know that he's doing it."

The detective speaking with Shardene echoes the lesson about Freamon's quiet effectiveness: "Yeah, I know what you mean" ("All Prologue", 2.6). Though we learn once more how potent Freamon is, we never learn what moves Shardene to stay in this relationship with a man nearly old enough to be her father. Her actions remain unmotivated by anything other than by the force of Freamon's personality.

In subsequent seasons, Freamon continues as before, investigating political corruption along with street-level dealing through careful management of data and his knowledge of the local community and operation of city and state bureaucracies. He deals in paperwork more than in violence, but remains a dedicated cop, indifferent to the self-promotion and short-term payoffs rewarded by the bureaucracy of the police department. He focuses his attention on such crimes as systemic corruption and mass violence that tend to make life harder for the impoverished communities of Baltimore.

In the fourth season, he comes as close to open defiance as he ever does, when he threatens to go to a friendly judge for help in his resistance to bureaucratic efforts to shut his anti-corruption unit down. He faces off against the most politically savvy self-promoter among his commanders, who notes with amusement that, "if memory serves, this isn't the first time a deputy ops felt the need to bury you. You have a gift for martyrdom" ("Home Rooms", 4.3).

To this assessment of his martyrdom, Freamon shrugs and smiles in pride (see Figure 2). When the commander presses Freamon on his weakest spot, threatening young colleagues to whom Freamon is loyal, the detective relents. He loses his investigative unit and thus much of his real police work. Though defeated, he is also rewarded, both for his political concession and for his investigative skills, by reassignment to the prestigious homicide bureau. This plotting maintains the focus both on Freamon's admirable qualities and also on his losses to the power of the organization.

Figure 2: Freamon smiles in pride at having offended bureaucrats, and having endured punishment by one, in pursuit of his work.

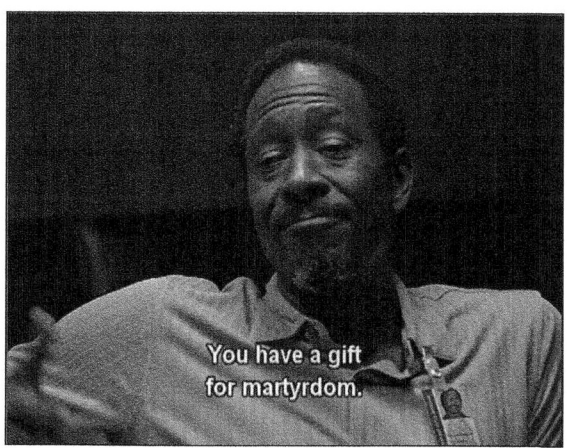

Source: DVD frame grab

In the fifth season, Freamon hopes to bring a case against mass killers of poor people in the drug trade, and decides to cooperate with a rogue colleague in a fraud that will enlarge their budget in the homicide bureau, so that he can do his real police work, serve the African American communities about which he cares, once again.[1] When the fraud comes to

---

1 The rogue cops manufacture evidence of sexual serial killing, to inspire newspaper coverage of the salacious details, and in turn mayoral support for the homicide unit. They then use the newly granted resources to track the actual killers of poor people in the ghetto.

light at the end of the season and series, he is banished once more to a non-investigative job, and elects to retire at that point. Celebrated by his former colleagues, he returns to making his dollhouse furniture at home. A brief moment during the show's final montage shows Shardene distracting him from his trade with a show of amorous affection. He appears to have retired, but only partially, to a life of financial security; a chosen trade; and physical pleasure with a much younger, very nurturing woman.

Figure 3: Freamon collects his reward at the conclusion of the show, an extremely nurturing partner in domestic bliss.

Source: DVD frame grab

This fictional retirement fits a pattern already documented in U.S. cop action movies, in which loss of job offends the performance-orientation of masculinity. In a previous study of cop action cinema produced in Hollywood (King "Old Cops"), I found that recent retirements by movie-cop heroes fit into three patterns: refusal, as in the case of cops who have announced plans to retire but who remain on the job regardless; death, in the case of corrupt cops who were nearing retirement; and compensation, in the form of glamorous romance. In the latter, most common pattern, actresses (most of whom have worked as models in the past and thus represent the highest end of Hollywood beauty) play opposite actors who are older than they are, in stories that end in romantic union for the retiring heroes, who appear to take satisfaction in the domestic bliss after the loss of their professional prestige. In all three cases, the lesson is that retirement is bad: to be avoided, interchangeable with death, tolerable only under conditions of romance that elevates, or at least celebrates, the high status of the men. If they cannot be taken care of very well by subordinated women, then these men prefer not to retire at all. The genre includes acknowledgement of the fact of occupational aging, as when heroes at forty years of age remark that they're "too old for this shit" (*Lethal Weapon* movies); but retirement remains a poor choice for them.

Such storytelling assumes that the female characters who devote themselves to the care of much older lovers have no qualms about serving in these subordinating roles, even though daily life in the U.S. middle class features little of this cross-generational romance. The vast majority of heterosexual married couples in the U.S. today are within several years of being the same age. And large gaps in age have been associated mainly with patriarchal family forms, in regions where women have extremely low status (Casterline, Williams, and McDonald).

I found that this subordination of women had little to do with the organization of retirement among police officers in the U.S. and looked more like the careers of aging Hollywood stars instead, in which retirement from the glamorous profession can feel like a social death, for which very wealthy stars compensate by taking very young lovers as signs of their high status. Because few women maintain stardom into old age, the vast majority of these aging bearers of status are men, their partners usually much younger women.

Indeed, by pairing Detective Freamon with a sweet-tempered, beautiful, cooperative, experienced sex worker nearly a generation behind him in age, who allows him to push her to become, of all things, a nurse, the writers of *The Wire* have given him a form of unpaid care and support at home that one would typically find in a patriarchal community, one that subordinated women to enhance the status of powerful men. Absent an analysis of how such women wind up caring for such men, in a show known for its analysis of inequalities, the placement of Shardene in this role looks like a throwback to patriarchy, the provision of unpaid service to men by low status women. In other words, it looks like a screenwriter's cheat, an anachronistic provision of patriarchal status to an otherwise beleaguered, low status character for being heroic.

What distinguishes Freamon's retirement from the claims to male privilege in cinema is the defeat that brings his retirement about. Like his cinematic cousins, Freamon chooses a lover on the young side and does not appear to want to leave his job. As "real police", he hopes to see his job through. But the discovery of the fraud by which he and McNulty conned the city into funding their police work threatens to return him to the "paper unit" from which he had risen at the beginning of the show. No such threat to career occurs in cop cinema, in which heroes retire only as their bodies age, never because of punitive demotion.

This difference may owe to the PTS format, which allows for an extended look at organizational machinations. Detailed depictions of institutional inertia take time; and cinematic attempts tend to run long and draw few viewers (e.g., Sidney Lumet's *Prince of the City*, a well-reviewed but little seen film from 1981 that runs nearly three hours). By ending his story in this way, *The Wire* uses its PTS format to illustrate yet again how a character's indifference to the reward system of the bureaucratic career results in being shut down by the system. Politicians and officials more concerned than Freamon is with self-promotion see to it that his police work stops.

This addition, of a sense of defeat, to his retirement, owes not to some larger pattern in cop action but instead to the particular focus of this show, one made possible by the television production system and its output, the PTS. *The Wire* is justly famed for its portrayal of such bureaucratic operations. But it shuts down its own analytic operations when the matter of Freamon's reward arises. The ministrations of Shardene amount to its own utopian dream.

A Real Dream

Jameson joins a chorus of scholars by lauding *The Wire* for its realism; but he qualifies his praise by focusing on the utopian elements that makes that style, "the construction of the fictive, yet utterly realistic, events" (371), worthwhile. Those shattered dreams include an attempt to restore dignified work to the Baltimore docks; a legalization of drugs, which reduces violence against and legal processing of residents of poor neighborhoods; reinvestment in public schools in those neighborhoods; and the funding of investigation of crimes against the poor. Such utopian bids fail when bureaucracies, run with self-promotion in mind, grind them down. Those changes would not advance the careers of those who seek short-term public approval.

To these utopian visions, on which the show and Jameson focus their dialog and comments, we can add one that does succeed but goes unremarked. Drawn from the lifestyles of men in highly stratified groups, in which women remain subordinate, Freamon's retirement to Shardene's ministrations is a vision of job loss augmented by remunerative though optional employment, and affection provided by subordinated women who ask for little if anything in return. As a dream of lifestyles available to working class men, this is utopian in Jameson's sense. If presented within a rigidly realistic depiction of law enforcement in a U.S. city, it would appear as a fantasy or wish fulfillment. This is perhaps the fondest utopia of *The Wire*, in that the show does nothing to show how bureaucratic or other constraints keep these straight men's dreams from coming true. The glamorous, not-quite retirement of a heroic man is its real dream. It just happens, apparently because Freamon is the man that he is.

Simon sought to threaten an established order with this show; and I feel that it has been rightly celebrated for finding a way to make a study of organizational constraints engaging. The show deliberately analyses the racist, impoverishing outcomes of formal policies and their manipulation by agents of law enforcement, and it upends the clichés of cop TV shows by doing so. It avoids the Manichean dichotomies of good and evil and the romantic celebration of individual agency, to which cop television and cinema has tended.

Still, however, relations of gender and age go unexamined; and this depiction of retirement celebrates the high-status activities of straight men in much the same way as its movie cousins have, namely as the outcome of a hero's essential coolness. The show is revolutionary when mindful but just as prone to hetero-sex fantasy as any other depiction, once the unexamined relations of inequality hit the screen.

This intrusion of romantic cop-movie cliché into attempts at brutal honesty and genre subversion may owe as well to the ambivalent nature of a mass-media focus on workers who crave no attention to their personal agency. How does one celebrate those who cannot be celebrated, or depict the satisfaction and agency of those denied it by the organizations for which they work?

In the old-cop movies studied in my earlier research, no such tension arises; as the hero's mighty agency remains at issue throughout. In those movies, cop work compares not to organizational failure but to stardom instead. One hero (in the 2002 release *Blood Work*, starring Clint Eastwood) tells a friend that, before his retirement, he had felt "connected .... That's what it was, when I was at the top of my game. I felt connected to everything: the victim, the killer, the crime scene, everything. Just felt like it was all part of me." His encomium to cop work remains focused on the attention that he enjoys while doing it, the power that he feels on the job. The job has a glamour to it, one akin to acting on stage or screen, enjoyment of the focused attention of an admiring crowd. The movie then depicts the hero's return to the public eye through mass-media journalism. Good cops are stars, collecting, in the attention of young lovers, TV cameras, and curious crowds, the rewards of their stardom.

But this is not so, in *The Wire*, which instead depicts limitation and frustration, celebrates modesty and excoriates stardom, associating the latter with bureaucratic bungling and self-serving lies.

The paradox of *The Wire* is that the show uses actors on screen, aiming for the attention of the largest audience possible, to celebrate the virtues of working in the dark with little influence or reward. It invites prestige for characters who accomplish little and seek neither prizes, awards, nor public eyes. Such disavowal of praise is especially ironic given the focus of the show on organizational systems. This denial of the hunger for attention provides an example of the disavowal of ritual celebration that allows groups to fetishize their stars, gods, and other recipients of their tribute and adoration. That is, groups generate faith in the inherent goodness of the centers of their attention only by disavowing much of the work that they do to attain those states of adoration. Stars wishing to remain stars do themselves little good by calling attention to the hard work done by their fans. Their worship must seem effortless, merely unforced expression of love, for the fetishistic adoration to work.[2] The heroes and gods must seem inherently to merit our praise. Our organized efforts to excite ourselves over them must go unnoticed.

And so, to seem like a victim of social organization rather than its beneficiary (which status the show displaces onto lying politicians),

---

2 For a general discussion of fetishism, disavowal, and ritual, see Marshall.

Freamon must receive what privileges he finds as though they came to him without organizational effort, as a result of who he naturally is. Without finding a way to celebrate his character, the show cannot add the emotional appeal to its moral lesson in the dangers of bureaucratic self-promotion and virtues of service to the poor. Freamon is the show's self-effacing ideal of natural policing on behalf of communities who receive few favors; and the objectification of his age and gender privileges help the show to reward him on the sly while still dramatizing its sociological point about how bureaucracies grind him down. The work, the large-scale relations of gender and age that put him in the position to receive the lasting adoration of his young girlfriend, must seem like a gift given freely by a woman who does it purely out of love.

This paradox, of *The Wire*'s public celebration of self-effacement, gains a provisional resolution in the objectification of Freamon's goodness and personal success, dramatized with the aid of Shardene's extremely deferent and otherwise unmotivated nurturing. To the extent that voluntary retirement amounts, in these stories, to another form of self-effacement, added to that of his humble police work, then we celebrate it by piling unexamined privileges upon it. And that privileging turns out to be young women's work, accomplished by their subordination. To examine the systemic nature of what the Shardenes of the world give to the Freamons, for neither pay nor celebration, would be to make a very different show, about more kinds of inequality.

WORKS CITED

Altman, Rick. *Film/Genre*. London: BFI Publishing, 1999. Print.

Brooke, Libby and Philip Taylor. "Older Workers And Employment: Managing Age Relations." *Ageing & Society* 25.03 (2005): 415-29. Print.

Casterline, John B., Lindy Williams, and Peter McDonald. "The Age Difference Between Spouses: Variations Among Developing Countries." *Population Studies* 40.3 (1986): 353-74. Print.

Chudacoff, Howard P. *How Old Are You?: Age Consciousness in American Culture*. Princeton, N.J.: Princeton University Press, 1989. Print.

Duncan, Colin. "Assessing Anti-Ageism Routes to Older Worker Re-Engagement." *Work, Employment & Society* 17.1 (2003): 101-20. Print.

Jameson, Fredric. "Realism And Utopia in The Wire." *Criticism* 52.3-4 (2010): 359-72. Print.

Kinder, Marsha. "Re-Wiring Baltimore: The Emotive Power of Systemics, Seriality, and the City." *Film Quarterly* 62.2 (2008): 50-57. Print.

King, Neal and Toni Calasanti. "Men's Aging Amidst Intersecting Relations of Inequality." *Sociology Compass* 7.9 (2013): 699-710. Print.

King, Neal. "Old Cops: Occupational Aging in a Film Genre." *Staging Age: The Performance of Age in Theatre, Dance, and Film*. Eds. Valerie Barnes Lipscomb and Leni Marshall. New York: Palgrave Macmillan, 2010. 57-81. Print.

Laws, Glenda. "Understanding Ageism: Lessons From Feminism And Postmodernism." *The Gerontologist* 35.1 (1995): 112-18. Print.

Linkon, Sherry, Alexander Russo, and John Russo. "Contested Memories: Representing Work in the Wire." *The Wire: Race, Class, And Genre*. Eds. Liam Kennedy and Stephen Shapiro. Ann Arbor: University of Michigan Press, 2012. 239-61. Print.

Marshall, Douglas A. "Behavior, Belonging, and Belief: A Theory of Ritual Practice." *Sociological Theory* 20.3 (2002): 360-80. Print.

Mittell, Jason. "Narrative Complexity in Contemporary American Television." *The Velvet Light Trap* 58.1 (2006): 29-40. Print.

Ndalianis, Angela. "Television and the Neo-Baroque." *The Contemporary Television Series*. Eds. Michael Hammond and Lucy Mazdon. Edinburgh: Edinburgh University Press, 2005. 83-101. Print.

Newman, Michael Z. "From Beats to Arcs: Toward a Poetics of Television Narrative." *The Velvet Light Trap* 58.1 (2006): 16-28. Print.

Pietilä, Ilkka, Hanna Ojala, Neal King and Toni Calasanti. "Ageing Male Bodies, Health, And the Reproduction of Age Relations." *Journal of Aging Studies* 27.3 (2013): 243-51. Print.

Porter, Michael J., Deborah L. Larson, Allison Harthcock, and Kelly Berg Nellis. "Re(De)Fining Narrative Events: Examining Television Narrative Structure." *Journal of Popular Film & Television* 30.1 (2002): 23-30. Print.

Simon, David. *The Wire: A Dramatic Series for HBO*. *The Wire* Episode Scripts: 101 - The Target, Springfield! Springfield!, 2000. Web. Feb. 2014.

Thompson, Kristin. *Storytelling in the New Hollywood: Understanding Classical Narrative Technique*. Cambridge, Mass.: Harvard University Press, 1999. Print.

TELEVISION

Badge 373. Director Howard W. Koch (1973).
Blood Work. Director Clint Eastwood (2002).
Busting. Director Peter Hyams (1974).
CSI. Creator Anthony E. Zuiker, CBS (2000-2015).
Dirty Harry. Director Don Siegel (1971).
Electra Glide in Blue. Director James William Guercio (1973).
Homicide: Life on the Street. Creator Paul Attanasio, NBC (1993-1999).
Magnum Force. Director Ted Post (1973).
NYPD Blue. Creators Steven Bochco and David Milch, ABC (1993-2005).
Prince of the City. Director Sidney Lumet (1981).
Southland. Creator Ann Biderman,N NBC (2009-2013).
The French Connection. Director William Friedkin (1971).
The New Centurions. Director Richard Fleischer (1972).
The Wire. Creator David Simon, HBO (2002-2008).

Heroine and/or Caricature?

The Older Woman in *Desperate Housewives*

Ros Jennings and Maricel Oró-Piqueras

Desperate Housewives (ABC 2004-2012) is a successful US-produced television text that focuses on the lives, concerns, and struggles of a group of American women living in the fictitious suburban enclave of Wisteria Lane. Generically hybrid, the series encompasses elements of drama, comedy, soap opera and even gothic (Lancioni; Hill) and together with *Ally McBeal* (Fox 1997-2000) and *Sex in the City* (HBO 1998-2004), *Desperate Housewives* forms part of a trio of key television texts that have received close attention with regard to issues of postfeminism, femininity and female identities (Chicharro Merayo; Kaufer Busch; McCabe and Akass 2006; Akass and McCabe 2006a). The narrative struggles of the four central female characters in *Desperate Housewives* – Lynette Scavo (Felicity Huffman), Susan Mayer/Delfino (Teri Hatcher), Bree Van der Kamp/Hodge (Marcia Cross) and Gabrielle Solis (Eva Longoria) – represent, as Elizabeth Kaufer Busch argues "[t]he unfeasibility of the twenty-first century happy housewife heroine" (95). Aged between their late thirties to early fifties, the four main female protagonists encapsulate Rosalind Gill's definition of "postfeminist sensibility." Within the overall narrative of *Desperate Housewives*, their individual stories interweave and combine with each other to demonstrate that for the four pre- and peri-menopausal heterosexual women at the heart of the text "notions of autonomy, choice and self- improvement sit side-by-side with surveillance, discipline and the vilification of those who make the 'wrong' 'choices' (e.g. become too fat, too thin, or have the audacity or bad judgment to grow older)" (163).

The overwhelming preoccupation of existing research on *Desperate Housewives*[1] to engage only with characters who are involved in a 'desperate' battle to conform to the postfeminist ideals as delineated by Gill has worked to exclude and devalue the importance of characters who are not similarly portrayed. Female characters who have made the 'wrong choices' by not just growing older but more specifically by not trying to defy and disguise their age through the representational and cosmetic processes of youthification have so far attracted little academic attention. Because postmenopausal women fall outside the scope of postfeminist concerns the role of the older women within *Desperate Housewives* has largely gone unnoticed. This paper attempts to reverse this omission by offering an analysis of one of *Desperate Housewives'* older female characters, Karen McCluskey (Kathryn Joosten). The following analysis explores the role of Mrs McCluskey both as an older woman within the series and as an example of how older women are perceived, represented and understood within American and Western society more generally.

Although there are other older women characters around the same age range as Mrs McCluskey in the series, such as Ida Greenberg, Karen's best friend during the first seasons of the series, McCluskey is the only older woman character who is present throughout the whole eight seasons of the series and whose character is developed in any depth. Running over eight seasons, which amounts to a fictional time span of thirteen years, with a five year gap inserted into the series continuity between season 4 and 5, *Desperate Housewives'* serial format facilitates the viewers' ability to observe both the process of character ageing and also the cultural attitudes at play in relation to it; diegetically within the text and intertextually in their own viewing responses. During the span of the series, Mrs McCluskey ages from her mid-sixties to her late-seventies and, because her character also moves to a more central role within the community life of Wisteria Lane and the TV series overall, her representation becomes an important focal point for an analysis of the representation of the older woman within the series.

---

1 For instance Karen McCluskey is only mentioned very briefly in a few sentences on two pages throughout the whole of McCabe and Akass *Reading Desperate Housewives*.

Old Age, Television Genre and *Desperate Housewives*

The "generic fusion" of *Desperate Housewives* creates a complex textual space where "incongruity, idiosyncrasy, exaggeration and absurdity are used to foreground the polysemy of a particular scene, situation or character" (Lancioni 133). The suburban location of *Desperate Housewives* underpins the overall ambivalence of the text. On a geographical level, the suburbs can be understood also as a marginal space positioned, as they are, between the city and the countryside. On the surface, the retro inflected white picket fence mise en scene of Wisteria Lane conforms to the ideal of the American dream but below the surface, within the confines of the pristine domestic spaces, things are less benign (Hill). Wisteria Lane is a liminal space where realities are multiple and often contradictory (Lancioni) and characterisation is always in productive tension rather than homogeneous or unified. When conceptualised within a notion of productive tension, an analysis of Wisteria Lane's oldest female residents, Karen McCluskey provides an important instance of an older woman presented as more than just a one-dimensional stereotype.

Serial complexity (Creeber) also plays its part and, over the span of *Desperate Housewives*, characters are able to be developed rather than remaining static. Ultimately, what shapes Karen McCluskey's textual depiction is a process of mutual dynamics which link televisual representations to "the broader currents of practical consciousness of thinking and feeling, active within culture" (Corner 126). In *Desperate Housewives*, the complexity and uniqueness of its serial narration is made evident from the very first episode when it becomes clear that the narrator of the series is actually dead. The voice-over narration is from Mary Ann Young, a friend of the four main desperate housewives, Lynette, Bree, Susan and Gabrielle, who had just committed suicide. The hybrid and multi-storyline construction of *Desperate Housewives* work to transgress and challenge discrete boundaries from the outset by combining elements from different television genres; by bridging the separation of life and death and by calling into question limited and fixed understandings of identities. The following sections will discuss how the complex textual strategies of the series construct Karen McCluskey and more especially the ways that this is done in relation to some of the key cultural tropes that shape understandings of older women in Western society.

Negotiating Binary Approaches to Ageing

During the course of the eight seasons of *Desperate Housewives*, Karen McCluskey moves from being credited as a "guest star" to being credited as "also starring"[2]. Her role is transformed from marginal figure to that of a central supporting character as she becomes more and more entwined in the storylines involving the four main protagonists. In the process of this transition her life story, emotions and motivations become more known to the audience and other characters. At the same time, the representation of her character becomes more nuanced and moves beyond her initial depiction which conforms to what Margaret Cruickshank suggests is the "characteristic mark" of the older woman: "an alien creature, costly and crabby" (5).

When Karen McCluskey is first introduced in season 1, she is presented in stark contrast to the text's four central protagonists. The first episodes in which Mrs McCluskey appears seem to reinforce many of the limiting stereotypical conceptions of the older woman in Western culture. She is portrayed as a lonely and irritable old woman who lives alone with her beloved cat (Lancioni). She is presented as being outside or 'other' to the hegemony of the youthful postfeminist heterosexual ideal. In many ways she corresponds to deep-seated myths and conventions of the post- menopausal crone[3] (Ronn and Dausgard). A widow in her late sixties, her concerns and circumstances seem at the outset to be quite different from those of her younger neighbours.

As Featherstone and Hepworth indicate, a negative cultural lens dominates the representation of older age. In their view, "images of youth become positively charged with connotations of beauty, energy, grace, moral fortitude and optimism, whereas images of old age become negatively charged with ugliness, idleness, degeneration and moral failure" (252). Mrs McCluskey is introduced as a difficult and disruptive character. In season 1, episode 14, entitled "Love is in the Air," she accuses Lynette Scavo's children of having stolen her clock. Audience sympathy is directed towards the more established central character, the overworked and overtired mother of four. Lynette's desperation as a housewife is rooted in her inability to con-

---

2 In season 7, she is credited as "starring" in the episodes that she appeared in.
3 In season 3, when news of her husband's body being found in the freezer becomes public, the neighborhood children paint "Witch" on her door.

trol her children despite previously managing a high-level business portfolio. With no responsibilities except to her cat, Lynette treats Mrs McCluskey as a crazy old woman with no demands on her time. As Markson puts it "older women are at particular risk of madness, decrepitude, death or murder: visual reminders of the loss of mobility, loss of mind, loss of functional capacity, and possibility of lingering or sudden death is associated with aging" (93):

McCluskey: Your little criminals snuck into my house and stole my wall clock.
Lynette: What?
McCluskey: It was a hand-painted, purple and white wall clock. My son made it.
Lynette: Are you sure you didn't displace it. No offence, but you probably forget where you put things.
McCluskey: No offense, but you should be sterilized.
Lynette: Look, my boys do not break into people's houses. Sure they may have stolen your flowerpot.
[*Later in the episode.*]
McCluskey: Maybe it's my dementia but I still haven't found my white wall clock.
Lynette: Nobody in my family knows or cares where your stupid clock is. ("Love is in the Air", 1.14)

As Eva Krainitzki argues, "[a]geist stereotypes express predominant ideas about the ageing process, constructing ageing as a process of decline and reifying ageism as acceptable" (35) and it is these ageist assumptions that underpin Lynette and her children's initial attitudes and responses. Lynette's default response is steeped in a predominant cultural stereotype of old age that automatically equates it with mental decline even though their exchange presents Mrs McCluskey as quick-witted and also clearly aware of the cultural tropes that Lynette is employing against her.

By the end of the episode, the audience is invited to shed its initial perceptions of Mrs McCluskey as a selfish old woman unable to sympathise with Lynette's difficult situation. Not only does she turn out to be correct, Lynette's children had actually stolen her precious clock[4], but when Lynette's children go round to apologise she invites them in for tea and

---

4   We learn that the clock was given to her by her son who died when he was 12 years old.

biscuits. The audience is given a glimpse of a more humane and less irascible side to her character. However, when the Scavo boys come to apologise, as the following exchange between them and Mrs McCluskey demonstrates, the underlying interplay of chronological, social and individual understandings of age in operation between the boys and the older woman illustrates just how much perceptions of age are culturally inscribed and highly subjective:

Boys: We're sorry.
McCluskey: That's it uh? Didn't you know that stealing is wrong? How old are you anyway?
Boys: We're six.
McCluskey: And how old are you?
Parker: Five. [...]
Porter: And how old are you?
McCluskey: How old do you think?
Porter: 150. ("Love is in the Air", 1.14)

Roles and Representation: The Older Female Body

Cruickshank suggests that, culturally, "old women are seen as old bodies, physical appearance encompasses their whole being" (4). For women, menopause is considered to be 'the change of life' which transitions them into old age (Sontag; Greer; de Beauvoir). According to critics such as Kaplan (1999) and Woodward (1999), the negative stereotypes associated with old age and the older body serve to make the loss of youth especially traumatic for women.

In *Desperate Housewives*, the dominance of the postfeminist sensibility (Gill) reinforces negative associations with becoming an old woman. For the series' main protagonists, Bree, Lynette, Susan and Gabrielle, every day is a perpetual battle to maintain the "sleek toned controlled figure [which] is normatively essential for portraying success" (Gill 150). The less than perfectly groomed Karen McCluskey provides a constant reminder to her four neighbours of the work involved in maintaining appropriate youthful femininity. The ongoing project of 'successful ageing' that Bree, Lynette, Susan and Gabrielle are engaged in, requires both the disavowal of old age and the physical abilities and material circumstances to do so. As John

Bell's analysis of the television series *Murder, She Wrote* and *The Golden Girls* concludes, despite the fact that both programmes have older women as their main protagonists, they are imbued with specific characteristics which make them difficult models to achieve by the rest of the population. In the same way as the central protagonists of Wisteria Lane, the protagonists of *Murder, She Wrote* and *The Golden Girls* are powerful members of their communities, they live in an affluent environment and are affluent themselves. In addition, they are generally healthy, socially active and quick-witted. An important contrast between the desperate housewives and the postmenopausal protagonists in Bell's study is that "they may be sexy but not sexual" (308-309). Bell argues that although the representation of successful ageing in television drama "may satisfy fantasies of many older or younger viewers, it hardly presents an accurate picture of American life" (310). As Cruickshank argues, successful ageing is a limiting concept despite the apparent positive overtones of the term as it is embedded in the neoliberal capitalist context where profit defines success. As such, "the often substantial differences in aging created by ethnicity, class and gender are covered up by the falsely universalizing phrase 'successful aging'" (3).

Mrs McCluskey's circumstances exclude her from pursuing the goal of successful ageing. From season 1, we learn that she has had quite a difficult life; she had endured the loss of a son, a failed marriage and her last husband had died. She was living on a fixed income which did not allow her many luxuries and, above all, she was suffering from arthritis which she had to keep under control in order to keep mobile and maintain her independence. The realities of Karen McCluskey's precarious financial situation is explored in true *Desperate Housewives* serio-comic style in season 3, when it is discovered that she kept the body of her dead husband, Gilbert, in her freezer so she could cash his pension cheques, as he had signed his pension over to his first wife. By means of this plot device, Karen McCluskey's own 'desperation' to keep her independence is made clear.

It is significant that once women have gone beyond their fertile years and have raised a family, their fictional roles have been traditionally limited to those of the mother or motherly figure (Markson; Coupland). Throughout the series, Mrs McCluskey is not portrayed as the mother or grandmother, the stereotypical positive image of the older women as pointed out by Markson. Despite the fact that she occasionally babysits for her neighbours, she never actually takes that role. In fact, any time she takes care of

Lynette Scavo's children, she asks the Scavo's for some kind of economic compensation. In the beginning, Tom and Lynette Scavo are sceptical that an older woman will be able to keep their children under control, especially when Lynette struggles to do so herself:

Lynette: A million teenagers in this street and you hire McCluskey?
Tom: What's the big deal?
Lynette: Well, for starters, she's ancient.
[*Later in the episode, McCluskey and Lynette*:]
McCluskey: What exactly is it you look for in a baby-sitter? I may be ancient, like you said, but I've never gotten drunk and lost track of three kids.
Lynette: What?
McCluskey: I smelled wine on Bree Van de Kamp when she was looking for your boys. ("Thank You So Much", 2.15)

In this episode, Mrs McCluskey confronts Lynette's limiting conceptions of old age and makes clear that being old does not make her incapable but rather gives her certain experiential advantages. One of the advantages of *Desperate Housewives*'s serial format is that, by virtue of a narrative and generic complexity that is developing over time, it constructs a televisual space where the four main younger women protagonists gain greater understandings of themselves as well as others. In this sense, as the series advances, the four desperate housewives understand that Mrs McCluskey's blunt and bold character is the result of having to survive in an environment in which entering old age and being female are no longer valuable categories. In the particular episode between Lynette and Mrs McCluskey mentioned above, as well as in other small fights between these two characters, Lynette is ultimately the one who has to confront her own fears about the fact that she herself is ageing in a society in which being old equates to decline, loss and disempowerment. As Cruickshank explains, "aging in North America is shaped more by culture than biology, more by beliefs, customs, and traditions than by bodily changes." (ix). Lynette's interactions with Karen McCluskey therefore provide important counterpoints for self-reflection.

Karen McCluskey's age, her lack of conformity to postfeminist notions of appearance and neo-liberal constructions of successful ageing result in her abilities being consistently underestimated by the residents of Wisteria

Lane. The often-discussed concept of the invisibility of older women in society (Lövgren) frequently works to Karen McCluskey's advantage within the plot lines of *Desperate Housewives*. On some occasions, she is portrayed as an amateur sleuth in the tradition of other fictional older women such as Jessica Fletcher (*Murder, She Wrote*) and Agatha Christie's Jane Marple. For instance in season 5, enlisting the help of her sister Roberta (Lily Tomlin), Karen McCluskey solves the mystery of Edie Britt's (Nicollette Sheridan) new husband, Dave Williams (Neil McDonough) and his unstable behaviour, discovering that Dave's ex-wife and daughter were killed in the accident that involved Mike and Susan Delfino.

As she moves from peripheral character to a central supporting character through the course of the eight seasons, it becomes clear that although she eschews the role of a nurturing motherly type, she is loyal and protective of her neighbours. She is a source of bold and wise advice to the younger women protagonists and does not sugar-coat the realities of life in her advice. Above all she is proactive on their behalf, utilising, as discussed earlier, her older woman's 'cloak of invisibility' to go unnoticed and garner important information whilst also drawing on culturally denigrated attributes of the older woman busy body, such as gossip to alert them to dangers that might befall them.

Ironic and sarcastic on the outside but generous and understanding on the inside, Karen McCluskey is a complex character rather than a one-dimensional stereotype. She encompasses Karin Lövgren's conceptualisation of the 'tant,' who is a contradictory older woman figure in Swedish culture. Like Karen McCluskey, the 'tant' is at one and the same time an admirable figure and a frumpish gossip.

Postmenopausal Sexuality

As Julia Twigg contends, the aging body is "not natural, is not prediscursive, but fashioned within and by culture" (60). Consequently, despite the increasing visibility in recent decades of older characters in films, their portrayals have generally strengthened, rather than lessened, the cultural associations that connect older characters with notions of unattractiveness, decline and abjection (Krainitzki; Chivers). To a great extent this results from the cultural celebration of the physiological exception. The exceptional ageing body has taken a certain hold in the public imagination through the celebration of glamourous older women stars who look 'good for their age'[5]; their presence acting as a fetish against the "toxicity" of decay and decline (Twigg 61). At the same time, actresses who go under, or are suspected of going under, the plastic surgeon's knife are vilified in the press and on social media for taking their own more concrete steps to avert the perceived bodily ravages of age.

In terms of the physical signs of ageing and her ageing body, Mrs McCluskey does not try to make her body look younger or fitter than it is. She does not police herself about her appearance in the same way as the four main protagonists. Referring to Bree, Susan, Lynette and Gabrielle, Janet McCabe suggests that: "Of course, none of the ladies violate our contemporary obsession with bodies obedient to the social norm, the toned, waxed, slender youthful-looking female body" (76). In season 5, Karen McCluskey celebrates her seventieth birthday. This inscribes her age as being different to that of the central female protagonists and marks her chronologically as older. It also confirms that she crosses, if only just, into the broad age spectrum that would place her in the parental generation in relation to the others. The concept of age and generation also corresponds to common debates in relation to feminism and postfeminism and as Christine Holmlund explains, "postfeminists are generally young; a few are middle-aged; none seem old (Botox helps)" (116). In terms of chronological age, at seventy, Karen McCluskey corresponds to the age profile of women who might have been directly involved in second wave feminism's battles for women's liberation. Her fierce independence and the fact that she does not subject herself to the appropriate level of appearance anxiety dictated by postfeminism would also connect her to the legacy of second wave feminism. Her humour and desire, however, contradict postfeminist assumptions about sex-hating humourless second wave feminists and this also positions her within the dominant framework of ambivalence that *Desperate Housewives* manipulates as its core approach.

Although the situation is gradually changing, feminism has said little so far about old age (Woodward 1999) and the older female body (Twigg). Preoccupied with issues of reproduction, objectification and desire, feminism has concentrated on the premenopausal body – a younger, sexy, desired and desiring body. Arber, Davidson and Ginn argue that "although

---

5   For instance British actress Dame Helen Mirren.

sex has assumed a greater importance within society than perhaps ever before, old age remains outside this sexualized world, with the stereotype of an asexual old age pervading not only popular culture, but also policy, practice and research" (64). When forced to confront the actuality of sexual activity in older age, Bouman et al. suggest that three of the most common cultural responses are silence, distaste and tunnel vision (i.e. limited and narrow definitions of heterosexual intercourse). Karen McCluskey's role in *Desperate Housewives* serves to challenge the negativity of these discourses on several levels. In contrast to her younger conventionally heterosexually attractive neighbours, Mrs McCluskey frequently jokes about her lack of sex appeal and the fact that she is no longer attractive in the way that she was when she was younger. She is still, however, a sexual and desiring body. She is not coy about the fact that she misses sex. In season 6, she starts dating Roy Bender (Orson Bean) and they embark on a relationship where sex is an important component. In the following conversation with Gabrielle it becomes apparent that not only is sex in older age almost culturally inconceivable but there is additionally a high level of cultural squeamishness involved when younger people are forced to consider the older sexually intimate body:

Gabrielle: I think it's sweet that you've found a companion at this stage of your life.
McCluskey: Roy's no companion. The man has seen Paris. That's right. I'm back in the saddle. See, it started one night when Roy asked if my bathtub was big enough for two.
Gabrielle: Hey, hey, hey! You want me to crash the car? Cause I will. ("Nice is Different than Good", 6.1)

Within *Desperate Housewives* much of the humour generated in relation to Roy and Karen's relationship stems from dominant cultural attitudes coming face to face with the realities of postmenopausal sex and desire which, as people live longer, will need to be reconsidered. Qualitative studies of later life sexuality and sexual practices (Arber, Davidson and Ginn; Gott and Hinchliff) suggest that sexuality remains an important aspect of identity and well-being. Increasingly, however, the neo-liberal project of 'successful ageing' extends to notions of successful or active later life sex (Katz and Marshall) which suggests that the four postfeminist protagonists will need to be as obedient and disciplined in their pursuit of postmenopausal sexual 'fitness' (Marshall) as they have been in the pursuit of appropriate feminine grooming and style.

The humour displayed when Karen McCluskey shares that she has a fulfilling sex life with her younger female neighbours is in sharp contrast to the pathos present in the scenes in which Roy and Karen express their feelings for each other. When later life sexuality is analysed in academic research, there is a tendency to discuss it merely in terms of the 'performance' of a narrowly defined act of heterosexual sexual activity (Bouman et al.; Katz and Marshall). As Bouman et al. indicate, this overconcentration on sexual intercourse obscures more holistic understandings of sexuality, namely that: "Sexuality, in the old as well as the young, encompasses far more than this. It includes all the physical intimacies" (151).

Ageing, Illness and Death

In Eva Krainitzki's study of older lesbians in cinema, she identifies that one of the main narrative cinematic devices to disavow older same-sex desire is to desexualise these relationships through notions of illness and the reduction of physical intimacies to those of nursing and caring tasks. Research (Bouman et al.; Gott and Hinchliff) suggests that, although illness and infirmity is likely to have discernible impact on both sexual desire and expressions of sexual desire, it does not necessarily end them. When Karen McCluskey's lung cancer returns in season 8, and is found to be terminal, the negotiation of everyday sexuality that encompass expressions of "loyalty, passion, affection, esteem and affirmation of one's body and its functioning" (Bouman et al. 151) can be identified in her relationship with Roy. To achieve this, the narrative requires the characters and also the audience to navigate their way through the implications and assumptions that underlie both the wider cultural constructions and also the internalized cultural conceptions of age and narratives of dependency and decline (Cruickshank). As indicated earlier, the complex generic style adopted in *Desperate Housewives* dictates that the exploration of Karen McCluskey's cancer is addressed along a spectrum of approaches and emotions that range from black humour to exquisite tenderness.

In American culture, self-reliance is a key element of personal and national identity and moving to a stage where help is needed "often brings anguish and humiliation" (Cruickshank 10). Over the course of the series,

Karen McCluskey has been as constructed as valuing her independence and as she faces this final stage of her life she wants to remain autonomous. She decides initially not to tell Roy because he has already endured the death of his first wife and does not want to put him through a similar situation. She decides to commit suicide so that she can take control of what will happen to her. This results in a range of darkly comic and farcical scenes[6] all of which are ultimately foiled and end in failure. By considering suicide, Mrs McCluskey is resisting what Cruickshank, among others, have defined as the overmedicalisation and institutionalisation of old age. In the last episode of the final season of *Desperate Housewives* Karen McCluskey is fully embraced into a community of women at the heart of the Wisteria Lane. This comes about once Roy assures her he is strong enough to be with her to the end and Bree, Lynette, Susan and Gabrielle insist on taking care of her so that she can die at home with minimal medical intervention. As the voice over articulates: "she was pleased to discover, after all those years, that they thought of her as a friend" ("Give me the Blame", 8.22).

Admittedly the affluent context of Wisteria Lane provides her carers with time and resources to support her and also a comfortable environment in which to do it, but the material circumstances do not lessen the overall psychological and cultural impact of the act itself. This engagement with an impending death dismantles some of the fears and cultural barriers related to disease and death in Western society (Twigg). As highlighted earlier, the audience is able to see that Karen and Roy's relationship is one that continues to find new forms of sensual and emotional expression; particularly in her deathbed scene when Roy tenderly kisses to the strains of Johnny Mathis's *Wonderful, Wonderful* playing on the record player. This diegetic use of music rather than using the underscore of a non-diegetic musical soundtrack emphasises the choice, consideration, pleasure and love that they are able to share even at this final stage. The intergenerational friendship that is forged between Karen and her neighbours is also significant and counters what Norbert Elias denounces as the fact that, in an increasingly individualised society defined by economic and social 'success', the old are

---

6   Her various methods, from asking Bree to help her commit suicide while Bree makes up silly excuses to avoid the situation to finally lying down behind Lynette's car and waiting for her to leave the house and run her over.

now generally left in institutions rather than spending their last years amongst families and friends.

The fact that as an older woman character, Karen McCluskey is the only person in the series who dies due to disease rather than murder, accident or suicide is not a signifier of the usual stereotypical construction of older age and decline so common in film and television dramas. The final narrative trajectory is primarily driven by the intertextual circumstances of the actress who plays Karen McCluskey, Kathryn Joosten, who at the time was herself suffering from terminal cancer herself. Joosten died only 20 days after the screening of the final episode, at the age of 72[7]. In terms of the portrayal of illness and older age in *Desperate Housewives*, until the terminal cancer storyline, Karen McCluskey is shown as a stoic character who needs to manage her chronic arthritis but who was determined to live as full a life as possible. The diagnosis of Lynette's Hodgkin's lymphoma in season 4 also suggested that cancer, and indeed illness in general, can strike at any stage of the lifecourse rather than being the preserve of older people.

Heroine and/or Caricature?

The final episode of *Desperate Housewives* would seem to direct the audience towards viewing Karen McCluskey as a heroine. Shortly before her death, and knowing that she has nothing further to lose, Mrs McCluskey decides to accuse herself of having killed and disposed of the body of Gabrielle's abusive father, Alejandro, and thus, save Gabrielle's husband and the younger woman protagonist from being charged with the crime. The overall fictional space of *Desperate Housewives*, however hinges on ambivalence. The space and openness afforded by the series' hybrid synthesis of different generic conventions produces complex and contradictory characterisations that are open to a high degree of interpretation. None of the female characters are purely positive or purely negative and Karen McCluskey is no different. By means of her sharp tongue and her complaints, she conforms to the stereotype of the grumpy old woman but simultaneously her quick wit and keen observations force both her neighbours and the audience to question their gut ageist beliefs and assumptions. Mrs

---

7   See *Guardian* obituary, 4 June 2012, http://www.theguardian.com/tv-and-radio/2012/jun/04/kathryn-joosten.

McCluskey's role in *Desperate Housewives* is in some ways the token older women who bears the burden of representing understandings and misunderstandings of older age in Western culture. She does not conform to the docile restrictions of the selfless nurturing mother or granny figure or to the postfeminist ideal of disciplined and glamourous body. In addition, despite not conforming to the standards of the sexy older woman she is shown as a sexual woman and thereby confronts dominant notions of older women being asexual and beyond sex.

The dominant mode of ambivalence that operates throughout *Desperate Housewives* constructs Mrs McCluskey as both caricature and heroine, and does so by letting the contradictions of the two positions play out at multiple levels and in multiple interactions with the other characters. Rather than investing Karen McCluskey with the status of a heroine of older age, her character and role aligns closely with Sandberg's notion of affirmative old age, where she "does not aspire to agelessness or attempt to reject and fight old age, but instead seeks a conceptualisation and acceptance of old age in all its diversity, from active to sedentary, from sexually vibrant to sexually indifferent" (35).

WORKS CITED

Akass, Kim and Janet McCabe, eds. *Reading Sex And The City*. New York: IB Tauris, 2004. Print

Arber, Sara, Kate Davidson, and Jay Ginn. *Gender And Ageing. Changing Roles And Relationships*. London: Open University Press, 2003. Print.

Bell, John. "In Search of a Discourse on Aging: The Elderly on Television". *The Gerontologist*. 32.2 (1992): 305-311. Print.

Bouman, Pierre et al. "Nottingham Study of Sexuality & Ageing (NoSSA I). Attitudes Regarding Sexuality And Older People: A Review of the Literature". *Sexual And Relationship Therapy*. 21.2 (May 2006): 149-161. Print.

Creeber, Glen. *Serial Television. Big Drama on The Small Screen*. Trowbridge, Wiltshire: Cromwell Press, 2004. Print.

Chicharro Merayo, Mar. "Representaciones de la Mujer en la Ficción Postfeminista: *Ally McBeal, Sex And The City* y *Desperate Housewives*" Papers. *Revista de Sociología*. 98.1 (March 2013): 11-3. Print.

Chivers, Sally. *The Silvering Screen. Old Age and Disability in Cinema.* Toronto: University of Toronto, 2011. Print.

Cruikshank, Margaret. *Learning to Be Old. Gender, Culture, And Aging.* Maryland: Rowman & Littlefield Publishers, 2009. Print.

De Beauvoir, Simone. *The Second Sex.* Parshely, H.M. trans. London: Vintage, 1997. Print.

Elias, Norbert. *The Loneliness of the Dying.* New York: Basil Blackwell, 1985. Print.

Featherstone, Mike and Mike Hepworth. "Images of Ageing." *Ageing in Society. An Introduction to Social Gerontology.* Eds. John Bond and Peter Coleman. London: Sage Publications, 1990. Print.

Gill, Rosalind. "Postfeminist Media Culture: Elements of a Sensibility." *European Journal of Cultural Studies.* 10.2. (May 2007): 147-166. Print.

Gott, Merryn and Sharon Hinchliff. "How Important is Sex in Later Life? The Views of Older People." *Social Science & Medicine.* Vol. 56. (2003): 1617–1628. Print.

Greer, Germaine. *The Change. Women, Aging And the Menopause.* New York: Alfred A. Knopf, 1991. Print.

Hill, Lisa. "Gender And Genre: Situating Desperate Housewives." *Journal of Popular Film And Television.* 38. 4. (2010): 162-169. Print.

Holmlund, Christine. "Postfeminism From A to G." *Cinema Journal 44*, No. 2 (Winter 2005): 116-121. Print.

Kaplan, E. Ann. "The Unconscious of Age: Performances in Psychoanalysis, Film And Popular Culture." *Staging Age. The Performance of Age in Theatre, Dance And Film.* Eds. Leni Marshall and Valerie Barnes. New York: Palgrave, 2010. 27-56. Print.

Kaplan, E. Ann. "Trauma And Aging: Marlene Dietrich, Melanie Klein And Marguerite Duras." *Figuring Age. Women, Bodies, Generations.* Ed. Kathleen Woodward. Bloomington and Indianapolis: Indiana UP, 1999. 171-194. Print.

Katz, Stephen and Barbara Marshall. "New Sex For Old: Lifestyle, Consumerism, And the Ethics of Aging Well." *Journal of Aging Studies* Volume 17 (2003): 3–16. Print.

Kaufer Busch, Elizabeth. "*Ally McBeal* to *Desperate Housewives:* A Brief History of the Postfeminist Heroine." *Perspectives on Political Science,* 2009. 87-97. Print.

Krainitzki, Eva. *Exploring the Hypervisibility Paradox: Older Lesbians in Contemporary Mainstream Cinema (1995-2009)*. PhD thesis at the University of Gloucestershire, 2011. Unpublished.

Lancioni, Judith. "Murder And Mayhem on Wisteria Lane: A Study of Genre And Cultural Context in *Desperate Housewives*". Eds. Janet McCabe and Kim Akass. *Reading 'Desperate Housewives'*. London: I.B. Tauris, 2006. 129-142. Print.

Lövgren, Karin. "The Swedish *Tant*: A Marker of Female Aging." *Journal of Women & Aging*, Volume 25. (2013): 119–137. Print.

Markson, Elizabeth. "The Female Aging Body Through Film". Ed. Christopher Faircloth. *Aging Bodies. Images And Everyday Experience*. Oxford: Altamira Press, 2003. 77-102. Print.

McCabe, Janet and Kim Akass, eds. *Reading 'Desperate Housewives'*. London: I.B. Tauris, 2006. Print.

McCabe, Janet and Kim Akass. "Feminist Television Criticism: Notes and Queries." *Critical Studies in Television*. 1.1 (May 2006): 108-120. Print.

Marshall, Barbara. "Medicalization And the Refashioning of Age-Related Limits on Sexuality." *The Journal of Sex Research*, Volume 49, Issue 4 (2012): 337-343. Print.

Ronn, Vicki and Kaylene Dausgard. "The Crone Conspiracy: The Literary Evolution of the Aging Woman." *International Journal of Humanities*, 3.1 (2005/2006): 43-50. Print.

Sandberg, Linn. "Affirmative Old Age – The Ageing Body And Feminist Theories on Difference." *International Journal of Ageing And Later Life*. 8.1 (2013): 11-40. Print.

Sontag, Susan. "The Double Standard of Aging." *Saturday Review of The Society*. 1972. September 23, 29-32. Print.

Woodward, Kathleen, ed. *Figuring Age. Women, Bodies, Generations*. Bloomington: Indiana University Press, 1999. Print.

Woodward, Kathleen. "Performing Age, Performing Gender." *NWSA Journal*, Volume 18 (Spring 2006): 162-168. Print.

TELEVISION

Ally McBeal. Creator E. Kelley, Fox (1997-2000).
Desperate Housewives. Creator Marc Cherry, ABC (2004-2012).
The Golden Girls. Creator Susan Harris, NBC (1985-1992).
Murder, She Wrote. Creators Peter S. Fischer, Richard Levinson, and William Link, CBS (1984-1996).
Sex in the City. Creator Darren Star, HBO (1998-2004).

Temporality and Aging: Experiments with Magic, Narrative and Genre

"Vampires Don't Age, But Actors Sure Do"
The Cult of Youth and the Paradox of Aging in *Buffy the Vampire Slayer*

SALLY CHIVERS

This paper analyzes the figure of the vampire as portrayed in Joss Whedon's television series *Buffy the Vampire Slayer* (hereafter referred to as *Buffy*) to illustrate how the show comments upon and contributes to anxieties about population aging. Originally airing in the US from March 1997 to May 2003, *Buffy* inserts mythologies of the vampire into millennial teen television, complete with its own understandings of youth, age, and bodily difference, intensifying the commentary on aging that the vampire figure already invites. The vampire figure comes from a complex folkloric and literary tradition, adapted for each contemporary usage. Across traditions, vampires are typically immune to death from old age, maintain their age appearance from the time they were changed from humans into demons (though they cannot admire themselves in the mirror), and yet increase in strength and skill as they age into antiquity. As such, they offer an intriguing figure through which to separate a significant contemporary marker of old age – appearance – from a value that contemporary culture often ignores in older adults – experience.

In Whedon's mythic world, which fans call the Buffyverse, vampires have to avoid sun and Christian symbols (especially crosses and holy water), which would make them burst into fatal flames. They feed on blood (preferably human), typically maintain their youthful appearance, and become much stronger when they turn into monsters and even stronger if they age into extreme old age before being slain. *Buffy* makes explicit the paradoxical nature of the vampire as a demon that ages inside an apparently human body that does not. Vampires who inhabit the Buffyverse are descended from a race of demons intriguingly called "Old Ones." They cannot fly and can closely emulate human appearance, including adopting the clothing of the era (though some of them need to learn how to do so convincingly). Whedon adds to this world the figure of the Vampire Slayer, a young girl growing into womanhood, imbued with ancient powers that make her stronger than most monsters and fated to fight them. The show sets this role up as generational, repeating the refrain that the Vampire Slayer, currently the sixteen-year-old, pert, attractive Buffy Summers, is "the Chosen One," the only one born of her generation destined to "stand against the vampires, the demons, and the forces of darkness" ("Welcome to the Hellmouth" 1.1 and throughout the series). As this paper makes clear, intergenerational strife and fears of old age propel *Buffy*, but the human generations are most united in their fight to slay vampires, with the twist that it is a member of the younger generation who is most equipped to do so.

Writing before the *Buffy* phenomenon, Nina Auerbach asserts that the "appeal" of the vampire is "dramatically generational," explaining that in her courses about the evolution of vampires, "age differences" are "central" (5). Each generation, it seems, has its vampires (145). And each cohort sees different things in the vampiric worlds portrayed in popular culture. Auerbach contends that vampires capaciously represent contemporaneous fears, especially because they are "disturbingly close to the mortals they prey on" (6). They become repositories of cultural worries that take on immortal life unless slain by a hero. Vampires are almost human, but in *Buffy*, their monstrosity taps into the turn-of-the-century anxieties about the passage of time, enhanced by the near-Hollywood location[1], and the coming of demographic doom in the form of a disproportionately old population. *Buffy*, then, is significant for the range of ages to which it appeals. While *Buffy* undoubtedly deserves the label 'teen show,' its allure extends beyond that viewing demographic. As Mary Celeste Kearney points out, the Warner Brothers Network, which hosted the first five seasons of *Buffy*, "targeted a multi-aged market whose members shared a 'youthful' sensibility"

---

1   *Buffy* is set in the fictional town of Sunnydale, about two hours' drive northwest of Los Angeles.

(Kearney 19). While the fascination with vampire narratives is always in part a fascination with immortality and youth, *Buffy* offers many clichés in the representation of human aging, and fully participates in the youthful biases of Hollywood production. Though typical of the genre and location, that fascination and that bias become more interesting because they occur during a period intrigued by time. Buffy aired originally in the US over a period that included Y2K which made people very conscious of the calendar, 9/11 which led to strong voices for commemoration of the past, and an increased fear of the demographic imbalance potentially wrought by population aging, which continues to incite panic through dire predictions that the younger generations will pay the price for the older generations. *Buffy*'s emphasis on the fact that vampires have human bodies that do not age resonates with the dominant discourses of aging and ageism of its time. As such, it is worth examining as an example of how even relatively progressive woman-centered television struggles to transcend the pervasive ageism of contemporary media.

The fantastical demonic Buffyverse presents a combination of cliché and innovation in thinking through the construction of the aging process. This paper explores the contradiction posed by the figure of the vampire by interrogating the collision within the show over seven seasons of *Buffy* between the mythic fantasy of eternal youth posed by the demon in a human body, the cult of youth—especially but not only in terms of beauty standards—that dominates even this alternative transgressive feminist television show, and a fear of human aging on the part of teenaged characters.[2]

"When I Get So Worn and Wrinkly": Teenaged Projections of Aging in the Buffyverse

While *Buffy* deserves praise for its critical exploration of stereotypes about gender and sexuality, as well perhaps for its attempts to explore race

---

2   Whereas the film version of *Buffy the Vampire Slayer* (1992) showcases many tropes also present in the television series, such as the youthful superhero grossed out by old age and having to think about growing up too soon, it ends when the Slayer leaves high school, does not portray the graphic physical transformation of vampires into demon form, and is able to work with actors over a short time frame, not having to account for their physical aging.

through a mythic world of demons, it fails to offer the same liberating or even interrogative view of age. The teen perspective in *Buffy*, similar to what Julia Twigg refers to as the "gaze of youth,"[3] takes up the shallow perspective that older bodies have negative meanings encapsulated in what Margaret Morganroth Gullette refers to as decline narratives (Twigg 65, Gullette *Declining*). As Kearney points out, *Buffy* "[depicts] young people's social and cultural dominance of a community" (31). Further, the show buys into the simplistic notion that decline in later life, which comes quite early in *Buffy*'s projections, must be worse for women who face what Susan Sontag calls the double standard of aging, since their femininity is apparently tied to their youthful appearance. Despite imbuing a young pretty blonde female with superhuman strength, or perhaps *because* Buffy is so blond and so pretty, *Buffy* refuses the innovative rethinking of the category of aging femininity that its investment in the vampire myth promises.

Chris Richards explains that through Buffy's "fast and witty 'youth' speak, in her dress and in her insistence on the pursuit of a relationship with Angel, [Buffy] identifies herself as belonging to 'teen culture'" (127). *Buffy* incited a whole set of high school-based television shows, in part because it revels in youth and shuns age, offering repeated jokes about being old as simply negative and leaning on the assumption that old age, usually signified by wrinkles, is bad. When Buffy and her friend Xander fear the motives of a person their friend Willow meets over the then new internet, Xander jokes that it could be possible for him to pretend to be an "elderly Dutch woman." Buffy agrees, worrying that "this guy could be anybody, he could be weird, or crazy, or old or...he could be a circus freak," demonstrating through parallelism where older people fit in these teenagers' view ("I, Robot...You, Jane", 1.8). When Xander unwittingly falls for an Incan Mummy disguised as a beautiful young woman, the horror is partly that she is murderous, sucking the life out of younger people in order to stay alive herself, but even more so that she is a wrinkled corpse, matching the teenagers' view of old people, rather than being the nubile Latina young woman

---

3   Twigg explains that "we are accustomed from Foucauldian and feminist writings to the professional gaze or the phallic gaze, but there is also a gaze of youth. We have seen how the process of aging can be one of becoming increasingly subject to the corrosive power of such a gaze embodied in media imagery." (65)

she had appeared to be. As Jonathan, another of the Incan Mummy's near-victims, points out, "[Her] hands feel kind of rough" ("Inca Mummy Girl", 2.4). When Buffy's friend Ford reveals that he is dying of cancer, he explains his demise in deeply ageist terms, saying of his corpse, "It'll be bald and shriveled and it'll smell bad" ("Lie to Me", 2.7). Especially in the first few seasons, age feeds on youth and invites almost as much fear as the evil demonic world. The teenager characters, even when they later enter their twenties, continue to make quips about what they perceive to be the ludicrous nature of old people. For example, Xander says after learning that Genevieve Holt abused children residents of the home she oversaw, "This totally adds to my old people are crazy theory" ("Where the Wild Things Are", 4.18). Throughout *Buffy*, signs of aging are presented as though they are as disturbing and physically threatening as signs of danger from the demon world: both mark mortality and, before death, a carnal transformation into the monstrous.

The character Anya intensifies the age anxiety present in *Buffy*. As Cynthia Fuchs points out, "Anya is probably the series' 'youngest' character," in that she is repeatedly having to learn how to become a human adult" (106). Appearing first in season 3, Anya is a thousand-year-old vengeance demon, Patron of Women Scorned, who Giles, the school librarian who is fated to be Buffy's Watcher (a type of mythical mentor), inadvertently traps in the mortal dimension ("The Wish", 3.9). Anya's transformation from immortal to teenage girl furthers insight into the gendered paradoxes of aging promoted throughout the series. A character who misses the nuances in human speech and behavior, she has a procedural understanding of what being young should mean in the human world, telling her then boyfriend Xander, "I don't understand. I'm pretty, I'm young... I mean... Why didn't you take advantage of me? Is something wrong with your body... I saw that wrinkled man on TV talking about erectile dysfunction" ("Where the Wild Things Are", 4.18). She quips about her demon age, referring to her days as "a silly young thing. 700 years old," when she used to hang out with Dracula ("Buffy vs. Dracula", 5.1). When she is injured, she muses that she now has only about fifty years left to live. As Xander puts it, "You were going to live for thousands of years. Now you're going to age and die. That must be terrifying." She expresses her terror in notably ageist terms, "I'm going to get old. And ... you can't promise you'll be with me when I'm ... wrinkly and my teeth are artificial and stuck into my wrinkly mouth with an adhesive." As she heals, she expresses her relief by saying, "I anticipate many years before my death. Excepting disease or airbag failure" ("The Replacement", 5.3). When Xander and Anya announce their engagement to the rest of the gang, Anya explains, "Mortal life being so short, we gotta cram in as much marital bliss as we can before we wither and die," expressing the sentiment made more real in her song lyric from the musical episode quoted in the subtitle to this section ("All the Way", 6.6, "Once More, with Feeling", 6.7). In keeping with these simplistic ageist tropes, her fear continues to be that Xander will cease to love her when she ages as a mortal human. And before he does leave her at the altar, he imagines a future with her in fantasy scenes that project just the ageist view she fears the most. While the humorous tone of Anya's oblivious ageist ethos invites ridicule, her view so closely matches that of the teenage generation that it is funny for its blunt expression of what everyone is thinking rather than for being ridiculous in its content.

"Once Again I Teeter at the Precipice of the Generation Gap": Age Trouble and Age Appropriateness in the Middle Generation

Added to this fear of the aging body, the most pressing age anxieties of Buffy appear in the depiction of the generation gap between the teacher-parent middle-generation and the teenagers they feel responsible for, which Giles references in the lines quoted in the subtitle of this section. The two main middle-aged characters of the first half of the series, Giles and Joyce, Buffy's mother, can never quite understand the pressures Buffy faces: Giles because he ignores Buffy's social desires as a teenager and Joyce partly because she trivializes those desires but also because, for much of the time she appears on the series, she does not know her daughter is the Slayer. Joyce, not understanding her daughter's destiny, misinterprets Buffy's 'need' to go out one night (to save the world) as arising from the social demands on teenagers, saying, "I know. If you don't go out it'll be the end of the world. Everything is life or death when you're a sixteen-year-old girl" ("The Harvest", 1.2). In saying this, she unwittingly makes explicit the joke upon which the entire series rests – the world depends upon a seemingly frivolous, young, petite, attractive, blonde girl who feels the social demands on teenagers as acutely as she does her destiny as the Slayer. And the irony is increased because the grown-ups refuse to understand either set of demands and thus they behave irresponsibly, putting Buffy and the world in greater danger. Even though she has learned her daughter's destiny, perhaps frightened by it, Joyce under mystical influences spearheads a crusade with a group mockingly named "Mothers Opposed to the Occult" (MOO) to the extent of nearly burning Buffy and two of her friends at the stake ("Gingerbread", 3.11). Giles tells Buffy, "I make allowances for your youth," while actively trying to stop Buffy from pursuing activities particular to her age cohort, such as trying out for the cheerleading squad. Resentfully, Buffy tells her friends, "I'd say he should get a girlfriend if he wasn't so old," reminding viewers the age bias is decidedly two-directional ("Witch", 1.3). Perhaps worse than well meaning Giles and Joyce, Buffy's teenaged friends Xander and Willow's parents treat their offspring with differing types of neglect. Thus, from the very outset, the series establishes generational tensions: between teenagers and the middle-aged generation that just doesn't get it.

While Giles and Joyce are emblems of the meddlesome yet ignorant middle generation, many episodes in the first season offer examples of other adult figures that intensify the generation gap and that further the disgust with the older female body mentioned in the previous section. The episode "Witch" revolves around a body switch between a mother who had been a cheerleading star, and her daughter who is not. Forced to inhabit her mother's middle aged body so that her mother can use her youthful frame to have another shot at high school glory, Amy explains, "She said I was wasting my youth, so she took it." Cordelia, an over-the-top stereotypical popular girl, explains her desire to be on the cheerleading squad: "We have to achieve our dreams, Amy. Otherwise, we wither and die," equating an objectified physical aging with immediate death. When Buffy and her friends figure out the evil magic at play and force a reversal so that Amy is back to her teenaged body and her mother back to her older self, the mother exclaims, "That body was mine. Mine!" Buffy quips, "Oh grow up," revealing the series' ethos that the middle generation is annoying, but should learn to act its age. Her own mother Joyce demonstrates a deep horror at the notion of living as a teenager again, saying "Oh that's a frightful notion. Go through all that again? Not even if it helped me understand you" (1.3) As much as Buffy despairs at Joyce's lack of insight into Buffy's genuine struggle, the teenaged Slayer appreciates that her mother prefers age-appropriate behavior to yearning for lost youth.

Anxieties about age-appropriateness resurface in "Teacher's Pet," a first season episode that opposes two stereotypes of the older woman, the hyper-sexualized predator and the sweet old lady. The episode magnifies the stereotype of the sexually voracious older female, which has more recently come to be known as the "cougar" (Montemurro and Siefken, 35), into the form of a substitute teacher who genuinely is a monster. In monstrous shape, she becomes a creature akin to a praying mantis in that she must mate repeatedly and kill her lovers. To Buffy's disgust at his gullibility, Miss French easily catches sexually inexperienced and ungainly Xander. When Xander confidently explains that Buffy and Willow are "a little young to understand what an older woman would see in a younger man," Buffy retorts with, "The younger man is too dumb to wonder why an older woman can't find someone her own age, and too dumb to care about the surgical improvements," highlighting the physical attributes that Xander cannot see or does not mind are not genuinely part of the older female body he desires, while also gesturing to the catch-22 faced by older women in Buffyverse (1.4). They are potentially hideous if they show signs of age on their bodies, but artificial measures to prevent those signs of aging invite mockery.

Making Miss French, who is gorgeous and 20-something, monstrous in part because of her age reinforces the Buffyverse idea that, among humans, the middle generation invites ageism even before old age. When Buffy and gang later realize that Xander faces grave danger in Miss French's basement, they seek him at the house the school board records list as the substitute teacher's residence. Whereas the shooting script describes the Miss French teaching at Sunnydale High School as in her "late twenties," the Miss French who opens the door is considerable older (the script notes say 90 years old), and decidedly matches the stereotype of the "sweetest little old lady," on screen and as per the script notes. The younger (yet old to the teenagers) Miss French has stolen the much older Miss French's identity, making the previous jokes about the younger version of Miss French as an older woman hollow but still resonant for teenagers who perceive even the false Miss French to be of that amorphous group of adults known to be older but not wiser (1.4).

In the third season episode, "Band Candy" (3.6), the middle-generation characters are rendered youthful through the ingestion of mystically imbued confectionary and become, in fact, notably less responsible than Buffy and her friends are as teens without gaining the insight accorded to teen characters in the show. Even in their youthful state, Giles and Joyce do not understand Buffy's teenaged perspective because they go back to their youths rather than to the teenagehood that Buffy experiences in the 90s. To emphasize the reversal, the episode features Miss Barton, a substitute teacher played by an actress about thirty years older than the actors who play Joyce and Giles. This apparent gesture towards featuring an older character serves only to make more humorous her apparent return to behavior influenced by alcohol and marijuana. As the middle and older generations take over the local teenager hangout, the Bronze, the teenagers express their anxieties in relation to human frailty, with Willow saying, "I don't like this. They could have heart attacks." In the course of research, Willow decides to search for "disturbing second childhood," greatly exaggerating the situation, describing the 1960s youth counterculture behavior exhibited by Joyce and Giles in terms used for people with dementia. Cordelia is disgusted when her mother borrows her clothes because "there should be an age limit on lycra" and equally appalled by her father's open turn to pornography. The generational switch in "Band Candy" enables further ageist perspectives on the body and the mind amplified by the fact that this is a TV series so that, unlike age-reverse films such as *Big* or *Freaky Friday*, the show relies both on clichés about aging and on viewers' knowledge of the specific staid and neurotic characters of Joyce and Giles.

While the adults appear ridiculous as teenagers in this episode, their ridicule of teenagers in other episodes comes across as their misunderstanding, demonstrating that, as is so often the case, middle age is of the least interest to popular culture. As Buffy explains, "I was hoping not to get that cynical until I was at least 40," indicating where the age lines lie for her ("Beauty and the Beasts", 3.4). The disruption of the human age schema poses a threat to Sunnydale and to the teenagers' sense of themselves as empowered by youth. As Richards explains, "Ironically, of course, it is the 'grownups' with the most authority, the school principal and the mayor who are the most monstrous" (126-127). When Mayor Wilkins emerges as the demonic 'big bad' of season 3, the teenagers' distrust of the middle-aged generation is made manifest and dramatically slain. Gullette articulates the danger of positing such a false generation gap in explaining, "it undermines commonalities between parents and children. It pits them against one another as if they were unrelated social groups: silenced audience versus dominators of discourse, small fraternity against huge horde, poor youths versus rich adults" (*Aged by Culture* 57). Though Buffy is able to find deep commonalities with ancient vampires who physically appear to be close to her age, she rarely glimpses past the age divide to understand middle-aged human characters.

"The Earth Will Belong to the Old Ones": Ancient Evil As Supreme Strength

The inaugural episode of Buffy, "Welcome to the Hellmouth," sets up a further generational dichotomy between 'the old ones,' referring to a world of demons, and those living in the contemporary world. The Master, who is the 'big bad' of the first season, looks monstrous but also resembles, more than any other character on the show, an old man: he is bald and wrinkled even more than other vampires, with decayed but very pointy teeth. His ancient powerful evil starkly contrasts Buffy's youth and apparent obliviousness. To emphasize this, she humorously explains to Giles that she, at the age of sixteen, has 'retired' from her role as Slayer. When the Master asks his minion Luke to bring him "something…young," he means a young human on whom to feast. This portends his goal to ensure that once again, as Luke explains, "The earth will belong to the Old Ones," something Giles affirms in the next episode by explaining that "What remains of the Old Ones are vestiges" and that contemporary vampires, who are demons mixed with humans, are "waiting for the animals to die out," "and for the Old Ones" (who, unlike vampires, are pure demon) to return ("Welcome to Hellmouth", 1.1; "The Harvest", 1.2). As the show unfolds over a seven season arc, the biggest and oldest evil, known as The First, fights for this demonic desire to shed the contamination of human-demon hybridity and return pure demons to earth, in effect shuffling off the immortal coil of the apparently youthful human body for a similarly immortal but aesthetically less youthful visage.

In the Buffyverse, though vampires can typically pass as normal humans, sometimes with dubious 'carbon-dated' fashion sense, when they are attacking or feeling great passion, the signs of demonic possession show on their faces as wrinkled foreheads and pointed teeth, usually accompanied with guttural roaring. That transformation allows for in-jokes between Buffy and those who are in-the-know, often taking on an ageist tinge. For example, Buffy gibes a particularly vicious vampire named Darla, "You're older than him, right? Just between us girls, you are looking a little worn around the eyes," using the standard anti-ageist rhetoric that pervades the show to humorously describe the furrowed foreheads that vampires display on *Buffy* when they are in attack mode ("Angel", 1.7). When a nasty vampire who becomes a regular character, Spike, is unable to bite Willow despite the opportunity, he refers to his relatively young age, of 126, mocking the idea that virility only fades with age ("The Initiative", 4.7). Ageist jokes similar to those reviling human age apply to vampires within the show the moment there is a hint of any physical change, even though they are invulnerable to typical physical human aging.

For the most part, vampires are demon-human hybrids who appear as humans somewhat rejuvenated from the age when they were turned for the centuries. But in the Buffyverse, age does begin to show after extraordinary longevity: on figures such as the Master, who is almost batlike, and Kakistos, who has developed cloven hoofs. This differs from the weakening changes attributed to human aging. Whedon refers to this process as devolving towards a more animalistic state (qtd. in "Kakistos"). Thus there is a key difference between those younger vampires who can and mostly do appear human and those who do not, though the signs of age on the very few extremely ancient vampires come across as strength. The older the demons, the more evil they are, and their appearance reflects their evil through animalistic monstrosity along with no longer having to pass as human.

"I Ain't Getting Any Older": Angel's Youthful Longevity

Buffy's early love interest in the show's (first) vampire with a soul, Angel, best signifies the humor, pathos, and insight into contemporary views of aging afforded by vampires' invulnerability to human aging while appearing human. Before the great reveal that Angel is a vampire, he and Buffy almost express their feelings. He hesitates, explaining that "I'm older than you and this can't ever..." ("Angel", 1.7). Viewers assume he is at most in his 20s,[4] inappropriately old to be dating a 16-year-old but within socially accepted contraventions of romantic age difference, when the older person

---

4   He was turned into a vampire at the age of 26.

is the male. Despite his warning, they give in to a kiss, and as the kiss becomes more passionate, Angel's demon emerges, most evident in his transformed face. Buffy thereby learns that he really is too old for her, though relatively young...for a vampire. The discomfort that may accompany an adult dating a 16-year-old is overshadowed by the insider knowledge that the union between Buffy and Angel challenges boundaries well beyond the idea that he is an adult male taking advantage of an innocent teenager. Once the others learn that Angel is about 240 years old, Willow points out that, besides the fact that Buffy is destined to kill vampires, there is another painful paradox: "It is kind of novel how he'll stay young and handsome forever, although you'll still get wrinkly and die" ("Angel", 1.7). Though Angel does have a decidedly wrinkled face when his demon shows, for the most part he will always appear to be the slightly older, tall, dark, handsome man Buffy first met.[5]

The age difference between Angel and Buffy, signaling the different forms of chronological aging featured in the show, often becomes the source of wry jokes rife with dramatic irony. When Willow frets about her potential boyfriend, Oz, being a couple of years older than her, Buffy quips, "You think he's too old 'cause he's a senior? Please. My boyfriend had a bicentennial" ("Surprise", 2.13). In "The Prom," Buffy assures Angel that "lots of girls have older boyfriends. You'll blend" (3.20). Later in the series, when Buffy tries to explain how she knows Spike to her college boyfriend Riley, she describes Spike as "totally old...well not as old as my last boyfriend was" ("Something Blue", 4.9). In the final season, when Buffy has a date with the new high school principal, her friends point out that though Robin is ten years older than Buffy, he is at least a hundred years

---

5   The book and movie series *Twilight* deals with a similar disparity in a shallow manner. The difference is that the mortal female character, Bella, is upset when she finally passes the age that her vampire boyfriend, Edward, will remain forever. Like Buffy, she does not want to physically age while he remains young and flawless. The key difference is that in Buffy, vampires are portrayed as paradoxically appearing relatively young while being old. Angel is always the older man to Buffy. In *Twilight* vampires are depicted as staying the age that they appear. Thus Bella begs to be turned into a vampire in part to maintain her youth. Buffy, on the other hand, would never seek that change and matures rapidly because of her supernatural role as the Slayer.

younger than her type ("First Date", 7.14). The age difference between Angel and Buffy offers intermittent fodder for humor and for the expression of anxieties about the future that are already present because of the tension between Buffy's desire to be a 'normal' teenager who anticipates a career, marriage, babies, etc. and her calling as a Slayer, which does not guarantee her a long life since she continually faces mortal peril.

Angel worries he is not an appropriate love interest for Buffy, quipping that she could have a "less not normal" life with a different boyfriend ("Bad Eggs", 2.12). But Buffy assures him that she cannot think about the future in normative terms, though she has moments throughout the series of desiring as normal a life as Sunnydale would allow. As Kathryn Hill points out, Angel and late Spike are "variations on [a] popular culture trope, both are 'bad boys,' perpetual teen rebels, neither aging nor accepting the world as it is. At the same time both these characters are variations of that sexy, romantic, vulnerable figure of teenage revolt" (126). How do you date a teen rebel for the rest of your mortal human life? Because, as Angel says, he "ain't getting any older" ("Chosen", 7.22). Buffy remains torn between a desire for normalcy and the understanding that it would lack appeal. When a potion has diminished her powers, she panics about the potential of growing old without superhuman strength, saying, "What if I just get pathetic? Hanging out at 'The Old Slayer's Home' – talking people's ears off about my glory days" ("Helpless", 3.12). Joyce reminds Angel that he cannot offer Buffy what she deserves in terms of a future, prompting his move from Sunnydale to Los Angeles, which offers the premise for the spin-off *Angel* ("The Prom", 3.20). In a cross-over episode of *Angel*, concurrent with season 4 of *Buffy*, the "powers that be" offer Angel his mortality, along with a release from his duty to save humanity. While this would make him vulnerable to human age and death, it would also mean that he and Buffy could finally return to being lovers. They decide together that their duty to protect the world from evil supersedes their desire for a normal human love relationship, continuing the tortured notion of impossible love that haunts the series ("I Will Remember You", 1.8).

Buffy will always be over two centuries younger than Angel, but her body will eventually become marked by age in a way that his never will. Even in this mythic world, the physical marks of aging are as frightening as the evil presented by demons, so the prospect is especially alarming. The season 3 'big bad,' Mayor Wilkins, goads them about this, saying, when Angel points out that the Mayor is not his elder,

And that's just one of the things you're going to have to deal with. You're immortal, she's not. It's not easy. I married my Edna Mae in aught three and I was with her right until the end. Not a pretty scene. Wrinkled and senile and cursing me for my youth. It wasn't our happiest time. ("Choices", 3.19)

Even when Angel spends the equivalent of hundreds of years in a hell dimension, where time moves differently, his age in relation to Buffy remains consistent, so the hell years appear not to count for the mythology of the show, which depends on a consistently exaggerated age gap. Buffy ribs Angel about the couple being in a vampire-slaying rut, asking, "So this is our future? This is how we're going to spend our nights when I'm fifty and you're...the exact same age you are now?" ("Choices", 3.19). The fear that Buffy may not have a future at all due to the danger of her destiny is eclipsed by the fear that she might become physically older than her boyfriend.

"We Won't Be Young Forever": Growing Up in a Mythical World

When Buffy and her friends go through 'vocational aptitude' testing in high school, Willow is the only teenaged character who does not think the tests are a waste of time because, as she puts it, "We won't be young forever" ("What's My Line", 2.9). That double episode picks up on Buffy's anxieties about having a normal future and foreshadows the questions posed by the end of the series about what will happen to the Slayer and her friends as they mature into middle age. Giles points out to his love interest and fellow teacher Jenny Calendar, that "The Slayer rarely lives into her mid-twenties. It follows that she'd exhibit signs of maturity early on. Her whole life-cycle is accelerated" ("Surprise", 2.13). At college, Buffy's psychology professor discusses Buffy's apparent maturity with Giles, saying, "I think it can be unhealthy to take on adult roles too early" ("A New Man", 4.12). Kearney argues that this aspect of the Slayer's identity adds to *Buffy*'s appeal to viewers beyond the teen demographic (34-36). Through sleight of magic, Buffy gains a younger sister, Dawn, in season 5, a cunning way to introduce a new teen generation as Buffy becomes more mature. The weight of the duty to save the world is less comic in the last few seasons largely because of Buffy's responsibility for her sister and for the quotidian details of suburban life. As The First emerges as the ancient evil threatening yet another apocalyptic confrontation, Buffy herself matures, somewhat prematurely, into adulthood, ready to lead the forces against the biggest oldest evil to date.

Buffy's move into adulthood begins in "Helpless," a third season episode in which the Slayer's eighteenth birthday becomes an occasion for her to unknowingly be submitted to a cruel rite of passage by the Watcher's Council, a stuffy group of mostly men who make the rules from the UK. While Buffy ingeniously passes the test, Giles fails in his role as watcher because he shows too close an emotional attachment to Buffy. The council fires him, and Giles's increasing redundancy begins at this point. Once the high school has burned down, eliminating his other employment as school librarian, Giles's idleness becomes the butt of character and episode jokes. He tries to hang out at the Bronze with the teenagers, sings power ballads at cafés, becomes hooked on *Jeopardy*, having previously been a reader over a TV watcher, and buys a red convertible sports car. As Xander says to Anya, watching Giles perform, "If we grow old together, remind me to skip the midlife crisis" ("Where the Wild Things Are", 4.18). The introduction of Dawn's teenage perspective intensifies the view of Giles as aging. As she writes in her diary, "I think it's 'cause he's just so...old. I'm not sure how old he is, but I hear him use the world 'newfangled' one time. So he's gotta be pretty far gone" ("Real Me", 5.2). The focus is not on Giles's body, but on his mannerisms and vocation. For example, Spike gibes Giles for not being able to handle being surpassed by his student, Buffy ("Touched", 7.20). Buffy's maturity comes at the cost of Giles's value.

After her mother dies, and with Giles increasingly redundant, Buffy is forced to take on roles, previously ludicrous to her, of the middle generation. While her physical aging is not accelerated, she is prematurely aged in terms of the roles she has to take on. For example, Buffy plays the sexualized older woman role mocked in the early seasons of the show. A high school student, on whom Buffy's younger sister has a crush, also attracts twenty-two-year-old Buffy's sexual attentions due to an enchanted football jacket. Buffy describes herself to the object of affection, R.J., as "not really older at all, actually. Just like you, but with sexual experience and stuff." R.J. points out that she is like a teacher, but it does not stop his sexual advances. After the others find out about her inappropriate romance, she tells them that she is "extremely youthful. And peppy." As the sisters reconcile, Dawn explains, "You're older and hotter and have sex that's rough and kill people. I don't have any of that stuff." While Buffy has mocked Miss French for her sexual behavior, Buffy remains sexy without ridicule at about the same age ("Him", 7.6). The show does not progress to an insightful commentary about aging but it does set aside its prejudices when they would apply to the previously teenaged generation. The viewfinder of the youthful gaze may begin to shift with Buffy and her friends, but the idea that old age is frightening and undesirable never goes away. They do not redefine for themselves what it will mean to grow older, and they persist in striving to seem youthful.

Over the last couple of seasons, Buffy comes to realize that slaying is not going to provide the type of income necessary to maintain a middle class lifestyle, so the show begins to offer some sympathy for the more middle-aged difficulties of facing unemployment, a sympathy that Gullette points out the imposed generational war often functions to eradicate (*Aged by Culture* 57). Gradually, the show reveals the work required to rebuild the house when it is destroyed in the course of fighting evil, something that earlier seasons glossed over when responsibility for the house fell to Joyce. Previously, Buffy had briefly abandoned her friends in Sunnydale, her role as the Slayer, and her mother's comfortable home, and had to take up regular work to get by. The episode, "Anne," presages the relationship the show forges between hard work and aging. A demon captures vulnerable humans and steals them away to do hard labor in an underground world where time is accelerated. As Buffy puts it, having come to terms with the schema once she too has been kidnapped, "So you just work us till we're too old and spit us back out." Freed slaves wander the streets too exhausted and destroyed to remember their past selves and unrecognizable to those they knew only moments before because they have aged many years down below compared with a few hours by the time measured above ground. Buffy rescues the slaves and does not succumb to the seemingly accelerated aging, but the episode makes clear that the effect of work is accelerated physical aging and the physical aging comes with the loss of a sense of self, though this is not a depiction of dementia (3.1). Later, Buffy discovers that as a college dropout, her lack of qualifications limits her employment options. After a series of portrayals of the drudgery and terror of working in the fast food industry, her mythic role as the Slayer lands her a job in her previous high school as a counselor for troubled teens, cementing her transformation towards the middle-aged group, even though she is only in her twenties. Her new job presages the role of mentor that Buffy takes on for the climactic final episodes of the seventh season.

The final season of Buffy is preoccupied with showing the ways in which Buffy is the only one now suited to lead the younger generation rather than fixating on her as the sole Slayer of her own generation. Because of the duration of the show, over seven years, Buffy has to age into adulthood. Because of her role as Slayer, that aging is preternaturally fast. The show finally introduces an entire generation of 'potentials,' teenage girls who are proto-Slayers, ready to be transformed when the existing Slayer dies. This is a dramatic transformation from Buffy's solitary role as the one Slayer of her generation, destined to slay or be slain, fated to give up the trappings of happy teenage life in order to make them possible for others. The potentials gather in Sunnydale under Buffy's watch, emphasizing her precocious shift into the grown-up parent-like role she has previously mocked. She does not develop the wrinkled skin the teen characters continually revile but she does adopt the annoying adult position without which the teens would be lost. The season demonstrates the teen potentials' frustration with her, but, unlike her own teenaged generation, the potentials are always wrong and Buffy remains strong. She does a much better job than do the adults from the previous seasons, having previously been preternaturally more mature while also relentlessly an otherwise typical teenager. The idea that adulthood might entail some power and insight becomes at least a possibility at the end of *Buffy*, but the problem of aging flesh has not been eradicated. Her plan to defeat the First, in the final episode, by sharing her power with the proto-Slayers, dramatically advancing their development, offers a feminist revisioning of Whedon's already feminist myth of the Slayer. Rather than needing to step aside into retirement, Buffy comes up with a way for everyone called to be a Slayer to share the burden and the work.

Where Are They Now? Revamping the Vampire

Buffy launched a series of supernatural teen shows, including other vampire narratives, that share some of the same preoccupations and concerns including the aging of humans versus the longevity of demons. The most interesting from an age studies perspective, *True Blood* (2008-2014), introduces faeries to the mythology. They are not immortal but one is described as "halfway to being an elder" at the age of 500. Nonetheless, their aging into adulthood is accelerated so that they can quickly become characters who dress in provocative clothing and drink alcohol, not so that they can save the world, like Buffy. Bill, a central vampire in *True Blood* frequently appears in flashbacks that emphasize his longevity but remains 30-something in human appearance. He represents the Old South, betrayed by the Civil War that 'turned' him. While *Vampire Diaries* (2009-present) offers immortal vampires who do not age, it does little to investigate the implications in constructive or complex ways.

Creators of vampire television series face a particular challenge because, while vampire characters ought not show their chronological age, the actors who play them over several years of television serialization do visibly age. *Buffy* can rely on repeated jokes about old people, with only slight variations, over an extended period of time, but it also has to account for or hide the aging of its cast. My title, "Vampires Don't Age, But Actors Sure Do," is taken from media discussions of the dilemma faced by fans who would like to see *Buffy* and its spin-off *Angel* come back to the small or big screen (Wilson). The question remains whether such a return could dramatically open up the show's contemplation of aging into adulthood to reconsider age as a category as worthy of interrogation as gender. *Buffy* seasons 8 and 9 have appeared in comic book form without offering that insight, but that genre does not face the challenge of working with aging actors. Fans are certainly skeptical that 40-something David Boreanaz (who plays Angel) could ever play a character he already struggled to play as static in age when he was only in his late 20s and early 30s. To have Angel return, played by Boreanaz, would require a more dramatic shift to the conceptualization of vampires' physical aging. While Sarah Michelle Gellar's (who plays Buffy) age, 36, might present a challenge to ageist Hollywood norms for leading ladies were she to return as the Slayer, it should not be insurmountable within the transgressive Buffyverse. The show would have to continue to shift its perspective to match the aging of the central characters, Buffy and her closest friends, and take more interest in middle age in the process.

While *Buffy* clearly influenced subsequent vampire televsion shows, none offers the figure of the Slayer. Whedon created the transgressive figure of the young Vampire Slayer to challenge the sexist sensibilities of the horror genre. He then transformed his entire mythical universe in the final episode by allowing Buffy's power to be shared among all the again young potentials. Since Buffy is that rare Slayer who lives into adulthood, what gains could be made in presenting her now as a genuinely middle-aged female superhero? And what might happen if David Boreanaz returned as Angel, physically aged through some act of magic or with animalistic signs of age, but fighting for good? Rather than separating the experience gained over the years from the appearance of aging, such a revamped vampire and Slayer could play with attempts to match appearance to experience, potentially yielding a different set of ageist stereotypes but also, perhaps, finally undoing them.

WORKS CITED

Auerbach, Nina. *Our Vampires, Ourselves*. Chicago: University of Chicago Press, 1995. Print.

Fuchs, Cynthia. "'Did anyone ever explain to you what "Secret Identity" means?': Race and Displacement in Buffy and Dark Angel ." *Undead TV: Essays on Buffy the Vampire Slayer*. Ed. Elana Levine and Lisa Ann Parks. Durham,NC: Duke University Press, 2007. 96–115. Print.

Gullette, Margaret Morganroth. *Aged by Culture*. 1st ed. Chicago: University Of Chicago Press, 2004. Print.

Gullette, Margaret Morganroth. *Declining to Decline: Cultural Combat and the Politics of the Midlife* (Age Studies). Charlottesville: University of Virginia Press, 1997. Print.

Hill, Kathryn. "S/He's a Rebel: The James Dean Trope in *Buffy the Vampire Slayer*." *Continuum: Journal of Media & Cultural Studies*. 27.1 (2013): 124–140. Web. 6 Jan 2015

"Kakistos." *Slayerworld Offline Library*. (original statement from *Bronze*, Oct 1998) Slayer Network, 8 Sept 2004. Web. 7 Jan 2015.

Kearney, Mary Celeste. "The Changing Face of Teen Television, or Why We All Love Buffy." *Undead TV: Essays on Buffy the Vampire Slayer*.

Ed. Elana Levine and Lisa Ann Parks. Durham, NC: Duke University Press, 2007. 17–41. Print.

Montemurro, Beth and Jenna Marie Siefken, "Cougars on the Prowl? New Perceptions of Older Women's Sexuality." *Journal of Aging Studies.* 28 (2014): 35–43. Web. 7 Jan 2015.

Richards, Chris. "What Are We? Adolescence, Sex and Intimacy in Buffy the Vampire Slayer." *Continuum" Journal of Media & Cultural Studies.* 18.1 (2004): 121–137. Web. 6 Jan 2015

Sontag, Susan. *The Double Standard of Aging.* Toronto: Women's Kit, 1972. Print.

Twigg, Julia. "The Body, Gender, and Age: Feminist Insights in Social Gerontology." *Journal of Aging Studies.* 18.1 (2004): 59–73. Web. 6 Jan 2015.

Wilson, Emily. "Slay it Again." *The Guardian.* Guardian News and Media Limited, 2 April 2007. Web. 7 Jan 2015.

TELEVISION

Angel. Creators Joss Whedon and David Greenwalt (1999-2004).
Buffy the Vampire Slayer. Director Fran Rubel Kuzui (1992).
Buffy the Vampire Slayer. Creator Joss Whedon (1993-2003).
True Blood. Creator Alan Ball, HBO (2008-2014).
The Twilight Saga. Directed by Catherine Hardwicke (1), Chris Weitz (2), David Slade (3), Bill Condon (4-5) (2008-2012).
Vampire Diaries. Creators Julie Plec and Kevin Williamson, The CW (2009–present).

In the Twilight of Their Lives?
Magical Objects as Serial Devices and Catalysts of Aging in *The Twilight Zone*

MARTA MIQUEL-BALDELLOU

Introduction

The Twilight Zone was an American anthology series which presented a succession of different stories, pertaining for the most part to the genres of fantasy and science-fiction, with a plethora of characters and situations that changed in each episode and delved into aspects of the human condition. The original series ran on CBS for five seasons from 1959 to 1964, attracting popular and critical praise on equal terms and was rerun through syndication decades later, attaining outstanding renewed public acclaim. From a contemporary perspective, *The Twilight Zone* is considered a landmark series in the history of television, surpassing the status of a television show to become part of popular culture by virtue of the extraordinary magnetism it has exerted through years on audiences worldwide.

As critic William Boddy argues, in terms of its format, as an anthology series *The Twilight Zone* involved a negotiation between the dramatic values that characterised the television in the Golden Age and the structure that shaped the thirty-minute film series, thus blending features of the 1950s live drama with the format of modern telefilms (99). In fact, it could be claimed that this series has more in common with the single-play dramatic anthologies of the early 1950s than with the modern continuing-character episodic series, since it lacks continuing characters, settings, and plots. Nonetheless, as Boddy further admits, this series presents continuities through important narratological elements such as its narrative voice, its characterisation, and its ideological discourse (107). Among these continuities, in particular, there is the characteristic structure that recurs along the series, which, throughout time, proved to be extremely effective to engage the attention of the audience. In this respect, as Stewart Stanyard claims, each story introduces the viewer to a group of characters caught up in an ordinary situation when, suddenly, this realistic perspective shifts into a surrealistic framework, which frames the series within the genres of fantasy and science fiction, until an unexpected twist brings the story to a close (162).

Precisely, with regard to the genres this series mostly belongs to, critics such as Keith Booker have considered *The Twilight Zone* the series that marked the maturation of science fiction television as a genre (6). In fact, as J.P. Telotte claims, it made it possible that typical science fiction themes were used to comment upon the American contemporary culture of the time (12), thus turning the genre of science fiction into a valuable tool to create socially critical drama in a way that, according to Rodney Hill, would not unleash the concern of network executives, advertising agencies, corporate sponsors, and congressional committees (124). As Telotte further contends, *The Twilight Zone* made use of the speculative power that lies at the core of science fiction to lay bare the constructed nature of all things (4). In fact, drawing on Erik Mortenson's thesis that science fiction exploits the disturbing potential of a shadowy zone where rules are disrupted, *The Twilight Zone* explicitly makes use of this shadow imagery to explore liminal spaces of ambiguity that challenge any conventional or dualistic thinking (55).

According to Eric Barnouw, *The Twilight Zone*, being an anthology series, places a great emphasis on diversity (154), and explores an inventory of themes within the genres of fantasy and science fiction that recur throughout its different seasons and pave the ground for a thematic categorisation. In this respect, critics such as Stanyard have devised a catalogue of themes, which are frequently tackled in the series and encompass issues, mostly pertaining to science fiction, such as alternate universes, space travel, aliens, and time machines (33-56). Drawing on this plethora of themes, this article aims to address aging as another important topic within this group of issues related to the genres of fantasy and science fiction that *The Twilight Zone* explicitly deals with. As a matter of fact, in the context of a conference given at the UCLA in 1971 and upon being asked whether he could identify any pervasive theme in *The Twilight Zone*, the creator of the series, Rod Serling, referred to "the syndrome of age" and the issue of "age versus youth" as important threads that he believed recurred throughout the series. Similarly, in a 1995 documentary directed by Susan Lacy, which was meant to honour Rod Serling, it is claimed, with regard to the authors that contributed their stories to the series, that "it is amazing that these writers, who were in their thirties, were able to write with such understanding about old age," while it is also mentioned that "Serling often dealt with people in the twilight of their lives," thus evincing that aging was significantly present throughout the series.

In fact, reasons related to Rod Serling's biographical background as well as the historical context in which the series originated may account for the pervasive presence of aging in different episodes of *The Twilight Zone*. To use Marc Scott Zicree's words, "the theme of old age interested Rod Serling enough" (290), mostly because, owing to the fact that he had fought in the Second World War, Serling felt that he had been dispossessed of his youth too early and had been made to age before due course. Conversely, in his maturity, describing himself as a "middle-aged kid," Serling envisioned his writings for TV as a sort of refuge in an attempt to regain his lost youth at a later stage of his life. Serling's views on aging, which would ultimately find their reflection in some episodes of *The Twilight Zone*, mostly called into question the constructed separate categories of youth and old age, leading him to consider age as a mostly fluid category. This perception of aging as a pervasive thread in some episodes of the series also responds to the historical context in which *The Twilight Zone* came into being. According to F.M. Hodges, *The Twilight Zone* reflects the power struggle between the older and younger generations, and the growing polarisation of American society along generational lines (175). The age group known as 'baby boomers' – who were the first to grow up with television and became the first generation to watch *The Twilight Zone* – were regarded as an eminently liberal and as a particularly 'youthful' group. Actually, as Terhi-Anna Wilson claims, when the 'baby boomers' grew older, they claimed that they felt subjectively young, , thus contributing to reconstructing what age meant through concepts such as 'subjective age' rather than through 'biological age' (644). Some episodes of *The Twilight Zone* already envision age as a mainly ambivalent and socially constructed concept, and explicitly address the generational struggle between youth and old age.

Taking into consideration that aging is a thread that recurs in some episodes of the series, this article aims at portraying how the overall theme of aging is articulated throughout *The Twilight Zone*, paying special attention to the serial devices that join all the episodes that address aging, and how these elements of repetition and seriality contribute to constructing the different discourses of aging developed in the series. Even though *The Twilight Zone* clearly belongs to the television genre of anthology drama, it still presents significant aspects of seriality, since, as Tudor Oltean argues, not only does the concept of seriality stand for the characteristic system of serial narratives, but it also refers to the process whereby viewers reconstruct the textual interconnectedness of a series (20). In this respect, it can be claimed that the presence of 'thematic connections' among different episodes underlines the narrative sequential process of the series, while a system of interconnectedness is also achieved by the cyclical presence of magical objects that function as 'narratological links' through the episodes addressing the same theme. The analysis presented in this article focuses on sixteen episodes of *The Twilight Zone* which have been selected on a tripartite basis: the main characters of the story are aged individuals, the topic of aging plays an important role in the development of the plot, and the conclusion reached in each episode contributes some significant reflections on the discourses of aging. From a thematic perspective, the study of each episode within each thematic category will explore how aged characters are perceived, what kind of reading of aging is offered to the viewer, and whether this perception given changes or evolves through episodes pertaining to different seasons but included in the same thematic category. From a narratological perspective, the analysis of the magical objects that pervade the episodes selected will look into the concept of seriality and the effect it has on the discourse of aging developed along these episodes. In the context of postmodernism, Jean-François Lyotard argues that serial transformation becomes the means of continuous composition and decomposition of grand narratives (31). In this sense, the concept of seriality in this series will be tackled through the analysis of the presence of magical objects taken both as serial devices that provide cohesiveness to the series and as catalysts of ageing with the aim to judge whether they contribute to perpetuating commonly established categories of aging or whether these serial elements rather problematize pre-established categories in age studies such as the traditional dichotomy between youth and old age.

Categories of Aging as Thematic Connections, and Magical Objects as Narratological Links and Catalysts of Aging

As a result of the analysis of sixteen episodes of *The Twilight Zone* that deal with aging, it is possible to come up with six different thematic categories and, within each of them, there is a succession of magical objects that work as serial devices and provide cohesion among the different episodes classified in each section. In this respect, some episodes approach aging from mythical, cultural, social, technological, anthropological, and psychological perspectives, thus giving shape to six different categories of aging in the series. The episodes that address aging within each category also resort to the presence of some objects that turn into magical items and catalysts of aging, disrupting the normal functioning of reality such as ancestral tokens, domestic devices, scripts and lectures, technological gadgets, avatars, and houses that become extensions of the body.

Ancestral Tokens from the Past: Elders in Search of Eternal Youth

As Herbert Covey points out, the search for ways to extend the life-span or recapture youth has remained a long tradition in Western history (53), while, in the context of postmodern culture, Mike Featherstone and Mike Hepworth claim that the hope of an endless life has been revived by means of consumer images of perpetual youth and the blurring of traditional life course boundaries ("The Mask of Ageing" 371-390). In this context, some episodes of *The Twilight Zone* portray characters that manage to defy the boundaries of ordinary life expectancy and maintain an unusual youthful appearance in spite of their actual old chronological age. In stories such as "Long Live Walter Jameson" (1.24), "Of Late I Think of Cliffordville" (4.14), and "Queen of the Nile" (5.23), a history professor, a successful businessman, and a long-acclaimed actress attempt to attain eternal youth with the aim to achieve wisdom, wealth, and beauty, respectively. These three episodes from *The Twilight Zone*, pertaining to different seasons of the series, ultimately address the paradox comprised in the fact that, even though old age has hardly ever been regarded a desired state of being, individuals have conventionally aspired to live as long as possible and stretch the limits of longevity.

In addition to being thematically linked, as they tackle the mythical quest for eternal youth, these episodes are also narratologically correlated as they all present a series of tokens that refer back to the past, such as a history book, a legal contract, and an Egyptian scarab, but still have an important effect on the present. These tokens turn into magical objects that reverse the chronological passage of time and attest that characters move backwards and forwards in time and space, and manage to restore their youthfulness regardless of the passage of time. In turn, these tokens from the past also function as serial devices that join these episodes and contribute to replicating the theme of the quest for eternal youth. The presence of these tokens from the past reverberates along these three episodes and makes the virtual impression of extending the stories in time through different seasons of this television series, in analogy with the lives of their protagonists.

In the episode "Long Live Walter Jameson," a history book – insofar as it keeps record of a series of historical events in the past – serves the purpose of bridging the gap between the past and the present. This story focuses on an apparently young history professor, Walter Jameson, who talks about the past as if he had lived through the time he refers to in his classes. One of his colleagues, Samuel Kittridge, becomes suspicious when, upon reading a history book about the Civil War, he realises that Hugh Skelton, a distinguished officer during the Civil War, appears to be Walter Jameson's spitting image. To Kittridge's surprise, when he confronts Jameson about his findings, the young professor confesses that he is in fact Hugh Skelton and that he has managed to defy the barriers of time as, many centuries ago, he paid an alchemist for the gift of immortality. In the context of aging studies, it can be argued that Walter Jameson assumes the classical role of the sage who aspires to attain immortality in order to continue his everlasting pursuit of wisdom. This episode thus draws on the recurrent association of old age with deep knowledge, since, as Covey points out, in western art and history elders have often been regarded as individuals possessing great wisdom owing to their maturity and lifetime experience (61). In clear analogy with the character of Doctor Faustus, though, Jameson's purposes in the episode are deceitful, as he plans to marry Kittridge's young daughter in spite of knowing that, while she gradually grows old and ultimately dies, he will always remain young and will go on with his life. In an act of poetic justice, Jameson finally meets his death when one of the aging wives that he abandoned long ago comes back to take revenge. Accordingly, the character of Walter Jameson also personifies the archetypal character of the aging patriarch who intends to retain all knowledge and science in his own hands and use it exclusively to his own benefit. Hence, even though this episode contends that the quest for eternal youth has always fascinated humankind, it also condemns such pursuit as immoral, especially when it is clear that it responds to egoistical purposes.

In the following episode of *The Twilight Zone* that addresses the quest for eternal youth, "Of Late I think of Cliffordville," a legal contract becomes a magical token from the past that, back to the present, results in an ironic reversal of fortune. This episode revolves around aging executive William Feathersmith, who, one night in his office, meets Hecate, who works as the janitor of the company and happens to be from his same hometown, Cliffordville. This encounter awakens Feathersmith's nostalgia, as he finds himself wishing he could go back to his youth to start all over again. Owing to a contract he signs with the devil, Feathersmith goes back in time but, when he realises his past is not as fulfilling as he remembered, he begs the devil to take him back to the present. In order to get the money for the train ticket that will allow him to travel in time, Feathersmith feels compelled to sell young Hecate the purchase agreement of an oil-rich tract of land. Back to the present, to his dismay, Feathersmith realises that he is now the janitor of the company while Hecate has become its wealthy director. Within the framework of aging studies, Covey claims that elders have long been associated with miserly behaviour and that avarice has been regarded as one of the chief sins of old age, especially inasmuch as the elderly were believed to hold on to their possessions while the youth remained totally dependent on their seniors (51). Accordingly, drawing on this cultural stereotype related to old age, in this episode Feathersmith plays the classical role of the old miser who, blinded by selfishness and greed, tries to regain his youth in an attempt to become even wealthier. In his journeys to the past, the present and the future, Feathersmith is also somehow remindful of the classic Dickensian character of Scrooge, whose magical experience ultimately has a moral effect on him, as he eventually decides to leave behind his miserly behaviour. Nonetheless, as happens with Walter Jameson in the previous episode, Feathersmith also finds retribution as a result of his unlimited ambition since, in his will to quench his thirst for wealth and power, the tables are turned and he ultimately ends up in bankruptcy. Once more this episode of *The Twilight Zone* draws on a cultural stereotype traditionally attached to the elderly – as is avarice in old age – with the view to condemn it and underscore the belief that aged patriarchs have traditionally retained all wealth while younger generations have been compelled to remain in their shadow.

The serial device and catalyst of aging in the episode "Queen of the Nile" consists in a sacred scarab from ancient Egypt that allows a retired actress to remain young forever after, thus once more bridging the gap between the past and the present, and permitting an individual to attain physical eternal youth. As Covey claims, elders who try to cover and negate their aging traits have been traditionally ridiculed for their vanity, even though their attitude for the most part responds to cultural prejudices that have often equated beauty with youth (59). In the case of women, their vanity has been associated with trickery and deceit and it is in this context that aging women who endeavour to conceal their actual age have been habitually associated in cultural manifestations with gothic characters such as the witch or the vampire. In this episode, the protagonist, Pamela Morris, is significantly an actress, who indulges in a masquerade of youth and femininity on and off the screen, since, in her deceitful purposes, she attracts men and, by means of a sacred scarab, she drains their life and transfers it to herself in order to remain ever young. However, in contrast with eternally young characters from previous episodes of *The Twilight Zone* such as Walter Jameson and William Feathersmith, who are ultimately punished as a result of poetic justice, Pamela Morris is actually allowed to go on with her wicked plans. The conclusion to this episode can be interpreted as an ironic commentary by its screenwriter, who, well versed in the cinematic context, wishes to pay homage to the great actresses of the golden age and allows them to take revenge for having been banished from the screen far too early for the simple reason of being considered too aged. In fact, given the ageist and sexist prejudices to which Pamela Morris is exposed in her profession – as, in the world of cinema, women have been mostly celebrated for their physical appearance – it can be argued that

Pamela Morris has been made to bear what, in Susan Sontag's words, consists in 'the double standard of aging' (72-80), since, as opposed to men, she is culturally required to match up the image of a feminine adolescent ideal through all her life.

All along these three episodes, tokens from the past such as a history book, a legal contract, and a sacred scarab serve the purpose of addressing the devious quest of eternal youth, as, by means of the magical action that these devices bring about, characters undergo a process of physical rejuvenation and look much younger than they actually are. Accordingly, these three episodes ultimately present the mismatched dichotomy established between physical age and chronological age. As a matter of fact, the actors playing the roles of the main characters in "Long Live Walter Jameson" and "Of Late I Think of Cliffordville" present a profuse use of age effects through make-up and wigs that allow them to exhibit a considerable aged physical appearance that stands in sharp contrast with their rejuvenated physique. In this respect, Walter Jameson is first portrayed as an apparently young man who undergoes an abrupt process of aging once he is lethally injured, while William Feathersmith is initially depicted as an aged executive who goes back in time and suddenly transforms into a young entrepreneur. In both cases, their physical appearance does not reflect their chronological age and this divergence is further emphasised by the fact that Walter Jameson, in spite of his young looks, laments his forlorn existence as he is condemned to outlive all his friends, while William Feathersmith, in spite of looking as if he were in his thirties, also feels mentally exhausted as, chronologically, he is seventy-five years of age. Only Pamela Morris in "Queen of the Nile" appears to exemplify the fascinating utopia of eternal youth, as her physical age and chronological age seem to match one another. Her unusual longevity as an actress literally reflects that eternal physical youth can only be truly tenable through the fantasy of the screen. It is in this respect that the actress Pamela Morris is the only character exonerated, whereas Walter Jameson and William Feathersmith are punished for attempting to attain eternal youth.

Domestic Devices that Subvert the Cultural Dictates of Aging

In a series of episodes of *The Twilight Zone*, some ordinary objects and domestic devices acquire the role of mementos that allow aging individuals to awaken vivid memories from the past and from their youth. Domestic utensils such as a radio, a clock, or a can, and ordinary items such as a domestic screen projector acquire such evocative potential that turn into metaphorical time machines, even though it is rather the capacity of the aging characters to believe in magic what truly enables them to subvert the cultural dictates of aging and act against their age. Hence, in addition to displaying their evocative power, these objects also pave the ground to present aging as a culturally constructed discourse rather than as a primarily biological process. As an early indication of Margaret Morganroth Gullette's precepts that individuals are aged by culture and that aging cannot have a single universal meaning (11), these episodes show that the cultural dictates of age can be reconfigured, even if the process of aging has often been culturally associated with decline.

In the episode "The Sixteen-Millimiter Shrine" (1.4), an aging retired actress, Barbara Jean Trenton, decides to seclude herself in the private screening room of her mansion to spend her days running her screen projector and watching her old films. For this retired actress, the domestic screen projector turns into a constant reminder of the splendorous years of her youth, but it also becomes an alternate mirror of ageing that reflects the age she actually feels she is, especially when she realises that she is no longer offered the roles she would like to play on screen on account of her age. As a result of the serial device of magic that recurs all through the series, Barbara's screen projector acquires magical qualities that enable her to abandon her seat as a spectator, trespass the fourth wall and find herself back on the screen, once more playing a part in one of her old films. Accordingly, even though Barbara feels aged by culture, she decides to dismiss any prevailing cultural prescriptions about aging and, instead, holds on to the age standards that she has chosen to establish on her own. In this respect, critics such as Bryan Turner have referred to the disjuncture that takes place in the context of aging and identity, as the inner self usually remains youthful while the body becomes culturally and socially labelled as aged (250). In this episode of *The Twilight Zone*, the character of Barbara Trenton, aware of this disjuncture, envisions an alternate reality in which she is permitted to act the age she feels and is allowed to retain the roles that she used to play in her youth.

An antique radio acquires magical properties in the episode "Static" (2.20) and subverts the stratified periods of life and the prescribed behaviour that is attached to different age stages. In this episode, Ed Lindsay, an elderly bachelor who lives in a boarding house with other aging people – including Vinnie Broun, to whom Ed was engaged in his youth – finds an antique radio in the basement which can get access to stations that no longer exist and programmes that he used to listen to in his youth. When he calls Vinnie to come to his room and listen to the radio in his company, they find themselves back in time and are granted a second chance to resume their relationship. In this episode, an antique radio awakens memories from the past that still reverberate in the present and allows the protagonists to undergo a metaphorical journey in time and revert to a life stage that they felt was utterly lost. As the limits of time frameworks are blurred by virtue of this magical radio, it is implied that, as Mike Featherstone and Andrew Wernick claim, youth and old age, like all stages in the life course, are ultimately transitional statuses (8). In view of that, it is argued that life stages are not clearly separated from one another and, henceforth, it is perceived as pointless to attach any prescribed behaviour to any stage in life according to culturally determined dictates of aging. In this respect, even if in their old age, Ed and Vinnie believe their relationship is no longer tenable owing to social prejudices, through the action of magic and their metaphorical journey in time, they feel young again in their old age and ultimately resume their relationship.

The blurring of culturally determined life stages also becomes pivotal in the episode "Kick the Can" (3.21), in which a game for children involving a domestic can once more unleashes a world of fantasy that subverts culturally constructed perceptions of aging. In this episode, Charles Whitley is an aged man living in a rest home that witnesses how most residents have given up any will to have fun and spend most of their time complaining about their bleak situation. In the gardens outside the rest home, Charles sees a group of children playing a game known as "kick the can," which he also used to play in his childhood. Through his awakening memories, Charles realises that the secret of keeping young in old age simply lies in the fact of acting young and, to that end, he persuades all the residents to join him in the game. Out of magic, the act of playing becomes endowed with such transforming potential that literally turns its aged participants into children. Significantly enough, this surprising twist at the end of the episode underscores the controversial trope in aging studies that has traditionally associated old age with childhood. As Jenny Hockey and Allison James claim, second childhood consists in a cultural stereotype attached to aging whereby the dependent qualities of childhood are used to reflect a series of limitations that appear to characterise old age (137). However, the association of old age with childhood also grants the linear passage of time a cyclical nature that contributes to characterising old age as a turning point rather than a final stage in life. In this sense, even if they are also critical of this metaphor, Hockey and James also refer to the transformational power that lies in the metaphor of old age as childhood, even claiming that the elderly living in residential care may envision this image as a deliberate subversive strategy or as a form of resistance (146). As a matter of fact, it can be argued that even if it also contributes to perpetuating the metaphor of infantilisation in old age, the episode of "Kick the Can" also adds complexity to the metaphor of old age as second childhood, since, when the elders in the residential home literally transform into children, they actually follow their wish to subvert the cultural dictates of aging that strictly determine their behaviour and prevent them from engaging in any sort of game.

In the episode "Ninety Years without Slumbering" (5.12), a clock turns into a magical device that, paradoxically, serves the purpose of disrupting the established boundaries of time, which once more establishes a difference between culturally constructed precepts of age and the way individuals approach their personal process of aging. In the story, an aging man, Sam Forstmann, is convinced that when his grandfather's clock, which he has owned for all his life, stops, his life will also come to an end and, owing to this belief, he obsessively gets into the habit of regularly winding the clock. Upon realising that his relatives have sold his much appreciated token, Sam is convinced that he is going to die but, to his surprise, when the clock stops, he does not pass away but is rather released from his obsession and is metaphorically born to a new life in which the time that remains for him to live is no longer a matter for concern. In the context of cultural aging, Gullette claims that the concept of age identity comprises the collection of information about aging in general and of individual stories about one's process of aging, and it is as a result of these two sources that individuals construct their age narratives (15). In this episode, the aging protagonist has been indoctrinated in the belief that his life span depends on the effective working of his clock. His expectations about his life course and the way he approaches his process of aging have been influenced by this prejudice as, ironically, he believes that a magical clock that he has inherited from his family defines and determines his age. Nonetheless, it is this same clock that, upon stopping, allows the aging protagonist to metaphorically write his own age narrative as an individual, regardless of any cultural prejudice that determines the way he envisions his process of aging.

All the aging characters in these four episodes of *The Twilight Zone* are influenced by cultural prejudices about aging. However, in spite of the cultural constraints that request them to behave according to their age, these characters simply decide to defy age standards and act against their age. They encounter magical devices that, as mementos from their past, underline the passage of time and the characters' sense of nostalgia, but these objects also function as catalysts that urge the protagonists to make a change and construct their own age narratives. In this respect, despite the pervasive cultural requirements to act their age, Barbara Jean Trenton firmly believes that she can still play a leading role in a film, Ed Lindsay resumes his relationship with Vinnie, Charles Whitley transmits his capacity of enjoyment to all the residents in the rest home, and Sam Forsmann focuses on the present and no longer worries about the time he has left to live. All of them are portrayed as individuals that ultimately find out that aging is culturally determined and decide to subvert and reconstruct the dictates of aging to which they have been culturally indebted.

Of Scripts and Lectures on Aging:
The Social Prescriptions of Age

Some episodes in *The Twilight Zone* also portray aged characters that find themselves in the last years of their professional careers. Owing to social prescriptions of age, after a lifetime of commitment and hard work, these characters feel pressured to quit their jobs and begin to cast doubts on their capacity to work, even suspecting they are no longer the talented and skilful workers they used to be in their youthful years. Through the advent of magic, these characters are allowed to look back in time and take part in a symbolic life review that enables them to approach aging in a different light and acquire the courage they need to go through this new stage in their lives. In these episodes, an actor's script and a professor's lecture turn into magical devices that disrupt the sequential order of time frameworks and grant the aged protagonists entrance into a magical dimension. As a result of this fantastic experience, characters go back to the present and, having reconsidered their previous assumptions about age, they decide to face their aging process following their own scripts and attending to their own lessons, regardless of any social prescriptions about age.

From a historical perspective, Stephen Katz claims that the medical advances that conferred the aged body a fixed period of time also gave way to a governmental differentiation of old age, which ultimately had its reflection in the bureaucratic domain through the introduction of pensions and mandatory retirement (68). In this sense, Tamara Hareven argues that the social conceptualisations of old age have followed a process in which, first, individuals gained insight into the specific features of their stage in life, then professionals defined the conditions of that stage, and, as these conditions gradually became associated with a major social concern, public agencies ultimately turned old age into a institutionalised life stage (121). This institutionalisation of old age, which for the most part involved the introduction of public support systems, also had effect on the way individuals experienced aging, especially inasmuch as they felt constrained by the increasingly fixed timing of life transitions and assumed they had to follow a script that had been publicly written for them.

Drawing on the socially established concept of age, the episode "The Trouble with Templeton" (2.9) tackles the issue of following the script of age that social institutions have written for aged individuals. The story focuses on an aging actor, Booth Templeton, who feels that, at this stage of his life, he lacks the confidence that turned him into a reputed performer, mostly owing to external pressures coming from young stage directors in his profession. By effect of magic, Templeton finds himself back in the years of his youth and, when he goes back to the present, he brings with him a memento, which happens to be the script that his wife and the rest of actors were following during his short incursion in the past to help him regain his confidence. In addition to bridging the gap between the past and the present and thus call into question the division between different life stages, this magical script also serves the purpose of reminding Templeton that behaviour according to one's age is ultimately socially orchestrated. Accordingly, it is not only on stage but also in real life that aging individuals are required to follow a script that conditions the way they perceive their aging process and the way they should act. As a result of this magical experience, Templeton is enabled to approach his later stage as a performer in a confident way, well aware that his uneasiness responded to social expectations about how he was supposed to behave according to his age.

Social definitions of age limits implied that old age became marked by institutionalised rites of passage such as the advent of mandatory retirement and the introduction of public pensions. As Hareven claims, the social institutionalisation of old age also involved that the life transition into this stage of life became more rigidly defined to the extent that it often responded to specific age norms rather than to actual individual needs (130). Drawing on these age-specific regulations, in the episode "The Changing of the Guard" (3.37), Professor Fowler feels utterly disappointed when, after more than fifty years of teaching, he is informed that, following school norms and owing to his age, he should retire. In his desperation, one night he goes back to the school and, out of magic, he encounters the ghosts of a number of students that died in the war, who convince him that his lectures helped them enormously to mature. After this magical occurrence, Fowler gathers enough courage to face his retirement in a confident way. Through the episode, a series of lectures on behalf of different characters acquire symbolic meaning. In this sense, after years of giving lectures, Professor Fowler is compelled to bear the school director's lecture about mandatory retirement, while, in his desperation, Fowler is also metaphorically lectured by his late students, who remind him of his great worth as a teacher. Since the character of Professor Fowler is made to bear the effects of mandatory retirement, which is based on a rigid definition of old age rather than on the actual needs of aged individuals, this episode tackles the difference that can be established between social and personal definitions of old age, as social institutions draw on rigid parameters to define aging that often clash with personal considerations of old age on behalf of aged individuals.

These two episodes of *The Twilight Zone* address the issue that the meaning of old age cannot be merely defined from a social perspective as a specific stage in the life course since, as Hareven defends, the social meaning of old age varies according to psychological factors and is usually subjected to a series of variations (125). In this respect, despite facing their retirement, both Booth Templeton and Professor Fowler ultimately envision the last stages of their careers as a period of fulfilment after a lifetime of hard work. Even if they are pressured into abandoning their jobs at this stage of their lives, through the advent of magic, they go through a symbolic and personal life review that helps them reassess their present situation and envision their old age in a different way regardless of any prevailing social prejudices. Both as an actor and as a professor, they decide to write their own scripts and listen to their own lectures about old age. Hence, Booth Templeton takes advantage of his dilated experience on the stage and takes the rehearsals of his new play as a challenge, while Professor Fowler faces his retirement with contentment, pleased that his lifetime dedication to teaching has left a significant mark on his students.

Technological Gadgets and the Dystopian Approach to Old Age

As Katz claims, the characteristics of a technology-driven concept of aging derive from cultural industries that recast the life span in extraordinary ways by means of the masking of age and the fantasy of timelessness (69). Some episodes of *The Twilight Zone* make use of technological gadgets such as transplantation machines and rejuvenating serums that allow characters to live through the fantasy of living outside of time. By means of this approach to old age, gerontological writers draw attention to the positive images that refer to the vitality, creativity, and empowerment that can be attained in old age, in contrast with negative and stereotyped perceptions of aging as a stage of decline. However, as Featherstone and Hepworth claim, the concept of positive aging in the context of consumer culture also involves the tendency to scrutinise physical appearance in search of any trace of aging ("Images of Positive Ageing" 29) and, in this context, Katz further argues that elderhood has been reconstructed as a marketable lifestyle that joins the commodified values of youth with body-care techniques that ultimately mask the appearance of age (70).

As a case in point, in the episode "The Trade-Ins" (3.31), an aged couple, John and Marie Holt, have spent a happy lifetime together but are afraid that one of them, John, will soon pass away. Well aware of the current advances in science, the couple visits the company "New Life

Corporation" with the aim to transplant their personalities into youthful bodies, even though, given the cost of the operation, they realise they can only afford one operation. After the transplantation, John emerges in a youthful body and tells Marie about his exciting plans for the future. However, when John realises that Marie will not be able to share all his plans as he is bound to outlive her, he decides to return to his aged body and enjoy the rest of the years he has left to live with his wife. This episode shows that, through a dystopian approach to aging, images of old age as a necessary phase of bodily decline are undermined by virtue of biomedical and information technology, which proves that aged bodies can be reshaped, remade, fused with machines, and empowered by means of technological gadgets. Developments in information technology and virtual reality offer new modes of disembodiment and re-embodiment that re-inscribe the body in a youthful manner to the extent that, as Featherstone and Wernick argue, these virtual realities, even if not guaranteeing immortality, contain their own form of death denial (13). Nonetheless, the conclusion to this episode calls into question these 'positive' images of aging, ultimately considering them dystopian realities that contribute to dehumanising the individual in their attempt to 'normalise' aging by rendering it invisible.

Likewise, breakthroughs in the field of medicine have paved the ground to slow down or even reverse the biological clock to the extent that, as Featherstone and Wernick claim, the aging code, as we know it, may ultimately get disrupted (12). In this respect, the episode "A Short Drink from a Certain Fountain" (5.11) focuses on Harmon Gordon, an aging man very much in love with his young wife Flora, who, given the notable age gap existing between them, feels unable to cope with his wife's hectic rhythm of life and decides to resort to his brother, who happens to be a scientist that has been experimenting with a serum that may allow individuals to grow physically younger. As a result of the experiment, Gordon initially turns into a young man in his prime, but he soon realises that he looks younger and younger until he finally regresses into an infant. Accordingly, Flora, who has begun to neglect her responsibility to take care of her aging husband, now faces the duty of looking after him as a mother would take care of a helpless child. This episode underscores the dubious and even immoral consequences that may result from scientific experiments that seek to deny the physical effects of aging. In this respect, Turner has referred to the somatisation of the self, stating that, in modern societies, the consumer culture has turned the project of the body into our ultimate concern (257), as, in contrast with what happened in former times, when the body had to be subdued for the preservation of the soul, in modern societies it is the surface of the body which appears to carry the individual's inner moral condition. Accordingly, when by effect of age the outer body clashes with the youthfulness of the inner self, there seems to be the need to erase the traces of aging through resorting to the anti-aging policies that prevail in consumer culture.

In these two episodes, technological and scientific gadgets such as body transplantation machines and rejuvenating serums blur the boundaries between old age and youth, and contribute to recasting the life span through a dystopian fantasy of timelessness that ultimately ends up in a denial of aging. The ideological positioning of these episodes, though, defends an attitude of acceptance of old age rather than the will to resort to any technologically-driven fantasies of eternal youth. Actually, in "The Trade-Ins," even though John Holt indulges in the fantasy of becoming young again, he rejects such opportunity for the sake of growing old next to the woman he loves and is ultimately rewarded for that. Conversely, in "A Short Drink from a Certain Fountain," it is out of poetic justice that Harmon Gordon is punished for his will to regain youth, as he finds himself imprisoned in the body of a child, while his wife, in her reluctance to adopt an understanding attitude towards her aging husband, ultimately finds her retribution when she feels compelled to take care of him, since, as a child, he is perceived as being literally at her mercy.

Avatars of Old Age and the Conflict between Generations

From an anthropological perspective, Covey claims that the important role that aging people play in the family is one of the most important aspects in relation to old age (80). Historically, economic dependence has been one of the main reasons that account for the prevalence of the extended family, as young adults would sometimes stay with their parents out of economic necessity. However, these earlier sacrifices on behalf of aging parents were ultimately perceived as needing repayment by their offspring, since the family has been historically considered one important source of care for aging members. Some episodes of *The Twilight Zone* tackle this intergenerational conflict in families, especially when younger relatives are responsible for taking care of elders but are also economically dependent on them. In order to emphasise the authority that lies in the hands of the oldest members of the family, in these episodes, out of magic or science, elders devise strategies to extend their power even beyond their earthly existence. In this sense, aged family members resort to avatars or technological incarnations – such as toy phones, robots, and masks – that grant them a longer existence to continue exerting control on the younger relatives that have outlived them.

Historically, as Covey further argues, parental control declined with time and it was easier for grandparents to assume benevolent roles such as those of benefactors of their grandchildren (90). This issue is explicitly tackled and ultimately subverted in the episode "Long Distance Call" (2.22), which focuses on an extended family, comprising a young married couple, their young child Billy, and their grandmother. For the birthday of her grandson, Grandma gives Billy a toy phone, but she soon falls ill and passes away. Billy spends most of his time playing with his toy phone, ultimately confessing to his parents that Grandma has called to tell him he must come and pay her a visit because she feels lonely. Billy suffers a series of accidents until his father decides to speak on the toy phone and ask his late mother to spare Billy's life. This episode shows that grandmother and grandson have grown so attached to each other that when she realises that she will soon pass away, out of magic, the grandmother devises an avatar, a toy phone, through which she will be able to get in touch with her grandson. In spite of the evident affection between members of the older and younger generations, this episode evinces a noticeable intergenerational conflict since, owing to her possessive personality, the grandmother seeks to retain, at all costs, her affective control over her grandson.

Likewise, as a legacy of Puritan precepts, elders often perceived children as family members that were in need of discipline and control. In this sense, as Covey argues, members of the older generations felt they had to protect themselves from destitution and, to that end, they usually held a tight control over property, which used to aggravate intergenerational conflicts and contributed little to the goodwill of young members when it was their turn to take responsibility for the care of their elders (88). As a case in point, in the episode "Uncle Simon" (5.8), for many years Barbara has been taking care of her aging uncle, who, despite being a brilliant inventor, treats his niece with utmost loathing and disrespect. When her uncle passes away, Barbara believes herself released from her duties, but she is soon informed that, in his will, her uncle stated that she would only inherit his possessions if she agreed to take care of his last invention, which happens to be an annoying robot. After complying with her uncle's last will, Barbara realises that the automaton gradually takes on her late uncle's mannerisms and even assumes his voice, thus ultimately getting to know that, in spite of her uncle's absence, she will always remain under his long shadow. By its direct reference to the endless struggle between generations, this episode also underscores the historical context in which it originated, when social and political initiatives, which, later on, would ultimately give rise to the popular 'hippie' movement, sought to transfer the power from the elderly to the younger generations. Moreover, in this respect, according to Hodges, this episode also delves into the despotic rule of male gerontocracy, and how science can turn into a powerful instrument of control and oppression in the hands of aging patriarchs (177).

The struggle between young and old generations is also addressed in the episode "The Masks" (5.25), in which an aging man also makes use of an avatar – a series of masks – to extend his power and authority even after his death. Jason Foster is an aging wealthy man who believes his end is close at hand and decides to summon his young relatives to his house. Since it is the season of carnival, he asks them to wear a mask that he considers reflects their true moral values, while he puts on a mask that represents death. When the clock chimes twelve o'clock at night, Foster passes away and his relatives take off their masks but, to their consternation, they realise their faces have taken on the hideous features of the masks they were wearing. As Featherstone and Hepworth argue, the mask of aging refers to the inability of the body to represent the inner self adequately in old age ("The Mask of Ageing" 371-390), and this episode provides a wise reversal of the trope of the mask of aging insofar as, by virtue of the magical device of a mask, which truly reflects the inner self, the body ultimately represents the inner self adequately, as mask and body become fused into one. The avatar or representation ultimately becomes the true self, as the aging character playfully twists the trope of the mask of aging and obliges his younger relatives to undergo the same process for life.

Through the recurrent presence of magical avatars, these three episodes bring to the fore how the power and authority of elders and, especially, of aging patriarchs persists through time. Nonetheless, these episodes also reveal the complexity characterising the intergenerational gap, as the stories do not allow the audience to take sides in favour of the younger or the older generation. In this respect, in "Long Distance Call," the character of Grandma is portrayed as possessive, but also caring towards her beloved grandson. In "Uncle Simon," the aging scientist is demanding and egoistical, but his niece is also depicted as bitter and covetous. In "The Masks," the aging protagonist is characterised as whimsical, but his relatives are portrayed as greedy and totally heartless. Accordingly, these intergenerational relationships are revealed as intricate, even though, in all cases, the members of the older generation clearly exert a significant influence over those of the younger generation.

The Aging Body as a House: Opening the Door to Another Dimension

As Turner contends, given the fact that time is inscribed on our bodies, our embodiment is crucial to understand significant experiences subjected to time such as birth and death as well as to appreciate processes such as memory and identity (250). Some episodes of *The Twilight Zone*, such as "Nothing in the Dark" (3.16) and "Night Call" (5.19), present aging women who live in isolation and, metaphorically, envision their houses as extensions of their bodies and of their minds. As their house acquires the status of an embodied self, these aging women imprison themselves in their house with the aim to protect themselves from any threat that may deteriorate their physical or mental health. Despite their efforts to avoid any external influence that may propitiate their death or may awaken repressed memories from the past, a magical event such as a mysterious call or the unexpected visit of a stranger compel these aging women to abandon their house and, by extension, their embodied self, which ultimately causes their death.

According to Covey, old age has been historically associated with death, mostly because, owing to the improvement of the living conditions, death during old age was perceived as a timely death. Likewise, as Covey further argues, elders were the members of society traditionally considered as more capable of gaining insight into the meaning of death and, accordingly, they were often regarded as intercessors between this world and the next (146). In fact, as Covey claims, the association between old age and death has been so evident that old age has been occasionally used to represent death itself by means of the image of the 'crone' or the aging subject, who symbolically personifies a bringer of death (148). The episode "Nothing in the Dark" draws on a series of stereotypes that associate old age with death, but also contributes to endowing them with further complexity. In the story, an elderly woman, Wanda Dunn, lives alone in her house and, given her protracted age, she is extremely afraid of dying soon. In order to swindle death, she secludes herself from life outside her house until she receives the visit of a young man in need of help. Once she has let him in her house, she realises that he is Mister Death but, to her surprise, he is not a merciless destroyer, but rather a gentle young man that only asks her to take his hand and abandon her seclusion. This episode problematizes the traditional image of death as an implacable 'crone', since death is actually personified by an innocent-looking young man. Likewise, the episode turns into a metaphor of death itself, as, if Wanda's house symbolises her embodied self, when death intrudes upon it, she finally abandons the isolation of her house and is released from the seclusion of her body. The portrayal of death presented in this episode moves away from the protagonist's initial perception of the end of life as a shocking event to the approach to death as an ordinary occurrence in the process of living that must be accepted as part of the cycle of life.

As Covey further admits, the elderly have also been traditionally expected to reflect on death and the afterlife, and engage in a life review to examine their past at a late stage of their life (159). In the episode "Night Call," Elva Keene is an elderly woman who leads a quiet and lonely life in the seclusion of her house until she begins to receive a series of mysterious phone calls. Elva leaves the quietness of her house in order to discover who is calling her, and she ultimately finds out that the calls originate in a cemetery, as a result of a fallen wire lying on top of a graveyard that happens to be that of her late fiancé. This fantastic occurrence compels the aging protagonist to awaken her repressed memories of her youth regarding her relationship with her fiancé, as well as her guilty feelings upon realising that she always convinced her fiancé to do as she pleased. At this late stage of her life, Elva engages in a symbolic life review whereby she is requested to examine her past and face the guilty memories that she has been repressing for years. Likewise, in analogy with "Nothing in the Dark," when Elva leaves the safety of her house – her embodied self in which she feels protected from any external influence that may unleash her repressed memories – she is compelled to examine her life and accept the wrongs of her past, including the possibility that she might be to blame for the accident that caused her fiancé's death.

These two episodes initially draw on traditional images of the aged associated with death and with the contemplation of life at a late stage, but they also introduce an unexpected twist that complicates predetermined portrayals of old age. Both episodes resort to the metaphor of the house as an embodied self and as an extension of the body and the mind of the aging protagonists, who seek to enclose themselves in their houses for fear of death or of painful memories from the past. The magical experience that the protagonists undergo allows them to gain insight into another dimension that lies beyond death, which defies their initial fears and prejudices, as Wanda's ultimate encounter with death is quiet and peaceful, while Elva's symbolic awakening of her repressed memories is ultimately accepted as part of a necessary life review. In both cases, the choice of abandoning the seclusion of their metaphorical house – their embodied self – reveals itself as cathartic and even liberating.

Conclusions

The analysis of a significant number of episodes along the five seasons of *The Twilight Zone* evinces that aging becomes a pivotal theme that recurs in the series. All the stories that address aging in the series can be classified into different categories which present thematic and narratological connections. These different categories tackle aging from different perspectives and make use of diverse serial devices. In addition to functioning as narratological links to the episodes included in each of the categories of aging identified in the series, these serial devices also become catalysts of aging that also accomplish a number of purposes. These serial elements disrupt the normal functioning of reality within the story and enhance the advent of magic to provoke the viewer's response. Likewise, they contribute to reflecting the thematic focus of aging, as, in its disrupting nature, they problematize the dichotomy established between youth and old age, and underline the cyclical nature of life, thus mirroring the process of aging itself. Through their repetitive nature, these serial elements in the stories also contribute to, on the one hand, perpetuating commonly established beliefs about aging and, on the other hand, adding complexity and intricacy to pre-established ideas with regard to age. This dual function of serial devices is intimately linked with the ideological discourses in the series, as *The Twilight Zone* tends to sway between a moralistic and a rather dissident discourse. As a matter of fact, while some of the episodes classified within the same category of aging comprise a moralistic discourse, others rather embrace a more intricate positioning. In this respect, there are different narrative strategies used in the series that reinforce these two types of discourse, as is the case with Rod Serling's direct addresses to the audience and his voice-over, which is used to present each episode and put the story to an end. It could be argued that these narrative strategies back up the moralising discourse that prevails in the series insofar as these techniques are remindful of omniscient and authoritative narrators. However, Carl Plantinga claims that Rod Serling's voice-over also aids in laying bare the constructed nature of the episodes, thus contributing to encouraging critical thinking.

With regard to the moralising discourse that prevails in the series, critics such as Stanyard have regarded the episodes of *The Twilight Zone* as modern parables or contemporary morality plays (1), and similarly, Noël Carroll considers that many episodes of the series resort to poetic justice and envision situations in which ideal justice mostly prevails (26). As a matter of fact, episodes such as "Long Live Walter Jameson," "Long Distance Call," "Of Late I think of Cliffordville," "A Short Drink from a Certain Fountain," "The Masks," "Uncle Simon," and "Night Call" could be interpreted as cautionary tales with an eminently edifying purpose. Aging individuals are punished for daring to trespass moral boundaries when they attempt to achieve eternal youth, they exert a dictatorial authority on their younger relatives, or refuse to engage in a life review to expiate the wrongs they have committed and, as a result of their conduct, they are ultimately punished. It is often the case that these episodes also appear to resort to some stereotypical portrayals of the aged or contribute to spreading commonly established beliefs about age. However, it must also be acknowledged that, in most cases, these episodes avoid falling into a facile interpretation or allowing the viewer to clearly take sides with the members of the younger or the older generation. Even if in episodes such as "Long Live Walter Jameson," "Of Late I think of Cliffordville," and "Long

Distance Call," the aging protagonists are mostly portrayed in a negative way, there are episodes such as "A Short Drink for a Certain Fountain," "The Masks," and "Uncle Simon," which also describe the conduct of the younger generation with regard to their elders as particularly despicable.

Conversely, though, some episodes of the series move beyond a moralising discourse and rather put emphasis on the need to adopt a dissident frame of mind with the view to problematize certain assumed aspects of old age. In this sense, as Plantinga claims, some episodes of *The Twilight Zone* warn the viewer about the compliant acceptance of conventional thinking. In this respect, many of the episodes analysed underline this rather dissident discourse in the series, as they complicate fixed conceptualisations about aging, and present age as an ultimately fluid concept, since youth and old age are mostly characterised as blurred categories that become part of the same continuum. An important number of episodes thus call into question cultural dictates of aging and, to a certain extent, challenge social perceptions of age. Some of the episodes analysed such as "The Sixteen Millimeter Shrine," "The Trouble with Templeton," "Static," "The Changing of the Guard," "Nothing in the Dark," "Kick the Can," "The Trade-Ins," "Queen of The Nile," and "Ninety Years Without Slumbering" feature aged individuals who decide to defy cultural and social prescriptions of age, thus adopting their own perception of their process of aging and ultimately acting against their age.

WORKS CITED

Barnouw, Eric. *Tube of Plenty: The Evolution of American Television*. New York: Oxford University Press, 1990. Print.

Boddy, William. "Entering *The Twilight Zone*." *Screen* 25 (1984): 98-108. Print.

Booker, M. Keith. *Science Fiction Television: A History*. Westport: Praeger, 2004. Print.

Carroll, Noël. "Tales of Dread in *The Twilight Zone*: A Contribution to Narratology." *Philosophy in* The Twilight Zone. Eds. Noël Carrol and Lester H. Hunt. Chichester: Wiley-Blackwell, 2009. 26-38. Print.

Covey, Herbert. *Older People in Western Art and History*. New York: Praeger, 1991. Print.

Featherstone, Mike and Mike Hepworth. "The Mask of Ageing and the Postmodern Life Course." *The Body: Social Process and Cultural Theory*. Eds. Mike Featherstone, Mike Hepworth and Bryan Turner. London: Sage, 1991. 371-390. Print.

Featherstone, Mike and Mike Hepworth. "Images of Positive Ageing: A Case Study of *Retirement Choice* Magazine." *Images of Ageing: Cultural Representations of Later Life*. Eds. Mike Featherstone and Andrew Wernick. London: Routledge, 1995. 29-47. Print.

Featherstone, Mike and Andrew Wernick. "Introduction." *Images of Aging: Cultural Representations of Later Life*. Eds. Mike Featherstone and Andrew Wernick. London: Routledge, 1995. 1-15. Print.

Gullette, Margaret Morganroth. *Aged by Culture*. Chicago: The University of Chicago Press, 2004. Print.

Hareven, Tamara K.. "Changing Images of Aging and the Social Construction of the Life Course." *Images of Ageing: Cultural Representations of Later Life*. Eds. Mike Featherstone and Andrew Wernick. London: Routledge, 1995. 119-134. Print.

Hill, Rodney. "Anthology Drama: Mapping *The Twilight Zone*'s Cultural and Mythological Terrain." *The Essential Science Fiction: Television Reader*. Ed. J.P.Telotte. Kentucky: The University of Kentucky Press, 2008. 111-126. Print.

Hockey, Jenny and Allison James. "Back to Our Futures: Imagining Second Childhood." *Images of Ageing: Cultural Representations of Later Life*. Eds. Mike Featherstone and Andrew Wernick. London: Routledge, 1995. 135-148. Print

Hodges, F.M. "The Promised Planet: Alliances and Struggles of the Gerontocracy in American Television Science Fiction of the 1960s." *The Ageing Male* 6 (2003): 175-182. Print.

Katz, Stephen. "Imagining the Life Span: from Premodern Miracles to Postmodern Fantasies." *Images of Ageing: Cultural Representations of Later Life*. Eds. Mike Featherstone and Andrew Wernick. London: Routledge, 1995. 61-72. Print.

Lacy, Susan, dir. *Rod Serling: Submitted for Your Approval*. Produced by CBS Entertainment and WNET Channel 13. New York. Originally broadcast on PBS on 29 November 1995. Television.

Lyotard, Jean-François. *La Condition Postmoderne: Rapport sur le Savoir*. Paris: Editions du Minuit, 1979. Print.

Mortenson, Erik. "A Journey into the Shadows: *The Twilight Zone*'s Visual Critique of the Cold War." *Science Fiction Film and Television* 7.1 (2014): 55-76. Print.

Oltean, Tudor. "Series and Seriality in Media Culture." *European Journal of Communication* 8 (1993): 5-31. Print.

Plantinga, Carl. "Frame Shifters: Surprise Endings and Spectator Imagination in *The Twilight Zone*." *Philosophy in* The Twilight Zone. Eds. Noël Carrol and Lester H. Hunt. Chichester: Wiley-Blackwell, 2009. 39-57. Print.

"Rod Serling Speaking at the UCLA." *Archives for the UCLA Communication Studies Department*. 17 May 1971. Digitised in 2013.

Scott Zicree, Marc. The Twilight *Companion*. Los Angeles: Silman-James Press, 1992. Print.

Sontag, Susan. "The Double Standard of Ageing." *An Ageing Population*. Eds. Vida Carver and Penny Liddiard. London: Hodder and Stoughton, 1987. 72-80. Print.

Stanyard, Stewart. *Dimensions behind* The Twilight Zone: *A Backstage Tribute to Television's Groundbreaking Series*. Toronto: ECW Press, 2007. Print.

Telotte, J.P. "Introduction." *The Essential Science Fiction: Television Reader*. Ed. J.P.Telotte. Kentucky: The University of Kentucky Press, 2008. 1-34. Print.

Turner, Bryan S. "Aging and Identity: Some Reflections of the Somatisation of the Self." *Images of Ageing: Cultural Representations of Later Life*. Eds. Mike Featherstone and Andrew Wernick. London and New York: Routledge, 1995. 245-260. Print.

Wilson, Terhi-Anna. "Generation." *Encyclopedia of Consumer Culture*. Ed. Dale Southerton. California: Sage Publications, 2011. 643-647. Print.

TELEVISION

The Twilight Zone. Creator Rod Serling, CBS (1959-1964).

Wait For It...!

Temporality, Maturing, and the Depiction of Life Concepts in *How I Met Your Mother*[1]

CECILIA COLLOSEUS

> One day baby, we'll be old.
> Oh baby, we'll be old
> And think of all the stories
> that we could have told.
> ASAF AVIDAN

The format of the sitcom is, in many respects, quite intriguing. Its production process limits the creative liberties of authors and directors not only by technical means, and budget constraints, but also by the expectations of the producers, as well as standards and rules of the genre. Those rules are: a cyclical structure of single episodes (of about thirty minutes, airing on a weekly basis), in which stereotypical characters interact in a stage-like setting (Witthoefft 15). "The situation comedy" is a "humorous, episodic series of programs in which a well defined cast of characters, confined in one location or set of circumstances, respond predictably to new events" (Evans 479). Sitcom-characters usually do not develop (Witthoefft 11), and the audience can be sure that every problem brought up in an episode will be solved by the end of it, *because* the

---

[1] This publication was funded by the DFG-graduate program 2015 "Life Sciences, Life Writing."

characters act in their usual ways. While there are countless shows fulfilling most of these conventions and tanking after one or two seasons, few succeed finding an international audience. Supposedly, this success does not only stem from the expectations fulfilled, but from innovative or unique aspects that allow the audience to invest themselves in the narrative over a long time, either because they want to know the solution for a problem presented, or because they identify with the protagonists. This identification is not achieved by an attempt to realism, because a realistic representation of everyday life could not possibly fit with the necessities of sitcom storytelling. Instead, what sitcoms depict as 'everyday life' facilitates a reflected approach to what defines society, or a specific group of that society[2]. A sitcom can be seen as a way in which a society accounts for itself, "it both reflects and shapes" (Himmelstein 119). As such, it can and should be analyzed. The protagonists represent an assumed normal and acceptable behavior in a comical manner – including, of course, deviance –, and thus create the frame of reference for the particular generation addressed. The sitcom *How I Met Your Mother* (hereafter referred to as *HIMYM*) tells the story of a group of five 20-somethings in present day New York City, beginning in the year 2005. The plot is framed by the 52-year-old self of the protagonist Ted Mosby, telling his two teenage children – the year is then 2030 – the story of how he met their mother, and recalling all the events that led to meeting her. Every episode is opened by middle-aged Ted as an off-screen narrator introducing to his children and to the viewer what happens next.

Many of the specific traits of the series are linked to the fields of temporality and maturing. The passing of time is one of the most important devices of the show, and it is used on various levels. In a deductive approach, I will claim that *HIMYM*, like every other sitcom, has an affirmative function for its audience, and can thus be used as an avenue to current issues of the society depicted. It both mirrors and influences contemporary life concepts that are situated between the characteristic traits of a generation and traditional values, and adds the specifically new dimension of aging (of young adults) and temporality. Therefore I will look at the motifs and tropes of temporality and maturing in *HIMYM*, in single episodes and throughout the series. In the first section, the narrative

---

2   On the topic of the depiction of everyday life in TV series see Foltin.

framing will be presented, followed by section 2 that takes into view the life concepts of the show's characters. Section 3 discusses the meaning of temporality and maturing on the content level, and section 4 looks at some of the series' stylistic devices. Section 5 discusses how *HIMYM* can be used as a key to the generation it addresses, focusing on the phenomenon of digitalization, and section 6, finally, asks the question of how *HIMYM* is aware of the issues of its historic situation.

"If There's One Big Theme to this Story [...], It's Timing."[3]
– The Narrative Framing Device

There are several TV series using the device of an off-screen-narrator. In most cases, it is the older self of the protagonist, who recalls the events of a defining period in his or her life in a strictly chronological manner, and tells it to the audience of the show (e.g. *The Wonder Years*, *Call The Midwife*, *Everybody Hates Chris*). What is exceptional about *HIMYM* is that the 'past' of the story is actually the present of the audience. Both the story and the narrative situation of the story are being told, and they are actually incommensurable on a temporal level: While the telling of the story is stretched over nine years, and the development and aging process of the characters is depicted, the setting of a father telling a story to his children is always the same, and the kids do not age or alter at all. While the story is s tretched over a long period, time stands still at the moment of narration. Even in each episode, the passing of time plays an important role, while the time it takes to tell it does not. Another difference between *HIMYM* and other 'memoirs' series – and the sitcomgenre – is the use of flashback- and flashforward-scenes. There is no strict chronology, but a rather associative way of recalling the important events, with several stories inside the story. If the Deleuzian theory of cinema (Deleuze 1989) can be applied to TV series one could assume that *HIMYM* adapts Deleuze's view of images that are "haunted by a past and a future" (37), "a before and an after as they coexist with the image" (38) in a quite playful manner.

Additionally, different from other series that tell a story via an off-screen-narrator, Ted does not always remember every detail in the first place (or not at all) (e.g. "The Goat", 3.17, "The Leap", 4.24). This gives

---

3   "The Best Man" (7.1)

the narration an air of 'authenticity', as it seems quite realistic that not everything can be remembered after 25 years, and that a lot of 'memories' are merely constructions (see also Sielke 2013).

Another very intriguing characteristic of *HIMYM* is that it puts the anticipation and the reflection in one narration, meaning that in the narrated 'present', there is always an imagined moment in the future from which the present will once be remembered and narrated. Mark Currie presumes that this "anticipatory mode of being might be a characteristic of contemporary culture" (6), and he elaborates:

Narrative is understood as retrospection more readily than it is understood as anticipation, but it cannot really be one without also being the other. If, in order to look back at what has happened, we tell a story, we must also know that the present is a story yet to be told. The present is the object of a future memory, and we live it as such, in anticipation of the story we will tell later, envisaging the present as past. The present might be lived in anticipation of some future present from which it is narrated, but this may also entail the anticipation of events between the present present and the future present from which it is narrated which will also be part of that story. (5-6)

How this tendency to imagine life from a future perspective is acted out in *HIMYM* will be discussed in the next section.

What the narrator himself calls the "big theme" to his story, timing, is also very important for the narrative concept. In a tradition of creative storytelling – and different from the common sitcom –, pieces of information are not given away before they are due, keeping up a tension, without frustrating the viewers by letting them wait for the final clue. However, the narration is quite complex, and this meets the 'timing' of the watching habits of the young audience for whom the show is made. There is a continuity in the plot that makes it nearly impossible to watch single episodes out of context – even though they are, typically for a sitcom, more or less self-contained –, as there are references to the younger selves of the characters or flashforwards that give important clues, and some loose ends are not tied until the very last episode. This complex structure works better with contemporary concepts of media use (Ames 2012), like streaming, or 'binge watching', than it would with the 'traditional' concept of weekly episodes (though the series originally aired on a weekly basis). Usually, a sitcom does not put so much effort into the narrative. According to Mellencamp, the narrative is "only the merest overlay, perhaps an excuse" (91), while the focus lies on physical and, of course, situation comedy. Concerning the narrative, *HIMYM* can thus be seen as a development of the sitcom genre. But despite all the innovative elements, *HIMYM* still sticks with most of the sitcom conventions, like the thirty-minutes-format, the laugh track, running gags, and slapstick comedy. It also uses the device of the cliffhanger at the end of every season, and the settings are reduced to a minimum. The audience addressed can be imagined as those who grew up with the (domestic) sitcoms of the 1980s and 90s, and the creators might want to serve certain nostalgic feelings, while at the same time entertain with presenting contemporary lifestyles of young adults. While in *HIMYM* the focus is put on the narrative, most of the other aspects – including the underlying ideological pattern, which will be discussed more elaborately later on – stand in a tradition of sitcom storytelling.

„It's Like You're Trying to Skip Ahead to the End of the Book"[4] – Life Concepts Of The Main Characters

Though the story of *HIMYM* is told by a middle-aged man, the subject of the story is the defining, or better: in-between, phase of the late twenties and early thirties that sociologists call "liminal adulthood" (Raby 2012, Blatterer 2007). The characters have to deal with their lives in this stage of liminality. Every one of them has a different strategy to cope with their late coming-of-age situation, and it will be discussed how these strategies represent those of the young audience that *HIMYM* addresses.

All the characters are typical members of the "Generation Y" ("Generation Y Characteristics), or "Millennials" (born in the 1980s), in one or the other way. This generation is said to have a pronounced need to be loved unconditionally, to be ambitious in matters of career and lifestyle, but at the same time focused on a 'healthy' work-life-balance. They grew up with digitalization, and are said to have a great awareness of globalization. Their biographies are not as linear as those of the "Matures", the "Boomers", or even of their predecessors the "Xers", but characterized by frequent changes (Strauss/Howe 2000, Bund 2014). Therefore they are

---

4 "Shelter Island", 4.5

said to be flexible in every way, what is seen as a benefit in a globalized world. However, a rather negative preconception about the "Millennials" is that they cannot or do not really want to mature. They are imagined as 'kidults', who get stuck in liminality, getting older, but not wiser in terms of development and growth in personality. *HIMYM* captures the characteristics of the "Generation Y" in a quite nuanced way: the protagonists' everyday life is depicted as playful and at times even childish. On the other hand, all of the characters pursue ideals that seem not at all typical for their generation. On the contrary: some of the characters' dreams even read like a nostalgic wish to bring back a perfect 1950s domestic idyll. According to Kirk Curnutt "[i]n contemporary novels [...] youth's disaffected disposition is credited not to the oppressiveness of adult authority but to a lack of it" (94). What can be observed for novels holds also true for *HIMYM*: settledness and family are highly valued and the protagonists long for it. Additionally, even though the "Millennial's" adulthood is thought to be delayed, they still accept adulthood as a "default category" (Blatterer 26), and conform to 'traditional' life concepts. This underlying ideological pattern can be applied to all the main characters.

Most prominently it is found in the character of Theodore Evelyn "Ted" Mosby (Josh Radnor) whose wish to settle down is introduced from the very start of the series. Ted has a tendency to want to "skip ahead to the end of the book" ("Shelter Island", 4.5), and wants to get his "happily ever after" before it is due. This habit forces him to rush into things. As a result, Ted gets left at the altar (4.5), which leaves him traumatized. Yet his faith in romance is unshaken (Brost 2011). Before he finally meets his later wife Tracy McConnell (Cristin Milioti), Ted has uncountable relationships, and with every new woman he meets, he gives her the chance to be "the one". Ted's friends are annoyed by his naïve faith in romance – Lily calls him a "commitment junkie" ("The Front Porch", 4.17) –, and that he cannot live in the moment, but always thinks about what will or could be. At the same time, Ted is very nostalgic, and indulges in his memories. In "Vesuvius" (9.19), Ted is shown in a flashforward with Tracy in 2024, telling her another story from the time before they met. She tells him that he should give up "living in his stories" (9.19), and go ahead in his life. Her advice clearly points to her already being terminally ill, and that Ted will have to carry on when she is gone. But as the viewer does not know anything about Tracy's death at this point of the story it might just as well be another hint to Ted not being able to "live in the moment", but either in the future or in the past. Tracy and Ted also state that they do not have any more stories to tell each other, and that they are therefore "officially an old married couple" (9.19) what makes them happy and proud. They have been together for 11 years then, and they already have achieved a major goal in their life concept.

Ted is a fan of grand gestures. He wants to live up to his ideals, without any trade-offs, always balancing on the thin line of rushing into something, or waiting too long. He is playful and has a lot of eccentric habits, but at the same time, he eagerly pursues very smug ideals of family life.

Ted's friends Lily Aldrin (Alyson Hannigan) and Marshall Eriksen (Jason Segel) are presented as being in the most striking form of the young adult liminal state. However, they go through this phase together, aware that time will change everything. This awareness is pictured in the episode before the last ("The End of the Aisle", 9.22). The couple realizes that they are "different people than [they] were in 2007" (9.22), leading them to update their wedding-vows, because their original vows turned out to be "too romantic for real life" (9.22). This realism, however, is actually not a characteristic of the couple. Lily is a very manipulative character, who wants to create her ideal life by all means necessary. In "The Front Porch" (4.17), it is revealed, that Lily forces Ted into breakups, when his girlfriend does not pass the "front-porch-test" (4.17). This means, that Lily imagines her and Marshall's life, when they are old, sitting on the front porch of their third-age residence with Ted. If Ted's girlfriend does not fit into this imagination, she has to leave. Marshall does not share his wife's manipulative ways, but he is characterized as an idealistic and somewhat naïve person. His aim is to become an environmental lawyer to protect nature for the generations to come ("Life Among The Gorillas", 1.17). Generally, Marshall is very focused on the future, both of mankind and his own, and integrates his "future self" in everything he does.

Lily and Marshall strikingly act out the group's tendency to think life from the perspective of an imagined future, and they are also the most optimistic characters: as far as the story is told, their plans get carried out, their love and relationship last, and they both leave a legacy. Their domestic luck, depicted in the flashforwards and at the end of the series, does not have anything to do with their "Millennials"-selves. The Eriksens are then apparently mature – at least concerning their standard of living, which can almost be seen as that of a caricature of a bourgeois couple.

Ted's love interest Robin Charles Sherbatsky Jr. (Cobie Smulders), on the other hand, is portrayed as the opposite of the happy couple. She is an independent woman who – apparently for comic effect – repeatedly claims that she was brought up like a boy[5], and that she is therefore not interested in a 'typically female' life concept. Her career is her most important goal, and she does not aim for domestic bliss. Robin is not at all romantic, but agrees to become Ted's "backup wife" (5.17), in case they are not married before they are 40, implicitly giving in to a traditional life concept, but in a quite pragmatic way. Her affection for Ted grows over time, and when the two of them finally get together, it seems that the romantic concept of destiny and being meant for each other, has been replaced by a mature and rather prosaic interpretation of a relationship. However, Robin has got some romantic traces in her personality, and it is linked to the tendency of imagining life from the future. In "Something Old" (8.23), the viewer learns that a 14-year-old Robin once buried a locket in Central Park, intending to retrieve it, when she gets married one day, as her "something old". The retrieving of the locket tightens her bond with Ted, which is a major topic throughout the last season, as she realizes, that he is the one who actually meets her need for romance that seemingly got lost on the way from youth to adulthood.

Robin is presented as a person who sticks with her decisions, even if this first seems to result in an alienation from her peers. She is very much down to earth, and in various regards the exact opposite of Ted. As the series develops, however, Robin faces her emotional blockades, and she begins to show her vulnerability. Finally, even the childless career woman gets a late domestic bliss as the stepmother for Ted's children.

Barnabus "Barney" Stinson (Neil Patrick Harris) is the one member of the group whose life plans significantly differ from the others'. From the first episode onwards, his womanizing ways serve as a contrast to Ted's romantic life concept, and as a very questionable kind of comic relief throughout the series. He is not planning for his future – it is not even

---

5 Note her male and Ted's female middle name, hinting to their 'switched' masculinity and femininity.

revealed what he does for a living before the last season ("Unpause", 9.15) –, and just hedonistically living the moment. He has his own notion of temporality, with regard, for example, to his impatience when is interested in a woman ("A week? That's like a year in hot-girl-time!", 1.1), or waiting three days to contact a prospective love interest ("The Three Day Rule", 4.21). The only accomplishment Barney wants to make and look back on is sleeping with as many women as possible. His aging process is only brought into discussion when he considers that it might help him "picking up" girls with "daddy issues" ("Last Forever", 9.23-24), but apart from that, there is no real development of his character. The notorious womanizer cannot be imagined as a dignified old person. Yet, also Barney has a way of thinking life from the perspective of the future. And he very bluntly calls it "his secret to life" ("The Time Travelers", 8.20): "Every time I make a decision on what to do on a given night, I ask myself: What would make the best memory, twenty years from now? So I let 20-years-from-now Barney call the shots." (8.20). Barney's life concept does not change before he experiences fatherhood in the last episode. He is the only one, however, who does not opt for a traditional family-life, but for an alternative concept of single parenthood.

Even though the characters' life concepts may not be identical, they all have in common the wish to look back on their lives, realizing they have accomplished something. Their development is depicted on various levels, and it is made clear from the beginning that it will lead away from a playful youth to a rather smug lifestyle. (Old) age is never presented as something that has to be feared, but is expected by all of them rather joyfully. Not even their 30th birthdays are narrated as severe crises ("The Goat", 3.17) which is remarkable compared to other contemporary novels, films, or TV series, in which late-coming-of-age is negotiated (Wohlmann 14, 144). While the main traits of the single characters and the basic configuration of their relationships does not significantly change over the run of the series – which is typical of the sitcom genre where a stable setting of characters allows watching and understanding single episodes without having to know them all – this evaluation by their future selves is a specific trait of *HIMYM*, intertwining different levels of narration.

Becoming What One Has to Become – Aging and the Passing of Time as Major Aspects of the Narration

Kids, there is more than one story of how I met your mother. You know the short version. The thing with your mom's yellow umbrella. But there's a bigger story. The story of how I became what I had to become before I could meet her. ("Wait for it", 3.1)

On the content level, *HIMYM* deals with getting older above all. What starts as a typical story that a father tells his children about his "wild days" turns out to be a quite complex narration of how the passing of time is important to fully understand how and why things developed as they did. In "Pilot" (1.1) Ted states: "25 years ago, before I was a dad, I had that whole other life". By calling the time before he became a father a "whole other life" Ted distances himself from his younger self[6]. This is certainly a kind of an excuse or a justification for the rather promiscuous life he led. What happened to him when he was younger does not really belong to his person anymore. However, as the story develops, Ted and the viewer notice that all phases of life are connected (Segal 2013). In the end, it even turns out that the initial point of Ted's narration is not at all randomly chosen: The very last scene is equal to the scene in "Pilot" (1.1), when Ted meets Robin for their second date. It shows Ted waiting in front of Robin's house, carrying with him the blue French horn, while Robin is waiting at the window, surrounded by her dogs (9.23-24). The "two lives" – the life before, and after being a father – are finally united.

The concept of romance – not only in TV series – is usually captured as: "They are meant for each other, no matter what happens." *HIMYM* first seems to break with this convention of structure (Brost 2011), as Robin and Ted do not end up together, because of such mundane things as timing, and the clash of life concepts. But in the end, the whole 'will-they-or-won't-

---

6   It must be noted here that middle-aged Ted's voice is not the one of his younger self's actor Josh Radnor, but of Bob Saget who used to play the widower and father of three daughters Danny Tanner in the series *Full House*. It was inofficially discussed that *HIMYM* was thought as a kind of a prequel *to Full House*. But this is merely a theory, and has not at all been acknowledged by the creators of *HIMYM* (Browne, Writes).

they'-scenario set up between Robin and Ted from the first episode on is wrapped up by them getting back together, restoring the narrative convention of the romance plot: "But that's the funny thing about destiny: It happens whether you plan it or not" (1.1)[7].

Apart from romance, every other aspect of life is depicted through the development of the characters, and turning points in their lives clearly separate the earlier from the later seasons. Additionally, addressing selected external events, like hurricanes or the economy crisis, in how they influence the topical private life of the characters, also serve as a link to the passing of time. *HIMYM* captures how time passing is important for the development of the story and its characters, and does not just narrate the outcome of the development. As far as sitcoms go, this is a rather specific trait, implemented and symbolized by a great number of objects, places, and events, designed to create continuity.

The most intriguing of these continuity devices is "the mother's" yellow umbrella. In "Wait For It" (3.1) its significance for the story is mentioned first. The yellow umbrella is carried by a woman whose face is not shown. The narrator reveals that this woman is "the mother", and the viewer now has another thing to pay attention to (spotting the umbrella), when watching further episodes. In "No Tomorrow" (3.12), "the mother" – whose identity is not revealed in that episode either – leaves her umbrella at a bar. Ted accidentally takes the umbrella with him, which is shown again in a flashback in "How Your Mother Met Me" (9.16). In "Right Place, Right Time" (4.22), Ted is carrying the umbrella with him, when he runs into his ex-fiancé Stella, which by a devious route leads to Ted becoming a professor. It is Ted's first lecture, when "the mother" first sees Ted, as she is enrolled at the university as a student. In "Girls Versus Suits" (5.12), Ted dates "the mother's" roommate, and accidentally leaves the umbrella in the women's apartment. In "Big Days" (6.1) and "Farhampton" (8.1), the umbrella is shown, carried by "the mother" whose face is again not revealed. In "How Your Mother Met Me" (9.16), the story of the yellow

---

7 It must be argued, though, that the notion of 'destiny' in Ted's narration is reserved for everything concerning "the mother". His relationship with Robin is rather prosaic and pragmatic, leading me to the thesis, that "the mother's" death is a necessary narrative device of terminating Ted's romantic youth, letting him mature eventually.

umbrella is told from "the mother's" perspective. In "Last Forever" (9.23-24), it is shown, how the umbrella is involved in Tracy's and Ted's first meeting, when they tell each other their own story of how they lost and found the umbrella, which is used as a symbol of destiny and the good that is yet to come for Ted.

Another continuity device is introduced in season two ("Slap Bet", 2.9), when after a bet Marshall receives the right to slap Barney five times all in all, whenever he wishes, without temporal limitation. Throughout the series, this "slap bet" gets carried out ("Slapsgiving", 3.9, "Slapsgiving 2: Revenge Of The Slap", 5.9). Like in a fairytale where the hero gets granted three wishes, and the reader knows that the story can not be over before all three wishes are made, the viewer knows that the series can not be over before the last slap was performed, and this is not until the penultimate episode ("The End Of The Aisle", 9.22).

HIMYM depicts how life changes over nine years. The continuity devices help the viewer to keep track of the story and the characters' development. On a narrative level, this strategy very much meets the conventions of storytelling, and creates links to all kinds of genres, from fairytales to coming-of-age-narratives. It is obvious to the viewer that certain things will happen, but the audience has to wait for them to happen.

"Drumroll, Please" – Speeding Up, Slowing Down, Flashbacks and Flashforward Scenes as Stylistic Devices

> Kids, in life, there are a lot of big romantic moments, and they make life worth living. But here is the problem: Moments pass. And lurking just around the corner of those moments, is a cruel, unshaven bastard named Reality. ("Drumroll, Please", 1.13)

Ted's introduction to this episode is a hint to the unusual structure of *HIMYM*. It makes clear that this series is not one that fades out after the happy ending, giving the couple their 'happily ever after', but one that appeals to cherish the 'big' (romantic) moments, even though there is a cruel reality, with all its consequences. "Drumroll, Please" (1.13) is all about the right moments, and how they will be judged from the perspective of the future: Ted and Victoria meet, they spend an evening together, flirting, and getting to know each other, without revealing their names to each other. They seem to be a perfect match, as they are equally romantic and fond of creating special moments. Victoria insists on not kissing because she wants to make their relationship something special: "And then, when we're old and gray, we will look back on this night, and it will be perfect" (1.13). And later on: "Best part of every kiss is the lead-up to it. The moment right before the lips touch. It's like a big drumroll. How about tonight we just stick with the drumroll?" (1.13). The idea of 'taking it slow' when beginning a relationship is mirrored in the stretched narrative time of the episode.

In season 3, this concept of slowing down is contrasted by the device of speeding up both in content and in the narrative structure: Ted falls in love with Stella. As she is a single mother with little time, she does not want to date in the first place ("Ten Sessions", 3.13). For that reason, Ted sets up a "two-minute-date" that symbolizes very bluntly Ted's tendency to rush into things. While with Victoria everything is about taking it slow and waiting, it is the speeding up that defines Ted's relationship with Stella and that results in Ted being left at the altar (4.5).

The most intriguing use of speeding up and slowing down time is found throughout the series' ninth season. This last season wraps up the plot, and ties up loose ends from the preceding seasons, it reveals what will happen to the group, and it finally introduces the character of "the mother". The negotiation of narrative temporality is most striking here. No other season before used as many flashbacks and flashforwards as the ninth, and, above all, its framing is a paragon for stretched narrative time, as the episodes 1 to 22 of that season only narrate the 56 hours before Robin's and Barney's wedding. Despite the series' overall jolly mood, the last season is characterized by a certain melancholy, hinting both at the tragic ending of Ted's and Tracy's marriage, and to the phenomenon of the audience growing accustomed to a series, and finally having to 'say goodbye'. However, there are several ways in which it is pointed out, that the story must not be over, when it is over. For example, "Last Time In New York" (9.3) depicts elderly people, and how the main characters see them, always hinting to themselves getting older, too. The attributes that Ted and his friends apply to Robin's and Barney's elderly relatives that come to the wedding are the common clichés of old people. They are said to be slow, clingy ("They're like leeches", 9.3), spooky (creepy sound effects accompany their appearances), politically incorrect in a shrouded way

(Barney's brother James fears the elderly relatives' questions about him being black, gay, and divorced), too many, and practically living dead (Barney: "It's like we're in a zombie-movie!", Robin: "Chances are high that they chew your ear off", 9.3). Furthermore, this episode reveals Robin's and Barney's fear of becoming a fussy old married couple, and not having any erotic tension anymore, which changes into a hopeful view of the future when they witness Robin's great-grandparents having sex, after being married for 60 years. This depiction of old people can be seen as a symbol of all the aspects of a lifetime commitment: Growing old together does not only mean looking back on the good days of youth, but really *being* old and *living* old age with all the positive and negative consequences. By exaggerating the clichés of old age the viewers get confronted with preconceptions they themselves might have about aging as a process of decline, and can ironically distance themselves, while accepting that there might be some quirky traits in old people. Eventually, as the episode seems to suggest, it is mostly one's own decision what to become as an old person.

Another stylistic device that is used throughout the series – and especially in the last season – is going ahead or back in time within the narration. For example: In season 6, it is revealed that Ted will meet his future wife at Barney's wedding, but it is not known to the viewer before the end of season 7 that the bride is Robin. To make things more confusing, there are even mere imaginations of what might happen in the future, or what could have happened in the past. For instance, Ted and Barney summon the (imaginary) "20-years- and 20-hours-from-now Ted and Barney" (8.20) to discuss which decision Ted should make and Marshall and Lily summon their (imaginary) "2007 selves" ("Sunrise", 9.17) to end their current fight. In "The Time Travelers" (8.20), Ted also imagines what would have happened if he had gone to his future wife, before they actually met, which would have given him 45 extra days with her. In "Platonish" (9.9), Marshall tells Ted that Robin is still in love with Ted, and that they might be just 20 minutes away from their 'happily ever after'. Ted and Marshall then narrate a different version of what might happen in these 20 minutes. In Ted's version, he steals the blue French horn to give it to Robin as a present, already hinting tat the end of the series.

Evidently, the depiction of time passing is very important for the series' narrative concept. In contrast to other sitcoms, *HIMYM* aims to capture a realistic image of the development of its characters over the years. However, the use of temporality is a quite playful one, best captured in "The Rehearsal Dinner" (9.12), that contains a sequence, where the friends are making fun of Canada, while in the background, the life of a couple – from meeting for the first time, over getting engaged, and having their first child, to one of the partners dying – is being depicted, symbolizing bluntly how much time the group spends on making jokes[8]. This playfulness is in contrast to the rather traditional ideology transported throughout the narration: Ted's story is in fact a linear one, but the way his story is told makes it special and open in every direction.

Making Sense of One's Life – *HIMYM* As a Key to a Young Urban Digital Generation

While some aspects of a series may be seen as universal or 'timeless', others are very specific to a period. There are some striking parallels between *HIMYM* and the sitcom *Friends*, and one could even say that *HIMYM* is a copy of *Friends*. However, both shows address different audiences. The difference here is mostly about digitalization and a self-publicizing lifestyle that were not as current in the 1990s when *Friends* first aired. While there has always been a need to create continuity and meaning – from family chronicles to scrap booking –, the generation addressed by *HIMYM* satisfies this need quite excessively: The target audience of *HIMYM* is a cohort that is accustomed to the fact that Facebook documents the lives of its members in detail, that weblogs serve as public diaries, and that even Twitter enables its users to construct coherent stories. To live life to its fullest is nothing specifically new brought up by the "Generation Y", but the need to orchestrate and document all those perfect moments is something that defines them. *HIMYM* can thus be thought as an acted out Facebook-timeline – that is, as the name suggests, a rather linear way of telling a story –, presenting both mundane, funny things, and the major events of life. The latter can become quite excessive and season 9 seems to represent this focus on major life events by focusing entirely on a wedding.

---

8   This scene is the whole series in a nutshell: The friends are fooling around, while in the background it is being shown, what they all aim at, and what was the point of telling the story in the first place.

"The internet never forgets": This sentence normally used as an admonition might as well be a promise. Documenting one's life in an interactive and public way may be a way of making things that last for the members of a digitalized generation. It gives them an opportunity to leave a legacy. This aspect is not presented uncritically, though. In "Mystery Versus History" (6.7), the friends reflect on digitalization, stating that by "2011, the internet has taken a lot of intrigue out of life" (6.7), and referring to 2005 as "the dark ages without the smartphone" (6.7). Not only the characters develop, but there are also new milestones in technology that change the lives of the protagonists, and some think not for the better. Ted for instance, wishes himself back to the days when there was still mystery: "When my parents met, they didn't have the internet. They just went on a blind date, and fell in love" (6.7).

As the viewer accompanies the characters in their development and aging process, there is also a digital intertwining of the series with real life. Barney's blog, that is mentioned in various episodes, can actually be read on the internet (Stinson) and his "Play Book" and "The Bro Code" can be purchased[9]. Another aspect that influences most TV series nowadays, are online fan communities. Viewers from all over the world get connected to debate the latest episode, or speculate on what will happen next or how the series might end. *HIMYM* online discussion boards made way for all kinds of theories on the show's finale, from "The mother is dead" to "There is a Zombie Apocalypse going on" (Nadel).

On a formal level, the 'timelinification', that seems to characterize the attitude towards life of the "Millennials", still blends in with the traditional conventions of a linear narration. Concepts like the 'happily ever after' or 'destiny' are still part of the story; however, they are used differently. For instance, the wrap up of what will happen to the minor characters, is not part of the last episode, but comes on earlier ("Gary Blauman", 9.21); the 'happily ever after' is part of the story, but it is not told at the end of the story. The continuity that is constructed by Ted, throughout the series, is deconstructed in the open-in-every-direction ending of the last episode. In a way, *HIMYM* can be thought as an imagination of how storytelling will change for the first fully digitalized generation. It speculates on what will make the memories of the generation, and what will be left after 25 years.

---

9   See Amazon results.

Awareness Of Time: *HIMYM* in its Historic Situation

There is certainly a great number of questionable issues about *HIMYM* that cannot be treated profoundly within the scope of this essay, such as the fact that all the main characters of the show are white, straight, western, upper/middle class, successful, healthy young people, whereas supporting characters with an emancipatory political agenda are depicted as either rude or insane in their "ridiculous" deviance[10]. Furthermore, the story is told from a man's perspective [11], and women are represented in a quite ambivalent way. Barney's view on women and his behavior may be superficially frowned upon by some of his friends, but he is a crowd-pleaser exactly because of his misogynist ways.

Apart from that, it must be taken into account that "the mother" – as Ted's children remark in the last episode – "is hardly in the story" (9.23-24). Only "How Your Mother Met Me" (9.7) tells Tracy's story, summing up very shortly the eight years before she meets Ted, parallel to Ted's story (that is narrated over eight years!), from her point of view. Tracy is depicted as a mixture of a 'femme fragile' who is pure – suffering from the loss of her boyfriend she chooses to be abstinent –, childlike. She dies before her time and is a caring mother, giving her an air of divinity. Additionally, she does not show any affection for Ted, until he beats up her archenemy (9.7), acting out a very archaic concept of wooing. Tracy's illness and dying are not narrated in too much detail, either because of the children still remembering that time themselves, or because it is too painful for Ted to recall these events. Still, this narrative choice is a way of blanking out the female perspective. It can also be argued that generally older women are rendered invisible by the media, and that letting "the mother" die before she gets old – notice that she is only referred to by her 'function' throughout the story, by a notion that carries the whole traditional concept in it –, is just another example of predominantly showing women in their twenties[12].

Concerning contemporary societal questions one could say that *HIMYM*

---

10 Political activist and Ted's on-again-off-again girlfriend Karen, for instance.
11 There is only one exception to this rule: "The Symphony Of Illumination" (7.12) which is narrated by Robin.
12 For a more elaborate analysis of this phenomenon see Oró-Piqueras.

shows some kind of awareness of, but hints only very subtly at critical issues. To a greater part it sticks to traditional concepts and patriarchal standards. As far as *HIMYM* goes, the question if a sitcom can be innovative to a degree where it contains and addresses critical issues and still be a crowd-pleaser, must remain unanswered[13], but everything hints at the series functioning as an affirmation of bourgeois conventions.

Conclusion

If asked for the gist of *HIMYM*, Barney's catchphrase ("It's gonna be legen – wait for it! – dary! Legendary!") could be adduced as an instance. *HIMYM* is in great part about making (one's very own) history. It is about anticipating and actively waiting for a meaningful – or even "legendary" – life to look back on, and, later on, reflecting it in one's stories. As the German comedian Karl Valentin put it: "Heute ist die gute alte Zeit von morgen" ("Today is the good old days of tomorrow", translation mine), the characters of *HIMYM* always try to create their very own 'good old days', keeping in mind that they will be old one day. This concept is neither new nor outstanding, but the unique narrative structure of the series puts the anticipation, the experience and the reminiscence in one, creating a remarkable update of the sitcom genre. By simultaneously encouraging the mainstream life concept of the "Generation Y" and the heteronormative traditional values of nuclear-family-life, *HIMYM* ensures its lasting success. It highlights that 'the future' is the time where a successful life, in terms of having a good job and a family, lies waiting, and it does not give in to pessimism that current crises might evoke. Different from the usual depiction of aging as a process of decline, *HIMYM* celebrates aging, as the only way to make experiences, carry out one's plans, and find oneself. There is, however, the motif of 'time running out' that especially Ted has to deal with: Getting older has to be prepared while one is still young. The series' overall highly optimistic mood of making plans, growing older, and looking back on good times, is not marred until the mother's untimely death in the final episode, but also there, the series hints at the opportunities that middle or even old age offers for those left behind. *HIMYM* tells a series of events that makes the viewer think of a story with a 'happy ending' in the

---

13 For a more elaborate analysis of this phenomenon see Berman.

beginning but changes into a narrative of how life cannot be planned after all. It also tells its viewers that the story need not be over when it is over, but that one can start a new story at any point of one's life, which aligns with the life concept of the "Millennials" that is characterized by flexibility and provisionality (Blatterer 95).

If the premise is valid that sitcoms have an affirmative function for the society addressed, *HIMYM* shows that its target group is characterized by the need for a coherent story to look back on, and a rather bourgeois mindset above all. *HIMYM*'s playful, creative, and innovative way of narration meets its audience's expectations, while at the same time it tells a rather traditional linear (late) coming-of-age-story with an implicit appeal to become a neat US citizen enjoying a heteronormative domestic bliss. The "Millennials" are called on to let go of their in-between status and eventually become mature.

WORKS CITED

Ames, Melissa. *Time in Television Narrative*. Jackson: University Press of Mississippi, 2012. Print.

Berman, Ronald. *How Television Sees Its Audience. A Look at the Looking Glass*. Newbury Park: Sage, 1987. Print.

Blatterer, Henry. *Coming of Age in Times of Uncertainty*. New York: Berghahn, 2007. Print.

Brost, Molly. "Change the Structure, Change the Story. How I Met Your Mother and the Reformulation of the Television Romance." *Time in Television Narrative*. Ed. Melissa Ames. Jackson: University Press of Mississippi 2012. Print.

Browne, Kit Simpson. "The Dark Secret Behind The How I Met Your Mother Finale." *Moviepilot*. Moviepilot, Inc, 4 Apr. 2014. Web. 18 Jun. 2015.

Bund, Kerstin. *Glück schlägt Geld. Generation Y: Was wir wirklich wollen*. Hamburg: Murmann, 2014.

Curnutt, Kirk. "Teenage Wasteland: Coming-of-Age-Novels in the 1980s and 1990s." *Critique* 43.1 (Fall 2001): 93-111. *ProQuest*. Web. 2 May 2013.

Currie, Mark. *About Time. Narrative, Fiction and the Philosophy of Time*. Edinburgh: Edinburgh University Press, 2007.

Deleuze, Gilles. *Cinema 2: The Time-Image*. Trans. Hugh Tomlinson and Robert Galeta. Minneapolis: University of Minnesota Press, 1989. Print.

Evans, Jeff. *The Guinness Television Encyclopedia*. Enfield: Guinness World Records Limited, 1995. Print.

Foltin, Hans-Friedrich. "Alltag und 'Alltag' in den deutschen Fernsehserien. Am Beispiel der Serien 'Berlin – Ecke Bundesplatz', ‚Lindenstraße' und 'Gute Zeiten, schlechte Zeiten'." *Schweizerisches Archiv für Volkskunde* 95 (1999): 153-172. Print.

"Generation Y Characteristics." *Generation Y*. GAIA insights. Web. 18 Jun. 2015.

Himmelstein, Hal. *Television, Myth, and The American Mind*. New York: Praeger, 1984. Print.

Main, Douglas: "Who Are The Millennials?" *Live Science*. Purch, 9 Jul. 2013. Web. 18 Jun. 2015.

Mellencamp, Patricia. "Situation Comedy, Feminism and Freud. Discourses of Gracie and Lucy." *Studies in Entertainment. Critical Approaches to Mass Culture*. Ed. Tanja Modleski et al. Bloomington: Indiana University Press, 1986. Print.

Modleski, Tanja et al. (ed.). *Studies in Entertainment. Critical Approaches to Mass Culture*. Bloomington: Indiana University Press, 1986. Print.

Nadel, Nick. "The 10 Craziest 'How I Met Your Mother Fan Theories." *Mandatory*. AOL, Inc, 27 Mar. 2014. Web. 18 Jun. 2015.

Oró-Piqueras, Maricel. "Challenging Stereotypes? The Older Woman in the TV Series Brothers & Sisters." *Journal of Aging Studies* 31 (2014): 20-25. Print.

Raby, Rebecca. "Theorizing Liminal Adulthood and Its Consequences for Youth." *Times of Our Lives: Making Sense of Ageing*. Eds. Harry Blatterer and Julia Glahn. Oxford: Inter-Disciplinary Press, 2012. Web. 17 Apr. 2012.

Segal, Lynne. *Out of Time. The Pleasures and the Perils of Ageing*. New York: Verso, 2013. Print.

Sielke, Sabine. "'Joy in Repetition': The Significance of Seriality for Memory and (Re-)Mediation." *The Memory Effect: The Remediation of Memory in Literature and Film*. Ed. Russell Kilbourn and Eleanor Ty. Waterloo: Wilfrid Laurier P, 2013. Print.

Stinson, Barney: "Barney Stinson's Blog." *Barney Stinson's Blog*. Barney Stinson Blog. Web. 18 Jun. 2015.
Strauss, William/Howe, Neil. *Millennials Rising: The Next Great Generation*. New York: Vintage Original, 2000. Print.
Witthoefft, Brigitte. *Formen und Funktionsweisen von Komik in ausgewählten amerikanischen Comedyserien*. Master's thesis at the University of Hamburg, 1996. Unpublished.
Wohlmann, Anita. *Aged Young Adults. Age Readings of Contemporary American Novels and Films*. Bielefeld: Transcript Verlag, 2014. Print.
Writes, Corina. "HIMYM: The Mother Revealed, Theories Disproved & Clues To Still Possible Connections!" *Corina Writes*. Corina Writes, 1 Apr. 2013. 18 Jun. 2015
Amazon results for "The Bro Code" and "The Play Book". *Amazon*. Amazon.com, Inc. Web. 18 Jun. 2015.

TELEVISION

Call The Midwife. Creator Heidi Thomas, BBC 1 (2012-present).
Everybody Hates Chris. Creators Chris Rock and Ali LeRoi, UPN/The CW (2005-2009).
Friends. Creators David Crane and Marta Kauffman, NBC (1994-2004).
How I Met Your Mother. Creators Craig Thomas and Carter Bays, CBS (2005-2014).
The Wonder Years. Creators Neal Marlens and Carol Black, ABC (1988-1993).

Serial Cougars

Representations of a Non-Normative Lifestyle in a Sitcom, an Episodic Serial, and a Soap Opera

ANITA WOHLMANN AND JULIA REICHENPFADER[1]

Introduction[2]

The cougar, a "single, confident, female predator who likes to date younger men," is a relatively new phenomenon (Gibson 10). Even though women have been romantically involved with younger men long before the Canadian sex and relationships columnist Valerie Gibson coined the term in 2001, the catchy label has catapulted this sexualized version of an older woman on a new level of public attention. In her guide book *Cougar*, Gibson proclaims a "new, free cougar" who belongs to "a unique breed" of women who are "full of life," "single, older, and often divorced (at least once)" (16-17). The cougar is "a career woman or financially independent" and she has the time and the money to enjoy affairs with younger men without being interested in marriage or in procreation (17). Agewise, the cougar is usually 35 or older. The factor that makes a woman into a cougar is the age

---

[1] Our collaboration arose from discussions within the research training group „Life Sciences - Life Writing," which is supported by the German Research Foundation (DFG), under the grant 2015/1.

[2] We are very grateful to our reviewers who have helped us in shaping this chapter. We particularly want to mention the (repeated) feedback offered by Kristyn Gorton, who has supported us tremendously to render our analysis more grounded in television studies.

difference to her partner, which is typically a difference of 10 to 15 years (Kershaw). A wider definition of the cougar also encompasses women who consider marriage and children with the younger man they are dating.

A study by the *American Association of Retired Persons* (*AARP*) from 2003 on the lifestyles of mid-life singles, aged 40 to 69, finds that 34% of the women from the survey are dating a younger man (8).[3] According to Mark J. Penn, author of *Microtrends*, the *AARP* study proves that the cougar phenomenon is no longer scandalous but "has now become downright ordinary" (7).[4] If Penn is correct in his assumption, 'cougarism' would signify an important shift for age studies and gender studies: The double standard of aging would be overcome as female aging would no longer imply a decrease of attractiveness and sexual desirability; the scandalization of women who do not act their age and thus refuse to be placed "within the symbolic confines of birth, reproduction, and death" would be a matter of the past (Russo 21); and lastly, the linearity of standard life courses would be juxtaposed with temporalities that offer alternatives to heteronormative ideals.

In a study from Penn State University (2014), sociologists Beth Montemurro and Jenna Marie Siefken interviewed 84 women in their 20s to 60s, investigating their perceptions of older women's sexuality and, among others, their attitudes towards cougars. The study reveals that the perception of cougars is multi-layered. While 82% of the women had heard the term cougar before, this familiarity with the name did not indicate acceptance or reflect normality. On the contrary, the majority of the interviewees considered the term problematic and was irked by the pejorative and offensive connotations, such as women as "predators" or "flesh eaters" (40). They criticized that the term reinforces double standards. Other women welcomed the term and saw it as a "playful acknowledgment" of older women's desire. Interestingly, while most women of the sample rejected the

---

3   The cougar-typical age difference of more than 10 years was met by only 8% of the women who were interviewed. 15% dated a man 1 to 4 years younger, and 11% claimed to date a man 5 to 9 years younger.

4   Penn seems to misinterpret the data from the *AARP* study when he claims that "about one-quarter of those men [dated by women] are ten or more years younger" (7). In fact, 29% of the men date women ten or more years younger, while only 8% of the women date men with this age difference.

term cougar, they were less hostile towards the behavior associated with it (38). Journalists have commented upon the cougar phenomenon in similarly critical and differentiated ways. Sarah Kershaw argues, for instance, that the meaning of cougar, problematically, designates a woman who is "always on the hunt," "sex-starved," and who is "slinking through bars for young men to satisfy nothing but physical needs." And Maridel Reyes argues that while the media "glamorize" the cougar, they also "mock the archetype" of the sex-crazed cradle-robber.

Montemurro and Siefken stress the significance of images in popular culture and their effect on women's negotiation of sexual scripts: "[C]ulture shapes our feelings about aging," they argue and refer to the strong feelings they encountered during their interviews (43). In addition, Montemurro's and Siefken's study makes clear that the cougar is a polarizing cultural image of an older, desiring woman. Or, as Bill Lawrence, the co-creator of *Cougar Town* (2009-2015), maintains in an interview, it is a "noisy" and "zeitgeist-y" topic (Keller). But, apart from the associations that the term itself evokes and the numerous media appearances of cougars commented upon by journalists,[5] little has been said about *how* cougars are represented in fictional settings. Even though cougars have been featured quite prominently in recent fictional television series such as the sitcom *Cougar Town*, the multiple possibilities of characterizing, staging, and embedding cougars in fictional television narratives have not received much scholarly attention yet.[6]

Our particular interest in this article lies in the representation of cougars in relation to concepts of seriality. The way in which we use the term seriality here encompasses the format of the 'serial' (as for example in soap operas, where a continuous narrative unfolds over several episodes), the (episodic) series (such as sitcoms, where each episode is self-contained) as well as the many hybrid forms between serials and series such as mini-

---

5   See Klein, Montemurro and Siefken, Penn, and Reyes for enumerations of cougar-related media venues such as an Oprah episode dedicated to cougars, dating sites, reality TV-shows, cougar cruises, or cougar celebrities such as Madonna and Demi Moore.

6   There are, however, critical analyses of older-woman-younger-man representations in fiction film (see, for example, Wearing for an analysis of Something's Gotta Give).

series, episodic serials, sequential series, or flexi-narratives. How do different genres of serial narration shape and interact with the representation of the cougar? Which expectations do the individual genres raise in their viewers, and how does the narrative structure of these genres impact the representation of older, desiring women? If we follow Judith Butler, who argues that gender norms are constituted through "reiterative practices" (2), does the repetitive, circular nature of a sitcom, for example, normalize the cougar? The underlying question that guides our analysis is thus whether the 'serial cougar' perpetuates, challenges, or undermines stereotypes of age and aging.

In our analysis, we first provide a short background of contemporary cougar representations in American television. In drawing on concepts from gender studies, queer age studies, and television studies, we establish our theoretical framework on temporality, seriality, and television genres. We then discuss three test cases in which we focus on the representation of serial cougars in three distinct TV formats: the sitcom *Cougar*, the episodic serial *Damages* (2007-2012), and the German soap opera *Verbotene Liebe* (1995-present).

Serial Cougars: Norms, Seriality, and TV Genres

Regardless of (or maybe precisely because of) the ambivalences involved in cougarism, the cougar figure has become a notable presence in fictional television series. Prominent examples are Samantha Jones in *Sex and the City* and Gabrielle Solis in *Desperate Housewives*. Cougars also appear as secondary characters, for instance in *Damages* (as the partner to Michael Hewes, the son of Patty Hewes), in *Desperate Housewives* (as the affair of Porter Scavo, the son of Lynette Scavo), or in *Ally McBeal* (Jennifer 'Whipper' Cone, Richard Fish's girlfriend).

Two sitcoms stand out in their focus on cougars. In 2005, Fran Drescher, known as the nanny in the eponymous 7-seasoned sitcom, starred in a new show, *Living With Fran*, which revolves around a mother of two children and her young boyfriend (who is only five years older than her son). *Living With Fran* lasted for two seasons and was cancelled in 2006.[7]

---

7   The series has not been released on DVD. For this reason, we could not include it for an in-depth discussion.

The second sitcom, *Cougar Town*, features Jules Cobb, embodied by Courtney Cox, who is – more or less voluntarily – on the prowl for younger cubs. Jules, however, is actually too prudish and too insecure about her body to live up to the cougar stereotype. She dates a few younger men, but, by the end of the first season, Jules is romantically involved with her same-aged neighbor and marries him in the third season. The other cougar on the show is a secondary character, Barb, who is an exaggerated, even parodic version of the sex-crazed woman on the prowl and who reinforces all of the stereotypes associated with cougars. Barb's appearances in the series are regular, yet very short and always comic. Therefore, Emily Nussbaum argues that "Barb is less a character than a moral lesson. She's the cautionary cougar". While Nussbaum sees Barb as an example of an "older style of female humor, the self-loathing gags of Joan Rivers and Phyllis Diller," Barb's eccentricity and grotesqueness can also be framed as a type of "parodic displacement" (Swinnen 9), which reveals and tries to dismantle the artificiality and cultural construction of age norms, desire, and age-appropriate behavior (see next subchapter).

Beyond the comedy format, cougars also appear in drama series, such as *Desperate Housewives* and *Damages*, where their age-inappropriate behavior is provocative because it challenges normative age scripts. As mentioned earlier, for a cougar, sexuality is not necessarily associated with reproduction. While some cougars have children with their younger partners, for other cougars, procreation is no longer possible or no longer of interest (because she already has children from an earlier marriage, for example). Stereotypically, the cougar sees sex primarily as a source for pleasure and fun – an attitude towards sexuality that is not always presented in a favorable way.[8] Hence, the relationships of cougars, while they are

---

8   A character like Gabrielle Solis from *Desperate Housewives*, for example, who is married and has two children, walks a thin line when she dissociates sexuality from reproduction. On the one hand, her fooling around with a teenage gardener can be understood as a form of female emancipation and self-assertiveness (comparable to Samantha Jones in *Sex and the City*). At the same time, Gabrielle is, of course, also an adulteress, who risks her marriage and the nuclear-family-home to her children. As soon as a pregnancy is involved, the cougar-cub relationship becomes even more problematic. When, in the sixth and final season of *Desperate Housewives*, Porter Scavo (Lynette's teenage son) starts a

typically heterosexual, do not seem to conform to standard concepts of heteronormative temporality, which Judith Halberstam defines as "paradigmatic markers of life experience - namely birth, marriage, reproduction and death" (2). Queer time, according to Halberstam, implies "new ways of understanding the nonnormative behaviors that have clear but not essential relations to gay and lesbian subjects" (5). In understanding time as a social construction, Halberstam reminds us how normative concepts of time – such as "family time," "time of inheritance," "generational time," or "hypothetical temporality" (i.e. a form of risk management of the future through insurances) – do not only appear as natural but also shape how we respond emotionally to time and temporal logics (5-6). In this respect, the cougar might embody queer time: She is neither oriented towards the past nor the future. Instead, she focuses on the present, disregards or is no longer interested in conventional benchmarks of marriage and reproduction and seeks primarily the satisfaction of her desires. In dismissing cultural expectations of age-appropriate relationships, she challenges stereotypes about the negative impact of age on female life courses and identities. Therefore, following Halberstam, cougars might represent alternative "time horizons of possibilities" (2).

If we assume that cougars challenge normative timelines, how is their representation in television impacted by the particular temporal characteristics of TV series? How does seriality refract traditional notions of temporality and storytelling? In conceptualizing a general framework of seriality, Frank Kelleter argues that serial narration is characterized by repetition and variation, balancing two fundamental impulses of storytelling: the satisfaction produced by closure and the appeal inherent in renewal (11, 13). Serial narration is closely related to popular culture but does not simply echo the consumption practices encouraged by mass production and industrial manufacturing (12, 18-19). Instead, as Kelleter maintains, popular seriality repre-

---

relationship with Anne Schilling, the mother of one of his friends, Lynette does everything in her power to chase the cougar away from her son, particularly when she learns that the cougar might be pregnant. The representation of the cougar Anne Schilling is problematic on many levels: Not only does the narrative infer that her interest for Porter is an escape tactic (she suffers from an abusive husband), it also presents the relationship from the perspective of Lynette, who fiercely tries to get the couple apart.

sents a type of cultural work, which allows us to examine an esthetic process of modernization, which affects self-conceptions, identities and the various opportunities of people to assume different roles (22). Following Daniel Haas, today's television series have become a defining pattern in modern life. Their paradoxical logic of combining 'the familiar' and 'the new' promises both permanence and originality. However, as Haas believes, the originality and innovativeness of series should not be overemphasized: The defining criterion of series remains endless repetition and, as a consequence, implies stagnation. In her article "Joy in Repetition," Sabine Sielke takes a different approach to the concept of seriality as "repetition with variation" (38). She follows Gilles Deleuze's "sense of repetition as an operation not of sameness, but of singularity and variability" (44). Thus, in contrast to Haas, Sielke defines seriality as a pattern that emphasizes process and change, privileging "constellations of time over configurations of space" (49). In this sense, Sielke's conceptualization of seriality resonates with the demands voiced by scholars from age studies, who advocate a view of aging that looks for difference, singularity, and variability instead of generalized notions of sameness.

More specifically, when we take a closer look at how seriality is realized in television, it becomes clear that different formats or genres of serial storytelling, such as sitcoms, mini-series, or soap operas, each have their own relation to temporality. *Episodic series*, such as sitcoms, for example, are inherently circular because the storylines of each episode are always brought to an end within the same episode. The viewers can be certain that "whenever something drastic happened to a regular character [. . .], it would be reversed by the end of the episode and the characters would end up in the same general narrative situation that they began in" (Dolan 33). In this sense, sitcoms are not about change or development but about repetition, which in itself resists closure and is open-ended. Or, in the words of John Fiske: "The syntagmatic chain of events may reach closure, but the paradigmatic oppositions of character and situation never can. It is a requirement of television's routine repetition that its stories can never be finally resolved and closed off" (145). *Continuous serials*, such as soap operas, by contrast, have "a linear feel" (Dolan 33). They are characterized by their open-endedness. In contrast to traditional story arcs of beginning, middle, and end, the multiple storylines in soap operas are never fully resolved. Instead, they unfold across multiple episodes, intersect with other storylines, and are dramatically orchestrated through cliffhangers (Casey et al. 224; Fiske 179-180). It is "all loose ends" due to the soap opera's "infinitely extended middle" (Fiske 180). The soap celebrates narrative development and change without providing closure or an aim towards which the narrative develops.

According to Fiske, television has a unique sense of time "in its feel of the present and its assumption of the future" (145). Whether applied to sitcoms, soap operas, or the news, the "sense of future, of the existence of as yet unwritten events, is a specifically televisual characteristic, and one that works to resist narrative closure" (145). Television's "nowness" implies that the characters' future is still unwritten, inviting the viewers to "a more engaged and empowering reading relation than that offered by the novel or by film" (145). In this sense, television might provide an intriguing springboard for representations that show "life as an open-ended and unpredictable process of becoming rather than a rising, then falling staircase or curve," with the latter so often resulting in negative, static, and reductive notions of old age and aging (Gravagne 42).

Television and its genres are, however, more complex than the previous paragraph suggests. First of all, genres are usually neither simple, clear-cut formats, nor are they natural characteristics of a text (Mittell xi). Instead, we usually encounter hybrid forms of different genres. While sitcoms, for example, are based on endless repetition, sameness, and circularity, they usually also involve some kind of narrative development or change. Secondly, the narrative dimension of a television genre is not the only constitutive element of a genre: Instead, TV genres are shaped by viewing practices, audience expectations, scheduling decisions, and other choices by producers and the television industry (xiii). Therefore, Jason Mittell argues that television genres are cultural categories "constituted by clusters of discursive processes operative within texts, audiences, industries, and cultural contexts" (27). As a consequence, they represent fluid, relational cultural practices and not "deep repositories of hidden meanings, formal structures, or subtextual insights" (1, 25). Instead, we might ask how genres are culturally used in specific contexts. Similar to the categories of race, gender, and age, a discussion of television genres could thus enable us to "understand how genres work to shape our media experiences and how media work to shape our social realities" (28).

In the following analyses of three TV series, which can be roughly classified as three larger genres – the sitcom, the episodic serial, and the soap opera –, we will look at the ways in which each of them uses specific temporal frames (such as narrative arcs, closure, open-endedness, repetition, fragmentation, linear, and circular narrative) for the representation of a cougar character. The three analyses are not intended to be comprehensive or representative accounts of how seriality and the cougar inform each other. By examining a limited number of examples and by comparing American and German cougars, we cannot make any larger claims about how a specific genre, such as the sitcom, generally impacts the representation of a cougar figure. Instead, we see our analyses as test cases for thinking about possible links between specific realizations of television storytelling and the representation of a temporally-marked figure like the cougar. We are thus interested in exploring how serial storytelling theoretically harbor innovative temporal trajectories for stories about age and aging. Potentially, the representation of cougars in serial storytelling might not only herald non-normative temporalities but also enable alternative visions of age and aging, which no longer fall within the stereotypical, linear narratives of inevitable future decline and degeneration.

Jules and Barb in *Cougar Town*

Cougar Town was created by Bill Lawrence and Kevin Biegel[9] and is set in Florida. Similar to the sitcom *Friends*, to which *Cougar Town* is often compared, the series revolves around a group of middle-aged friends who spend most of their time with each other. In many ways, *Cougar Town* conforms to the characteristics of the sitcom, which Larry Mintz defines as a series

involving recurrent characters within the same premise. That is, each week we encounter the same people in essentially the same setting. The episodes are finite; what happens in a given episode is generally closed off, explained, reconciled, solved at the end of the half hour ... The most important feature of sitcom structure

---

9 Bill Lawrence also created *Scrubs*. *Cougar Town* makes many references to *Scrubs*, for example through repeated appearances of *Scrubs*-characters in *Cougar Town*.

is the cyclical nature of the normalcy of the premise undergoing stress or threat of change and becoming restored. (qtd. in Mills 28)

Cougar Town's premise consists in the eccentricities of Jules Cobb (played by Courtney Cox), the protagonist, and her loving, equally eccentric group of friends, family members, and neighbors who surround her. Jules is a recently divorced real estate agent in her early forties and mother of a teenage son, Travis, who tries to get out in the dating world to restore her battered sense of self. This aim leads to multiple problems, hurt feelings, and complications, but at the end of each episode, the original premise of the sitcom is restored: The conflict caused by Jules' peculiar, chaotic nature is resolved, and Jules is surrounded by her odd circle of lovable friends and family members. In this sense, *Cougar Town* presents a static, cyclical world which revolves around "the local, the small-scale, the familial and the domestic" (Mills 23).

This cyclical, small-scale world of the sitcom adds to the problematic portrayal of female age and aging in *Cougar Town*. The sitcom seems to repeat stereotypical notions of what it means to grow older for a woman. In contrast to her similarly aged neighbor Grayson Ellis, for example, who has numerous affairs with young women, Jules complains about the double standard of aging, which presumably makes it more difficult for women of a certain age to date younger men. The first episode of *Cougar Town* repeatedly emphasizes stereotypical notions about aging as decline and age as a source of humiliation for women. The show suggests that Jules is frustrated about her aging body and worries about her attractiveness on the dating market. Interestingly though, Jules' worries are not only exaggerated but also blatantly incongruous with what we see. Not only is Jules in spectacular shape and very attractive, she also starts to date younger, handsome men and turns into the cougar, which the title announces. This contradictory nature of *Cougar Town* could be construed as a sign of the progressive message of the show, along the lines of 'even though women may believe that their age is problematic, it's not.' As the seasons unfold, however, the incongruities continue, further solidifying conventional values over more radical alternatives.

Barb is the second cougar in *Cougar Town* and a cougar par excellence: She is always on the prowl, she continuously makes lascivious remarks which revolve around sex and which suggest that she is quite successful with younger men. Barb is like a sidekick to Jules. She usually appears when Jules is in a scene and only talks to Jules. Barb is a little older than Jules (Barb is 48) and she also works in the real estate business. She repeatedly appears throughout the sitcom, usually with a salacious one-liner:

Barb: "Morning, chicas. Drink in my new outfit."
Jules: "Barb, you look like a bobsledder."
Barb: "Well, I have sledded down a few Bobs." ("Mystery Man", 1.10)

Barb typically appears out of the blue and has a short scene in almost every episode. In this function, Barb's appearance is like a running gag: short and repetitive, yet always different and surprising. It is important to note, however, that Barb does not change or develop; she remains a flat character who only revolves around two topics: men and sex.

In the example of *Cougar Town,* the sitcom genre does not seem to offer progressive or innovative trajectories of aging. In continuously (and unconvincingly) repeating stereotypes about the negative implications of aging for women and the man-hungry oddities of a desiring older woman, the potentially radical cougar figure appears static and seems caught in self-deprecating humor and eccentricities. *Cougar Town,* however, does not strictly follow the genre definitions of the sitcom because the characters, to some extent, do change and evolve over the seasons. Even though it is generally referred to as a sitcom, *Cougar Town* thus also features story arcs that go beyond individual episodes.

A peculiar (and for our purposes quite relevant) example is the astonishing fact that even though *Cougar Town* starts out with a focus on cougars, as the series develops, both cougars (or rather their lifestyles) disappear. By the end of the first season, Jules has started to date her same-aged neighbor Grayson and Jules' affairs with younger men are thus replaced by an 'age-appropriate' relationship that leads to marriage in season 3 and a discussion about starting a family (another child is, however, not an option for Jules). Similarly, Barb gets married in season 3 to a man who seems a little older than Barb. From season 4 onwards, Barb never reappears on the show. This odd development of the sitcom, from a cougar-centered sitcom towards a cougar-free program, sparkled debates about changing the title of *Cougar Town* from season 2 onwards. The change was never realized because neither the producers nor the network (first ABC, then TBS) could agree on an appropriate title. During the second season, the opening credits sequence also comments on these discussions ironically by complementing the main title "Welcome to *Cougar Town*" with a new subtitle in every new episode, such as "Badly Titled: *Cougar Town*" (2.03) or "100% Cougar Free: *Cougar Town*" (2.05).[10] In a sense, the industry solidified the cougar theme externally by keeping the title, even though the content evolved beyond cougars. The label cougar thus becomes empty and in ironizing this fact through the commentaries in the title sequence, the producers and writers draw attention to the discrepancy between the static dimension of the title and the development of the characters.

In her quality as a recurring and (for most of the time) unchanging and one-dimensional character, Barb's radical potential seems stifled. By overemphasizing her sexual appetite, Barb appears like an overly adjusted version of the cougar on the prowl and thus, to some degree, she reproduces the stereotype of the lecherous, dirty old woman, who is out of control and scandalous in her sexual autonomy. From a different point of view, Barb could also be read as a hyperbolic and campy version of the cougar woman (also see Thomas Küpper's analysis of the ambivalences in Blanche from *The Golden Girls* in this volume). By purposefully overemphasizing her role as a 'dirty old woman,' *Cougar Town* would open up a space for a different kind of reading inspired by the subversive potential of mockery and queer theory. According to Miriam Haller, the disgraceful old woman ("unwürdige Greisin") is particularly interesting in this context because she inspires age mockery which carries the potential to breach norms and bring about "ageing trouble" (57-62). Drawing on Judith Butler's concept of "gender trouble," Haller understands grotesque representations of older women not as simple reproductions of problematic stereotypes, but as potentially subversive moments of destabilization and re-signification (60). According to Butler, "performativity must be understood not as a singular or deliberate 'act,' but, rather, as the reiterative and citational practice by which discourse produces the effects that it names" (2). Through their reiterative appearance on the screen, cougars, one could argue, challenge

---

10 For a list of the different title card jokes in the opening sequence, see <http://cougartown.wikia.com/wiki/Opening_Sequence_Subtitle?file=All_the_C ougar_Town_title_card_jokes>.

the conventional association of sexual desire with youthfulness and procreation.

In *Cougar Town,* Barb, for example, cites but also exaggerates the norms of age-appropriate behavior. She is repeatedly presented as a woman who frequently undergoes cosmetic rejuvenation treatment. In this sense, she references the common stereotype that women fear aging and feel obliged to fight wrinkles or saggy skin. Barb, however, does not try to conceal her attempts at passing for younger. Instead, she makes a spectacle out of her various treatments and their results. In "Don't Do Me Like That" (1.03), for example, we learn that she has had a vaginal rejuvenation surgery, making her look like 19 "below the belt". Barb exaggerates her actions in every way she can and, by drawing attention to the ludicrous effects of the youth cult, she transgresses the double standard of aging. From this angle, Barb invites us to laugh *with* her (and not *at* her) through "parodic displacement" (Swinnen 9-10). The fact, however, that Barb eventually marries a same-aged man so that her lifestyle becomes 'normalized' reintroduces an ambivalent note to the representation of this character. The comedic dimension of the sitcom thus opens a space for a more radical view, but this potential does not seem to be fully explored in *Cougar Town.*

To sum up, the cougar in the sitcom *Cougar Town* appears as a flat, one-dimensional and ridiculous woman. The sitcom's features of circular narration seem to solidify this impression. While *Cougar Town* is not a classic sitcom but also includes some degree of character development, the show does not use this hybridity to complicate or expand on the cougar lifestyle. Instead, the cougar vanishes and becomes domesticated within 'normal,' age-appropriate marriages.

Jill Burnham in *Damages*

Damages is a television show that focuses on the lawyer Patty Hewes and her relationship with her protégée Ellen Parsons, a young and gifted lawyer, and their fight against injustice, big corporations and against one another. *Damages* is a hybrid form of serial narration and is probably best described with the labels episodic serial or cumulative narrative. *Damages* is limited in length (each of the five seasons consists of 10 or 13 episodes). Within each season, the story arcs expand over all episodes and, similar to a serial, the storylines overlap. Some story arcs, particularly those that involve

Patty's family, expand over several seasons. *Damages* is particularly interesting for our discussion of seriality due to its narrative complexity and experimental use of temporality. Circumventing linear narrativity through repeated flashbacks and flashforwards, *Damages* starts each episode in the future, which is depicted as violent and to be feared. As the episodes unfold, we learn more and more about past events that lead to the 'result' in the future. The viewer has to be active and piece together the fragments of the discourse into a linear and causal chain of events.

One storyline within this complex narrative is a cougar-cub relationship that – like the narrative form – challenges normative and linear concepts of time. The relationship between Patty Hewes' 18-year-old son Michael and Jill Burnham, an accomplished gallery owner with a PhD,[11] evolves over the course of four seasons and interweaves the cougar Jill, who is a minor character in the series, within a complex network of power, concepts of motherhood, and normative temporality. Jill Burnham, as we gradually learn in the course of the series, is a successful and radiant businesswoman. She was married before and is the mother of two children, whom she can no longer see because she was declared an unfit mother by the court. Jill is not afraid of Patty Hewes and she refuses to be intimidated by Patty's manipulative strategies. On the contrary, Jill starts to get back at Patty by accepting Patty's money for leaving Michael without ever intending to keep her own part of the agreement. Jill is thus presented as a strong and complex woman, who is neither entirely good nor evil.

As it is typical for *Damages*, the story of Michael and Jill is about withholding knowledge, using knowledge, and disclosing it for manipulative strategies. By intertwining these negotiations about knowledge with temporal narrative experiments, such as flashbacks and flashforwards, which are a signature of the narrative structure in *Damages*, the series draws attention to how the discourse of the story and not so much the story itself constructs knowledge via "experiments with time" (Pape 165). According to Toni Pape,

the show demonstrates that, as law, time is a powerful tool that can be used and abused to one's interest. The show achieves this by means of a persistent correlation

---

11 The actress Wendy Moniz (alias Jill Burnham) was 40 years old when she played the role in 2009.

of its twisted, yet law-abiding temporal structures with the twisted logic of civil litigation. More precisely, the story of legal scheming continuously points to the 'temporal scheming' of the narrative itself. While, within the story, the show *explicitly* criticizes the legal system, the narrative discourse *implicitly* performs a critique of modern time (172).

According to Pape, the narrative structure of *Damages* both reproduces and critiques "an obsession with the future" (166). The show thus displays an awareness of the unreliability of knowledge when temporal continuity and linearity are undermined (167) as well as a critique of modern concepts of time, in which time is standardized, measurable and "split up into equal units" (170). Temporality – or rather the disruption of normative, linear temporality – therefore plays a major role in the series and provides a fascinating background against which the story about the cougar character and her relationship with Michael and Patty unfolds.

Jill Burnham is introduced in the series when she meets Michael's parents during a dinner. Before the dinner scene, the audience was led to believe that Michael's new girlfriend is an eccentric looking young woman with piercings, tattoos, and wild hair. The audience is thus misled on purpose for dramaturgical reasons. As viewers, we receive full disclosure of the identity of the girlfriend at the same time as Patty and her husband do. Patty's 'shock' moment thus falls together with the audience's surprise. Patty disapproves of the relationship from the very first moment and she continually tries to force Jill out of Michael's life. For instance, Patty wonders openly whether Jill is "mentally ill" because she cannot understand that a mature woman feels attracted to a "child" ("Uh Oh, Out Come the Skeletons", 2.10). Jill, in turn, frames Patty's behavior as that of a woman with an empty-nest-syndrome: Jill thus twists the accusation familiar to cougars, namely of being 'cradle-robbers,' and puts the blame on a mother who fails to realize that her son has come of age. To some degree, Michael, who has repeatedly tried to hurt his mother over the course of the first two seasons, also uses his age-inappropriate relationship with an older woman as a provocation with the purpose of punishing his mother. Fashioning himself as the only 'real man' left in his mother's life, Michael sounds the death knell for Patty, who discovered shortly after the dinner with Jill that her husband has had an affair with a younger woman. Out of spite, Patty then throws Michael out of her house and sends his belongings to Jill. In season 3, the dynamics between the timing of narrative disclosure and the viewers' and the characters' state of (not) knowing continues. Patty is now usually the last to receive crucial information. It is through other characters and the interlaced narrative structure that we learn, for example, that Michael has blatantly lied to his mother about his ongoing relationship with Jill, that Jill is pregnant, and that Jill has not kept her side of a deal. The challenging narrative structure seems to support the representation of the cougar Jill as a complex, multi-faceted woman.

In the finale of season 3, however, this representation changes and the cougar Jill falls prey to Patty's rancor. Crucially, Jill is not simply another victim to Patty's power games because, on a symbolic level, it is Jill in her role as a cougar who seems to be punished. She is arrested and accused of statutory rape due to a genetic test, which proves that at the date of conception of their child, Michael was 17 and thus a minor. With her incarceration, Jill is represented as a lawbreaker and a child abuser. Her relationship with Michael, which was initially staged as a provocation, is now presented as outright illegal. In season 4, we learn that Jill gave birth to her child in prison and Patty received custody of her granddaughter.

While *Damages* is radical and innovative in how the narrative discourse critiques modern temporality and legal epistemologies, the series seems to squander the opportunity to offer alternative temporal trajectories for its female characters. This is all the more unfortunate as the series does indeed provide a few narrative clues that might offer a more balanced or innovative representation of cougarism. When it comes to the legal question of Jill's and Michael's relationship, which the series unfortunately answers in an unimaginative accusation of statutory rape and thus a simultaneously literal and symbolic punishment of Jill, the previous plot actually facilitates a more complex reading. In the beginning of season 2, Patty had emancipated Michael, making him prematurely into an adult, when she had to realize that it would be best for her and Michael if she withdrew from his life altogether. By using a genetic test in season 3, Patty incapacitates Michael retroactively, claiming that Michael was still a minor when he had sex with Jill and thus taking full control over his life again. Regrettably, however, the series does not pursue this incongruity any further, which challenges so pointedly the artificiality and cultural contingency of legal age norms. Since the series partly admires Patty's wit in how easily she twists the law in order to make it meet her needs, *Damages* is inconsistent in its representation of the cougar Jill, pigeonholing her too easily as a lawbreaker and bad mother.

In a similar way, Toni Pape's auspicious statement about the series' innovative use of temporality does not fully apply to the representation of Jill or Patty, and thus to the nexus of older women and the legitimacy of sexual desire. While the narrative, as Pape argues, offers a critique of modern, standardized time through its narrative complexity, the series does not really explore alternative lifestyles that go beyond ageist stereotypes, even though there are some interesting clues for presenting alternative temporalities, such as the unpredictability of falling in love, disregarding age scripts, and age-appropriate standards or the fact that Patty becomes a loving mother way past her reproductive age. Unfortunately, *Damages* remains stuck in stereotypes about older, career-oriented women: Jill is not only an unfit mother, as stipulated by a court, her unusual love of Michael is condemned by her incarceration and erasure from the narrative. Similarly, Patty – who is presented as asexual throughout the five seasons – has become a substitute mother for her granddaughter through highly questionable means. Ironically, it is Patty now who has become a cradle-robber, and not the cougar Jill. She has become a late (grand-) mother by excluding sexual intercourse entirely.

Charlie Schneider in *Verbotene Liebe*

In contrast to *Cougar Town* and *Damages*, the German soap opera *Verbotene Liebe* was aired in the early evening, before the prime-time program.[12] As continuous serials, soap operas have a particularly interesting relation to time: According to John Fiske, "the narrative time [in soap operas] is a metaphorical equivalent of real time, and the audiences are constantly engaged in remembering the past, enjoying the future" (145). Soaps also have a unique narrative structure because "they have an indefinite run and, therefore, do not feature a final episode in which the *narrative* is closed or resolved" (Casey et al. 224). In contrast to the beginning-middle-end struc-

---

12 *Verbotene Liebe* had been broadcast daily on weekdays for twenty years. In February 2015, due to dropping viewing figures, the airtime was reduced drastically before the producers decided in June 2015 to discontinue the show entirely.

ture of, for example, a sitcom, the soap opera is characterized by an "infinitely extended middle" (Fiske 180). This implies that the soap opera never features a traditional climax that ends a story, resolves the conflict and reestablishes the previous status quo (Casey et al. 226). Instead, the narratives are ongoing and "all loose ends, and that is its attraction" (226). This particular narrative structure implies that soap operas evade closure (such as a happy ending that is often achieved through marriage in romantic movies). A marriage in a soap is thus never an end-point, but just one status among many others, which, as time progresses, evolves, deepens or fails (Fiske 181). Soap operas thus celebrate the process of life instead of concrete outcomes or achievements (of a competition, conflict or search, for example).

Soap operas have been discussed as a television format that particularly appeals to female audiences (Brown and Barwick 1987, Neale 2000). One of the reasons that Casey et al. mention is that the female characters in soap operas are usually strong and powerful; they are shown as individuals and not as types (225). Particularly interesting for our discussion of the cougar is Casey et al.'s finding that, in soap operas, "women, including older women, are often seen as having an active *sexuality* which they enjoy for themselves. Their sexuality is not simply represented as an object of male desire" (226; emphasis in the original). And Fiske adds: "In prime-time soaps the sexual power of the middle-aged woman goes hand in hand with her economic power in a significant reversal of conventional gender ascription" (184). Soap operas, despite their often domestic setting and focus on relationships, thus seem to open up a space to explore stories and characters of "female transgression" (Seiter qtd. in Fiske 181).

The German[13] soap opera *Verbotene Liebe* is an interesting example to investigate the cougar as a character of 'female transgression.' As the title of the soap indicates, *Verbotene Liebe,* or 'forbidden love,' narrates romantic relationships that are usually placed under a taboo. In the pilot, for ex-

---

13 We are aware of the fact that it is problematic to compare two American programs with a German one (see the commentary in the conclusion). The length of a successful soap opera, however, which can often span decades, makes it difficult for us as German researchers to access and credibly examine an American soap opera. In addition, we feel that the German example we chose is particularly interesting in relation to the topic of non-normative relationships and love stories.

ample, Jan and Julia meet and fall in love, only to find out later that they are brother and sister. Besides incest, the soap presents numerous adulterous relationships. And, *Verbotene Liebe* has become known for equating homosexual and bisexual relationships with heterosexual relationships and has featured the first homosexual church wedding in a German soap opera, which contributed to many viewers from LGBT-communities supporting the soap. Set in Düsseldorf, the soap's central topic is the gap between a middle-class family (formerly the Brandners, today the family Wolf) and their aristocratic counterpart (von Lahnstein). Over the course of the past twenty years, the members of each family have waged wars and have fallen in love with each other numerous times, so that the ties between the families are intricately interwoven.

Charlie Schneider, played by Gabriele Metzger (born in 1959), is the only character who stayed on the program since the first episode. She is one of the central characters, who belongs neither to the aristocracy nor to the bourgeoisie of the soap. Judging from her appearance, she can be seen as a member of the high society of Düsseldorf. Charlie is a typical cougar: She is financially independent and has numerous affairs with younger men. In the beginning of *Verbotene Liebe,* she was cast as a scheming secondary character. Over the years, she developed into a successful, buoyant, and generous businesswoman. She owns a restaurant and is appreciated and loved by her many friends. There is one aspect of Charlie's life that has not changed, however: her misfortune in romance. Charlie had numerous relationships with (often younger) men, who – sooner or later – cheated on her and/or lied to her. In episode 4350, Charlie 'eventually' marries the police inspector Frank Helmke (played by Christoph Kottenkampf, born in 1971).

Charlie's history and her lifestyle do not conform to the heteronormative plot of family formation. She has a daughter, Bella, for example, who – compliant with the central topic of the series – is the offspring of a taboo relationship: Her father is the husband of Charlie's sister. Charlie gave up her daughter for adoption shortly after she was born. When Bella's adoptive mother dies, the grown-up Bella looks for her biological mother, with whom she eventually establishes a loving relationship. Shortly after Charlie has 'become a mother,' she marries Frank Helmke. Being in her mid-fifties, Charlie thus eventually leads, to some extent, a heteronormative lifestyle, with a grown-up daughter (who was not raised by her) and a husband (who could almost be her son). This narrative development of the cougar Charlie was applauded in the media. With the headline "Charlie Schneider kommt endlich unter die Haube" ('Charlie Schneider finally gets married'), the female viewers of the soap were reassured that it is never too late to hope for a romantic happy ending. Interestingly, the media seem to celebrate Charlie's marriage without giving credit to the inherent open-endedness of the soap opera genre, in which the marriage will most likely be put to the test.

Charlie's and Frank's relationship is viewed favorably by most of the other characters in *Verbotene Liebe*. It is presented as a positive next stage in Charlie's individual development, who, due to her history of negative experiences, had suffered from commitment phobia before. Only one character openly criticizes this cougar relationship: Charlie's mother-in-law Elfriede Helmke, who appears in four episodes where she disparages the relationship by voicing prejudices against relationships between older women and younger men. The concern that Charlie could not fulfill her husband's desire for children is revealed as unjustified because Frank does not want to raise a family. At the end of her appearance on *Verbotene Liebe*, Elfriede's critique is revealed as envy and the soap stresses the similarities between Charlie and Elfriede: Both are successful, independent businesswomen of the same age. From the controversy with Elfriede, Charlie emerges as the stronger, more incorruptible woman and thus wins the 'battle' due to her natural authority. The implicit moral lesson is quite obvious: Since Charlie stays true to herself and masterfully defends her lifestyle against all kinds of attacks, she is able to win Elfriede's respect and affection.

The portrayal of sexuality and desire in middle-aged women is further underscored by the lingerie business that Charlie starts with her best friend Elisabeth (who also has a few cougar-cub relationships after her husband's death): The lingerie label is successful and *Verbotene Liebe* uses the business to discuss the meaning of age, aging and sexuality for mature women. The moral stance of the show is made quite clear when the only opponent, a young male photographer, Tim, eventually overcomes his ageist attitude and celebrates Charlie and Elisabeth when they model in their lingerie for a promotional campaign of their business. Tim is thus taught better and learns his lesson when he understands that his prejudices against older models are unfounded and that older women are attractive indeed. In contrast to the representation of Barb in *Cougar Town*, *Verbotene Liebe* does not use hyperbole, but features Charlie and Elisabeth as mature, desirable women.

Verbotene Liebe thus presents the cougar Charlie and her relation to aging in interesting ways. Charlie's life does not follow the 'normal' biography because she dates several younger men and did not raise children. Eventually, she enters the 'holy state' of matrimony and one can wonder whether or not this decision partly legitimizes her preference of younger men. The soap opera does not present Charlie's cougar lifestyle as particularly scandalous or unprecedented and puts those characters right who are critical or hostile towards her lifestyle. Charlie is everybody's darling, attractive, honest, successful, self-confident, funny, and helpful. It seems that her overwhelmingly positive character traits function as a means to make her cougar-lifestyle acceptable to the audience. In contrast to the 'comic grotesque' Barb in *Cougar Town*, whom Nussbaum describes as a cautionary cougar and moral lesson, the moralism associated with Charlie (and other relationships in *Verbotene Liebe*) advocates plurality of lifestyles and respect of unconventional desires. Charlie belongs to the main cast and represents a reputable and beloved character. Due to this representation, Charlie can be considered a role model for young viewers, particularly if Sabrina Hubbuch is correct in maintaining that soap operas function as a socializing instance (7).

Conclusion

The fact that the cougar Charlie is presented in such a positive way appears as an overall more progressive representation compared to the cougars in *Cougar Town* and *Damages*. This finding is all the more interesting against the background of the intended audiences of the three shows we have discussed here: While *Cougar Town* and *Damages* are prime time shows with TV-PG and TV-MA ratings and are thus intended for adult audiences,[14] *Verbotene Liebe* is aired during the early evening program and is also watched by younger audiences. From our observations here, crucial ques-

---

14 The TV Parental Guidelines are listed on imdb.com. TV-PG is a rating that suggests parental guidance as the "program contains material that parents may find unsuitable for younger children" (TV Parental Guidelines). TV-MA (Mature Audiences Only) indicates that the program "is specifically designed to be viewed by adults and therefore may be unsuitable for children under 17" (TV Parental Guidelines).

tions arise: Why did our two examples of prime time shows fail to explore more radical representations of non-normative lifestyles as opposed to the format that is aired during the day? To what extent is the more progressive representation of the cougar figure actually a result of the soap opera genre? The design of our analysis, unfortunately, does not allow us to provide generalizable answers to these questions. More research is needed to find out in how far a particular TV genre is generally more conducive to a particular representation. Our findings suggest that the soap opera might provide an intriguing narrative form. The fact, of course, that our soap opera example comes from a different cultural background as the two American examples raises the question to what degree cultural settings influence the representations we have studied.

What we set out to explore were the potential theoretical interconnections between narrative structures of seriality, of sameness, and repetition, in relation to the representation of a figure who is marked by non-normative notions of temporality. In our example of *Cougar Town*, the serial cougars Jules and Barb – though they do, mostly through humor, challenge reductive notions about (female) age and aging – do not appear as proud and assertive examples of female aging. They are either shown as self-deprecating or as exaggerated and grotesque. The circularity of the sitcom narrative and the repetitive nature of Barb's appearances seem to solidify the grotesqueness of cougar relationships and desiring older women. When *Cougar Town* goes beyond the sitcom's narrative structure of endless repetition by allowing some characters to develop, the program seems to exacerbate the problematic representation of the cougar figure by erasing the cougar life-style from the program altogether.

In the episodic serial *Damages* with its highly complex, fragmented narrative style, the cougar plot falls short of realizing its radical potential, too. Although the storyline involving the cougar Jill extends over several episodes and seasons and even plays with the show's central aesthetic concern of how temporality and (non-)linearity are related to knowledge and power, the cougar story is ultimately squashed and the non-normative female lifestyle is condemned and punished. The innovative narrative dimension of the show that is so tightly linked to concerns of temporality and linearity is not transferred to the representation of the cougar, nor to the representation of the protagonist Patty Hewes, who is after all a mature woman with power. And yet, the fascinating, multi-faceted heroine of the show is repeatedly represented as asexual, power hungry and man eating. In the show's finale, Patty appears as a lonely and deeply sad woman, as opposed to her younger rival Ellen, who has become a mother and has withdrawn from her job.

The soap opera *Verbotene Liebe* seems much more radical in its representation of the cougar. Not only is the format as such considered to be more welcoming to progressive representations of female power, age, and sexuality, the fact that a soap opera can feature characters who evolve, mature, and grow continually opens up a space to explore relationships and non-normative life courses not as static 'types' but as fluid and individual lifestyles that can and will change as time passes.

We hope that future research, in which the representation of a temporally marked figure such as the cougar is traced through several case studies of the same television genre (such as a comparison of the two sitcoms *Living with Fran* and *Cougar Town*), will help clarify to what extent the specific characteristics of a serial genre can be said to enhance, complicate or impair representations of non-normative lifestyles.

WORKS CITED

Brown, Mary Ellen, and Linda Barwick. "Fables and Endless Genealogies: Soap Opera and Women's Culture." *Continuum: The Australian Journal of Media and Culture* 1.2 (1987): N.pag. *Murdoch University School of Arts,* Web. 20 July 2015.

Butler, Judith. *Bodies That Matter: On the Discursive Limits of "Sex."* New York: Routledge, 1993. Print.

Casey, Bernadette, Neil Casey, Ben Calvert, Liam French, and Justin Lewis. *Television Studies: Key Concepts.* London: Routledge, 2002. Print

Dolan, Marc. "The Peaks and Valleys of Serial Creativity: What Happened to/on *Twin Peaks*." *Full of Secrets: Critical Approaches to Twin Peaks.* Ed. David Lavery. Detroit: Wayne State University Press, 1995. 30-50. Print.

Fiske, John. *Television Culture.* London: Routledge, 2003. Print.

Gibson, Valerie. *Cougar: A Guide for Older Women Dating Younger Men.* Toronto: Key Porter, 2001. Print.

Gravagne, Pamela. "The Magic of Cinema: Time as Becoming in *Strangers in Good Company*." *International Journal in Ageing and Later Life* 8.1 (2013): 41-63. Print.

Haas, Daniel. "Das kriegen wir schon auf die Reihe." *Zeit Online*. DIE ZEIT, 11 Oct. 2014. Web. 17 Nov. 2014.

Halberstam, Judith. *In a Queer Time and Place: Transgender Bodies, Subcultural Lives, Sexual Cultures*. New York: New York University Press, 2005. Print.

Haller, Miriam. "'Unwürdige Greisinnen:' 'Ageing trouble' im literarischen Text." *Alter und Geschlecht: Repräsentationen, Geschichten und Theorien des Alter(n)s*. Ed. Heike Hartung. Bielefeld: Transcript, 2005. 45-63. Print.

Hubbuch, Sabrina. *Mediale Wertvermittlung in Daily Soaps: Eine Studie zu Potentialen und Rezeption von Wertangeboten am Beispiel von* Verbotene Liebe. Dortmund: Universitätsbibliothek Technische Universität Dortmund, 2010. Web. 20 July 2015.

Keller, Joel. "Bill Lawrence Talks *Cougar Town*." *HuffingtonPost*. AOL-HuffPost TV Group, 23 Sept. 2009. Web. 10 Oct. 2014.

Kelleter, Frank. "Populäre Serialität: Eine Einführung." *Populäre Serialität: Narration – Evolution – Distinktion. Zum seriellen Erzählen seit dem 19. Jahrhundert*. Ed. Frank Kelleter. Bielefeld: Transcript, 2012. 11-46. Print.

Kershaw, Sarah. "Rethinking the Older Woman-Younger Man Relationship." *NYTimes*. The New York Times, 15 Oct. 2009. Web. 12 July 2014.

Klein, Rebecca. "Cougar Cruises Bring Younger Men To Older Women." *HuffingtonPost*. AOL-HuffPost TV Group, 7 March 2013. Web. 10 Oct. 2014.

Mills, Brett. *The Sitcom*. Edinburgh: Edinburgh University Press, 2009. Print.

Mittell, Jason. *Genre and Television: From Cop Shows to Cartoons in American Culture*. New York: Routledge, 2004. Print.

Montemurro, Beth, and Jenna Marie Siefken. "Cougars on the Prowl? New Perceptions of Older Women's Sexuality." *Journal of Aging Studies* 28 (2014): 35-43. *ScienceDirect*. Elsevier B.V. Jan. 2014. Web. 25 Oct. 2014.

Montenegro, Xenia P. "Lifestyles, Dating and Romance: A Study of Midlife Singles." *AARP The Magazine*. AARP, Sept. 2003. Web. 30 Sept. 2014.

Neale, Steve. *Genre and Hollywood*. London: Routledge, 2000. Print.

Nussbaum, Emily. "The Cougar Moment: The Best (Samantha Jones) and Worst (*Cougar Town*) of the Species." *NYMAG*. New York Magazine, 1 Nov. 2009. Web. 14 Oct. 2014.

Oxford English Dictionary. Oxford: Oxford University Press, 2001. Web. 15 Oct. 2014.

Pape, Toni. "Temporalities and Collision Course: Time, Knowledge, and Temporal Critique in *Damages*." *Time in Television Narrative: Exploring Temporality in Twenty-First-Century Programming*. Ed. Melissa Ames. Jackson: University Press of Mississippi, 2012. 165-177. Print.

Penn, Mark J. *Microtrends: The Small Forces Behind Today's Big Changes*. London: Lane, 2007. Print.

Reyes, Maridel. "Field Guide to The Cougar: Why Society Has Not Quite Accepted the May/December Relationship." *Psychology Today*. Sussex Publishers, 1 Nov. 2010. Web. 12 July 2014.

Russo, Mary. "Aging and the Scandal of Anachronism." *Figuring Age. Women, Bodies, Generations*. Ed. Kathleen Woodward. Bloomington: Indiana University Press, 1999. 20-33. Print.

Sielke, Sabine. "'Joy in Repetition'; Or, The Significance of Seriality in Processes of Memory and (Re-)Mediation." *The Memory Effect: The Remediation of Memory in Literature and Film*. Ed. Russel J. A. Kilbourn and Eleanor Ty. Waterloo, Ontario: Wilfrid Laurier University Press, 2014. 37-50. Print.

Swinnen, Aagje. "*Benidorm Bastards*, or the Do's and Don'ts of Aging." *Aging, Performance, and Stardom: Doing Age on the Stage of Consumerist Culture*. Ed. Aagje Swinnen and John A. Stotesbury. Münster: LIT, 2012. 7–14. Print.

"Traumhochzeit bei *Verbotene Liebe*: Charlie Schneider kommt endlich unter die Haube." *t-online*. Deutsche Telekom, 30 Aug. 2013. Web. 21 Oct. 2014.

"TV Parental Guidelines." *Federal Communications Commission*. 16 May 2012. Web. 26 Nov. 2014.

Wearing, Sadie. "Subjects of Rejuvenation: Aging in Postfeminist Culture." *Interrogating Postfeminism: Gender and the Politics of Popular Cul-*

ture. Eds. Yvonne Tasker and Diane Negra. Durham: Duke University Press, 2007. 278–310. Print.

TELEVISION

Ally McBeal. Creator David E. Kelley, FOX (1997-2002).
Cougar Town. Creators Bill Lawrence and Kevin Biegel, ABC (2009-2012); TBS (2013-2015).
Damages. Creators Todd A. Kessler, Glenn Kessler, and Daniel Zelman, FX (2007-2009); DirecTV (2010-2012).
Desperate Housewives. Creator Marc Cherry, ABC (2004-2012).
Living with Fran. Creators David Garrett, Jason Ward, Josh H. Etting, and Jamie Kennedy, The WB (2005-2006).
Sex and the City. Creator Darren Star, HBO (1998-2004).
Scrubs. Creator Bill Lawrence, NBC (2001-2008); ABC (2009-2010).
Verbotene Liebe. Production company UFA Serial Drama, Das Erste (1995-2015).

Sex and Desire
Through the Lens of Television Time

Still *Looking*

Temporality and Gay Aging in US Television

DUSTIN BRADLEY GOLTZ

The television series, as both a format of mediated representation and a tool for discursive intervention, carries the unique potential to challenge cultural meanings of aging in significant ways. Whereas Linklater's 2014 film *Boyhood* has garnered much discussion for allowing the audience to watch Ellar Coltrane grow up before their eyes, the expanded temporal workings of the television series regularly permit a similar audiencing position, relation, and perspective. The television series invites audiences to experience the aging processes of televised characters through a durational trajectory of multiple seasons, plotlines, and narrative arcs. With the unique temporal workings of this medium and format, television not only depicts a story of someone who ages, but it can temporally document the aging process through time. Put plainly, where shorter durational forms, such as film, can work to assert significant *meanings* around aging, the television series offers greater potential to reflect, inform and investigate aging *processes*. While now a cliché, and more of a metaphor (as TV series can be binge watched on mobile devices just about anywhere), television characters are welcomed into our living rooms and become a part of our social worlds, season after season. Television characters exist and linger, in and through our temporal lives, in a way that is qualitatively and quantitatively distinct.

Throughout this larger edited collection are examinations of a broad range of temporal possibilities unique to the medium of television, and how this form shapes and challenges our understanding of time and aging. Through television, we can follow as characters (and the bodies of actors in character) narrate the story of age, as well as experience the corporeal effects of age on the physical body. Across the temporal span of a series, we see characters transcend the confines of singular plotlines and narrative arcs. Before the days of binge watching, aging processes were paralleled with our own, wherein temporal bonds were forged through multiple season television series. For example, I went to high school at the same time as the kids in the original *Beverly Hills 90210* (1990-2000), we graduated together, went to college together (and the whole time, I was keenly aware that their bodies seemed much more mature than the bodies of my peers). Still, thirty-some years later, I can turn on *Days of Our Lives* (1965-present) on NBC and see how time and age has impacted the bodies of actors /characters I have known my entire life. Always running, alongside and in relation to my own embodied life, though not always temporally synched.[1]

This capacity for television to examine both the meanings and processes of aging is particularly significant when considering the discourses of aging and future mapped onto the gay male body. Foundational to this analysis, and to the argument set forth in this chapter, is a longstanding and highly durable set of cultural stories that write the aging gay male as a sad failure, if not a villainous monster. Homophobic mythologies in popular culture continually reify a deeply entrenched portrait of gay male aging as a tragic ritual of loss and punishment (Goltz "Queer"). Even when considering more 'positive' texts of gay representation, such as the GLAAD celebrated *Modern Family* (2009-present), the aging gay male is openly mocked, disparaged, and mostly erased (Goltz "Hollywood") from the youthism (Berger) that has come to define much of the mainstreamed gay male culture. With the near-absence of visible older gay male characters, gay future and aging are often constructed by how younger gay men discuss and narrate the meanings of aging – all too commonly as a process to be feared, fought, and resisted (Goltz "Harder", "Queer"). Future, as a system tied to the meanings and expectations assigned to our aging experiences, marks a contested and complicated system of meanings for gay men. Beyond merely equating age with loss of cultural value, the extreme fear and negative assignment of meanings to aging in gay male cultures has been tied to uniquely elevated fears, anxieties, disinvestment in longevity, and self-

---

[1] This phenomenon, in C. Lee Harrington's chapter in this volume, is referred to as SORAS (Soap Opera Rapid Aging Syndrome).

destructive behaviors (Kooden and Flowers). Historically, queers have been written in tension, if not direct opposition, to the stories and systems of future (Edelman; Goltz "Harder", "Queer"; Muñoz). However, these cultural and discursive cautionary tales that work to narrate gay male aging as tragedy, failure, and inescapable misery are not reflective of the research on the lived experiences of older gay men, as these myths are continually troubled by gay aging studies (Berger and Kelly; Brown; Dorfman; Ellis; Herdt and de Vries; Hostetler; Kertzner, Meyer, and Dolezal). While unfounded beyond cultural myth, these tales and assumptions about aging gay male meanings endure, functioning as lingering endorsements to the correctness of straight time. The aging gay male, in cultural representation, has a well-worn history of operating as a temporal scarecrow – a boogey man that makes aging and the future something to be feared and avoided.

Wherein a long lineage of negative and problematic meanings are signified and reproduced through representations of the aging gay body, the temporal opportunities[2] of the expanded format of the television series offer potent opportunities for rearticulating the process of gay male aging, and how gay males bodies are positioned in relationship to discourses of time and future. Where singular narrative arcs often follow punishing or normalizing structures and storylines for non-straight characters – working to reinscribe the correctness of straight temporal commitments – the expanded television series offers recurrent and extended opportunities for gay characters to be exist, negotiate, be uniquely situated in and be storied through a range of age and future narrations.

Decades of work by a community of scholars sits at the foundation of gay representation studies, which chronicles and analyses decades of representation in great detail (Becker; Dyer; Fejes and Petrich; Gross; Hart; Russo; Seidman; Tropiano; Walters). This project is deeply indebted to this expansive foundation, as this chapter will look at how the unique format of

---

2   The expanded durational format of the television series marks one of the many ways that the unique temporal opportunities of the television series can be examined. Although this chapter focuses on this singular element, this is not to foreclose or obscure the queer temporal opportunities afforded through repeated and nonlinear engagement with the series through reruns, the ongoing repetition of base plot structures, binge watching, or television series that experiment with non-linear narratives.

the television series shapes, informs, and potentially disrupts dominant understandings of gay male aging processes. Tracing appearances of gay characters on television series from the 1970s to today, this chapter theorizes the ongoing negotiated relationship between mainstream television representation, aging gay bodies, heteronormativity, and discourses of future. From rarely seen 'one episode' walk-ons in the 70s, to the increased normalization and appearance of gay bodies in the 90s, the television series offers a complex negotiation of gay aging cultural myths, mainstream assimilation, and the ongoing struggle to negotiate queer aging bodies through a dominant cultural lens. Shifting from the assertion of the *meaning* of gay aging to the representation of the *process* of gay aging, television navigates an extended history of cultural anxieties around the aging gay body and the gay male future. The chapter will begin with a theoretical set-up of the "space-off" as a guiding concept to navigate the sexual politics of televised representation. Next, the chapter provides a historical overview for how the aging gay male body has been introduced and negotiated throughout several television series in the last few decades. Finally, offering close attention to two current television programs representing older gay males, HBO's *Looking* and the PBS series *Vicious*, this chapter considers how the temporal process of gay male aging is being reworked and reconfigured through a variety of strategies and approaches.

Walk-ons, Space-offs, and Problems To Be Addressed

Feminist film theorist Teresa de Lauretis conceptualizes and spatializes an articulation of a queered cinematic gesture through her discussion of the "space-off," which marks the "blind spot" of representation – that horizon which is implied, but is not seen. The space-off asks us to look to the periphery of represented space for the ever-presence of queer potentiality. It calls to mind the out of frame events, lives, persons, and possibilities conjured by the narrative structure, but lingering just out of sight. In literal televised sitcom terms, where a sitcom has a set and cameras built to frame a specific location (the apartment on *Frasier*, the bar on *How I Met Your Mother*, etc....) the space-off exists (literally, but also metaphorically) just beyond that threshold of represented space. It can be alluded to and referenced, gestured to in a long stare, but is never fully situated inside the frame of the narrative. Wherein the space-off suggests the elusive space of queer presence/absence, the represented space (the *Friends* coffee shop; the *Rosanne*, living room; the *Mary Tyler Moore* office, etc....) is traditionally coded and organized through logics of heteronormativity and straight temporality. This is the space of mainstream intelligibility. The represented space is subject to the demands of linear temporal logic. It presents the space where events fall into a normative sequence, where relationships begin, marriages are proposed, babies are born, and the culturally accepted plot points of growth, maturation, kinship, and normative aging are reified. It is the domain of a linear narrative unfolding forward, carrying all the expectations, conventions, and generic formulas that define its form, its sequence, and its temporal movement. A queer temporality adopts a resistant and expanded approach to these limits of straight narratives, seeking out modes, stories, and trajectories beyond the linear and reproductively-driven path of straight time. Queer lives, queer stories, and queer temporalities resist the logics and expectations of the represented space, exposing the rigid normativity and limiting expectations of its conventions. Queer temporal interruptions can slow, stagnate, circle, and/or completely shoot wayward beyond the confines of the represented space, and thus the space-off, as conceptualized by de Lauretis, offers a queer resource. Enlisting the space-off, and its queering tension to the normativity of the represented space, this chapter will trace gay male representations (and more specifically gay male aging) through a historical negotiation between absence, presence, straight time and queer temporality.

The first images of gay-identified characters on a television series[3] may just as easily be defined by their departures, as their arrivals. Not unlike the history of representation of gay men in film (Russo), early gay characters on television never stayed around too long. While fleeting, at first, these short-lived appearances on television shows were not as regularly characterized by the tragic death, punishment, and suicide so common in Hollywood representations. The first walk-ons (and abrupt walk-outs) of gay characters on television series were navigated through the one episode story

---

3 The analysis in this chapter will focus specifically on recurring television series. Thus, while gay representation on television can take other forms (such as news broadcasts, TV movies, and talk shows), the chapter is specifically interested in looking at the temporal work of recurring gay characters over the span of multiple episodes, as well as seasons.

arc, including such shows as *All in the Family*, 1971-1979; *Barney Miller*, 1974-1982; *The Nancy Walker Show* (1976); *Alice* 1976-1985 (Gross 82). These "one shot appearances" (82) were more about a gay character entering the straight narrative (the represented space) and presenting/embodying a "topical issue" for the straight character to confront. "When TV does deal with gays it typically takes the point of view of straights struggling to understand" (William Henry qtd. in Gross 83). Gayness poses a 'problem' and a 'moral issue' to be dealt with by the lead, only entering the represented space for a brief moment, as if posing a question to be answered, but never to stay long. Within this 'problem' model of representation, there was no time or opportunity for the gay characters to grow or evolve (or age), as they were gone by the next episode. As a result, these walk-on representations were coded with static meanings that were not allowed to unfold or deepen across time or duration. Their presence was momentary within the unfolding narrative of the series. Thus, in the early days of 'one episode' representation, gay characters primarily lived their lives in the space-off, lingering beyond the intelligibility of normative narrative frames.

There is a temporal commitment and expectation upon the represented space that is scripted through heteronormativity (Goltz "Queer") and beholden to the hegemonic logics of straight time (Boellstorff; Edelman; Halberstam). Straight time, a guiding logic of narrative coherence (via courtship, coupling, marriage, procreation, grandparenting, etc.), continually stories mainstream cultural representation. This translates to the telling and retelling of narrowed definitions of 'correct' aging, growth, progress, success, and relational formation. It produced a hegemonic temporal map that enshrines the rightness of straight time, erasing the presence of queered temporal possibilities. Thus, even when gay characters began to appear on television series, this occurs in either straight-defined contexts (the heterosexual living room of our protagonist) or one-time outings to stereotypical gay contexts that provide a fleeting exotic and uncomfortable experience for the heterosexual characters. Regardless, when gay characters enter from the off-space, their presence is in the service of a straight narrative. This does not mean these quick appearances cannot work to challenge the meanings assigned to gayness, as any representation on television in the 70s was arguably 'progressive'. However, any element of fullness, completion, and satisfaction that does not reaffirm heteronormativity as inherently correct remained outside the frame, queerly haunting the margins. Perhaps this is why, when you consider the earliest gay television characters (and many contemporary ones), there is a constant struggle between remaining in the presented space and maintaining queerness. The longer a queer character lingered within the represented space of a series, it seemed, the less queer they became. This is not to say that their queerness simply became more familiar, but that their storylines actually turned more straight. We can refer to the characters of Jody Dallas (played by Billy Crystal from 1977-1981) on *Soap*, or Steven Carrington (played by Al Corley 1981-2, and Jack Coleman 1982-88), on *Dynasty*, who mark two of the first explicitly gay television characters on shows running for multiple seasons. Although the genre and style of these shows greatly differed, these two characters share several key traits, most notably how they 'straightened up' as the show went forward. On both shows, once the prescribed list of gay narrative plot points were dealt with through these characters (announcement of being gay, deal with straight characters coping with gayness, confronting homophobia where straight character nobly steps up, personal struggle with gayness and hatred of self), Jody and Steven start inching more in line with the logics of straight time. Marriage to women, procreating, raising children, commitment to their biological family, and more normative temporal narrative conventions come to define their storylines. Extended time on the cultural screen quite literally, straightened them out, softened their queerness, and worked to position them in more normative narrative conventions. The logic for this straightening can obviously be tied to pandering to mainstream audience sensibilities, yet there is a second way to make sense of this tension. By lingering within the represented space, rather than walking on for a brief moment, their presence highlighted the absence of a culturally intelligible story of gay living, gay aging, and a gay narrative. The shows, it seemed, had no idea just what to do with these characters.

The 90s, Building Temporal Identification, and the New Normal

The purpose of this chapter is not to trace the history of all gay television, but to highlight this significant and evolving tension around queerness, aging, time, and television. Although the space-off marks a space beyond straight time – opening a space and possibility for the potentializing of queer lives – the negative cultural myths and cautionary tales of gay aging remain unchallenged and continue to denigrate the lives of those who live beyond representation. Ghost stories work to write what happens out in the darkness. The push and pull of normativity and queerness is highlighted in this represented space/space-off tension, yet the television series provides a unique potential for disrupting this pattern through the extended element of time. The gay representational field broadened significantly through 1990s, where gay characters were appearing on television series with increased regularity, offering a wider range of gay characters navigating the process of aging on the cultural screen.

Wherein 'one episode encounters' did little to impact or disrupt cultural stories of gay aging, once the gay male character became more anchored in the unfolding represented space, the potential for television series to intervene in discourses of gay male aging became much more explicit. Suddenly, not confined to a future of doom and a perpetual fear of age, gay male characters were bridging themselves into intelligible discourses of future. This provided an opportunity for gay characters to not merely be present within a story but to age and evolve within an extended narrative arc. Slowly pushing past the confines of 'being' a gay character, television afforded a space for gay characters to continue on being, and thus grow and develop in and over time.

Will from *Will & Grace* (1998-2006), David from *Six Feet Under* (2001-2005), and characters across a broad range of shows such as *Spin City* (1996-2002), *Dawson's Creek* (1998-2003), *Sex and the City* (1998-2004), *Brothers & Sisters* 2006-2011), *Desperate Housewives* (2004-2012), and *Queer as Folk* (2000-2005) began appearing and reappearing as a lingering and progressive presence on the television screen. Similar to the mechanisms that worked to write Jody Dallas and Steven Carrington into the temporal logics of straight time, these newer characters shared several traits that aided in their mainstream appeal and acceptance. Differing from Jody and Steven, these characters were unwavering in their gay identity, but they were also unwavering in their endorsement, desire, and steadfast commitment to the pillars of straight time. These were men who testified to the correctness and ideal of heternormative systems.[4] Much like the popular show *Friends*, the friendship of *Will & Grace* depicted a liminal time of early adulthood on the way to the eventual (expected and hoped for) set-

---

4   For a detailed analysis and breakdown of this trend in 90s representation, see Goltz 2010.

tling down to marriage and kids. While straightening out gay characters, over time, works to rhetorically position heteronormativity as the inevitable and the ideal (upholding the myth that a life without a wife and kids would be empty and miserable), it also locates important distinction between more normalized and mainstream consumable gay characters and more contranormative queer characters. While gay characters that operate within straight temporal logics and commitments are becoming more and more common on the cultural screen, queerness merely lingers at the margins of the space-off of representation. This is one of the reasons why, historically on television, the most queer and resistant characters have always existed outside the central frame of the show. The quirky neighbor next store, the "ugly naked guy" across the street, or the playfully flamboyant Jack and Karen who are defined by their regular coming and going mark characters who resist the temporal commitments mapped onto television narrative arcs. As continual interruptions to the normative flows of the program, and arguably the queerest characters, Jack and Karen draw attention to the queer space-off beyond the normative longings of Grace and Will. Their off-camera adventures, referenced but rarely depicted, testify to the existence of a naughty, sexualized and deviously fun range of possibilities beyond the frame.[5] They become a queer trace and a gesture to the space-off. Gross identified an early version of this tension, in his discussion of the 1980s Showtime series *Brothers* (1984-89). Wherein Cliff, the gay brother with two straight brothers, "never does much that might be seen as, well, gay" (85), this is left to his more flamboyant and explicitly queer best friend, Donald. Gross writes, "Any resemblance to NBC's late-nineties *Will & Grace* should surprise no one familiar with Hollywood" (85). Framed in temporal terms, Jack McFarland from *Will & Grace*, much like Donald, can move in and out of the narrative frame with a defiance, sexualized, and unapologetic queerness, yet the gay character (literally as 'the straight man') situated more central to the story is more tempered and tethered to systems of straight time. We watch Will (and *Six Feet Under's* David, and many others in the 90s and 2000s) grow, and age, and plan for a future, and while it is remarkable to see gay men age and frame the process of aging in

---

5   See Goltz, "The Dinner Party: Queer Gesturing to Time and Future" in *Queer Temporalities in Gay Male Representation* for an extended analysis of Jack and Karen's queer temporal interruptions.

positive terms, these terms are also remarkably normative in their articulation.

Often criticized for their white, cis-gendered, middle class normativity, late 90s gay male representation also fell within an extremely limited age window of late 20s to late 30s (and a disproportionate amount of them were suit-wearing lawyers living in the expensive urban centers). Queer media critiques have routinely troubled the "progressive" framing of this period, by detailing how a broad range of social systems operate to construct a mainstreamed, familiar, likeable, and non-threatening primetime gay male (Battles and Hilton-Morrow; Brookey; Dow; Seidman; Walters). Seidman refers to this model as the "good sexual citizen," which offers a depoliticized gay (usually white and middle class) male whose primarily allegiance is to the heterosexual family and unit. A significant concern with these limited representations is the fact that they fail to bring forth alternative images of queer lives, designating those who do not subscribe to the inherent correctness of heteronormativity as, by default, the "bad queers." Beyond the limits of a white, consumable, middle-class, apolitical gay male who writes his future through allegiances to marriage and children, queer aging and alternatives for queers lives continue to only exist in the space-off.

The influx of 90s representation did little to disrupt the myths of gay aging, as older gays remained mostly absent and shadowed in the periphery (Goltz "Queer"). When they did appear, they were resistant to happiness, in the service of younger gay storylines, and lingering cautionary figures. For example, Uncle Vic on *Queer as Folk* was an HIV positive male who rarely left the house or took off his robe. He was a support system to others, but rarely had a story of his own (and when he did, the results were being arrested for public indecency and his death) (70-2). Vic, as a character, was defined only by his past and his lost youth, yet failed to be narrated in a way that told any additional stories about who he is or might be. Returning to the series narrative problem of "what to do with Steven Carrington or Jody Dallas," the cultural screen in the nineties became more comfortable with gay characters so long as their lives, desires, politics, identities, and futures looked much like the straight normative characters that proceeded them so long as they were under forty.

Recentering the Space Off: Promising Steps for Queering Age and Temporality

In 2001, in the season 1 finale of the groundbreaking showtime series *Queer as Folk*, Brian Kinney turns (gasp!) 30 years old. As turning 30 in the gay community, according to Brian, is (literally) the end of his life, his friends surprise him with his "death day" party (with a grave on his cake), and welcome him into the "Dead Faggots Society." Although his friends are attempting to offer some levity, and perhaps criticism to this youthist ideology in gay male culture, Brian seriously contemplates and attempts his own suicide as his birthday episode progresses. For Brian, 30 is the end. He wants to go out in a "blaze of glory," which includes suffocating himself while masturbating. When Michael catches him and stops him, Brian explains his general disinterest in growing old and getting wrinkles, wanting to die young and stay young forever. While the episode's invocation of gay cultural youthism (Berger), the devaluation of gay age, and the equation of gay men and suicide is hardly groundbreaking, the presence of this episode at the conclusion of the first season of the series is highly significant. Most notably, Brian manages to survive all the way to the end of the series, which continues for four more seasons. Even as he struggled to understand why his life, as he ages, would have value or meaning, the format of the television series allows us to watch and experience this ongoing question. Resisting marriage and the continual normative systems of meanings that are presented to him, we see Brian, at the center of the narrative space, fight to make sense of his queer existence as an aging gay male. Quite boldly, though somewhat sadly, Brian's story ends (as it carried on for so many years) with this lingering question and anxiety. At the end of season five, he's still tethered to, though skeptical of, a social life defined by gay dance clubs and youth worship. He's reluctant, he's growing, he's compromising, and he's changing, and this is something audiences experience with him over a five-year period (and four years after he, and the cultural narrative announced his finale). He's not Will Truman, or Steven Carrington, or any of the gay men who proceeded him, but while he knows who he is not, he struggles to make sense of what he is, what he does, and what his life can mean beyond these systems of straight time.

Thirteen years after Brian Kinney's death day party, the guiding and assumed logics of straight time in television continue to dominate narrative conventions. Yet, as gay characters have grown more commonplace, and often more normative, on mainstream television, individual texts and characters emerge that continue to push, challenge, and queer the temporal definitions of gayness, age, and future. Two specific texts that will be given specific attention in this analysis are the HBO series *Looking* (2014-present) and the PBS series *Vicious* (2012-present), as they each present different, yet complementary work in disrupting mainstream heteronormative scripts. As each show is very new, with a limited number of episodes to date (season one of *Vicious* was six episodes, and season one of *Looking* was eight episodes), their not-yet-tested promise offers productive sites to cautiously trace alternative temporal workings.

In a gesture that both mirrors and extends the Brian Kinney "Death day" party, *Looking* begins its first season with Dom, the older of the friend group, turning forty.[6] He says to his friend, "At 40, Grindr emails you a death certificate." Kinney-esque in his sexually active history and the narrative that he has, historically, been highly sought after around town, Dom struggles with aging as a defining narrative crisis in season one. Dom fears age, but his fear is not coded to the extreme suicidal panic that plagued Kinney. Rather he knows he needs a change, needs to mature, needs to face and deal with being 40. Yet, outside the number, Dom is not entirely sure what 40 is or can mean. Like *Queer as Folk*, the cultural "end" of his life is still the beginning of the series, allowing the space and time for the unintelligible – the aging gay male – to be negotiated within the cultural frame (without the conventional plot points of child, marriage, or maintenance of a biological heterosexual family). The show, early on, makes a bold move to upset Dom's "age crisis" through the introduction of Lynn, an even older (gasp) gay male, played by Scott Bakula (who, born in 1954 is now 60).

The two men, initially, meet in a steam room in a bathhouse where Dom is busy chasing some younger boys around. Upon initial meeting, subtle impulses of youthism and ageism appear as Dom assumes he is the desired, and implies a certain amount of power from this. Yet soon into the show and their friendship, Lynn is quickly and explicitly liberated from confining myths of the older, sad, and sexually desperate gay male. Lynn has a successful business, an active social network, and soon becomes

---

6   Murray Bartlett, the actor who plays Dom was born in 1971, and thus is a few years older than the age he is portraying in the show.

sexually and romantically sought after by Dom. In a scene where Dom kisses Lynn, it is Lynn who pulls back and reasserts that they are better off as friends. Lynn refuses to let Dom throw a tantrum and treat him poorly. In a significant flip from previous gay representation, Dom and his younger friends seem to struggle much more with the growing pains of age and maturity than the older and more self-assured gay men who populate Lynn's world. It is not unlike *Queer as Folk* with regard to the younger gay cohort struggling with age, yet Queer as Folk did not have an older presence of a gay community to balance/answer this anxiety. Beyond the homebound Vic, the aging gay men in *Queer as Folk* were cast to the space-off or enlisted in brief cautionary glimpses. Articulated through the concept of the space-off, *Looking* does not only acknowledge the aging older males that linger in the periphery, but eyes them with a degree of envy and hope.

A second text, with a very different aesthetic, is the British sitcom *Vicious*, starring Derek Jacobi (as Stuart) and Ian McKellen (as Freddie). Freddie and Stuart are a gay couple living in a London flat, which is the primary set for the show. Together for over forty years, Freddie and Stuart bicker, taunt, and constantly belittle one another with an understanding that beneath their vicious behavior towards each other is a longstanding love and commitment. Additional characters include Violet, their single and sexually assertive straight female friend who plays like a British Blanche Dubois, and Ash, the younger straight boy who lives upstairs. This cast of four sets forth a uniquely queered articulation of family. In many ways flipping the sexual representations of many previous sitcoms, Freddie and Stuart are the centralized represented space, wherein Ash and Violet float in and out of the scene. Their existence, outside of their relation to the couple, remains primarily in the space-off.

Unlike Dom, or Brian Kinney, where we are watching gay male characters struggle with the fear of facing age, Freddie and Stuart have aged to the point where the outside world makes little sense to them. In terms of perspective, this show flips the camera and viewpoint of much gay representation on its head by asking the audience to see with and through the older gay male perspective. Too often and for too long, the older gay male was only seen through the eyes of younger gay men, presenting a cautionary threat in the dark corners of the bar. In one subplot, where Ash is promoting a new hip club, Freddie and Stuart decide to accept his invitation to attend. Nothing about the experience fits, from their clothes, to their postures in the setting, to the volume of the music. It is a time warp. They are out of time and out of place. When some younger guys give Stuart some attention, Freddie gets jealous, and Stuart tries to hang out with the younger crowd. It becomes clear the younger guys expect Stuart to pay, and while Stuart is knocked down a few pegs in this realization, it does not devastate him. More importantly, because we are experiencing the story through Stuart's eyes, we see the younger men as somewhat trivial, and are given a perspective on Stuart that is rarely offered. Rather than reading the shadows and stares of these older men in the club as menacing and predatory, Freddie and Stuart rewrite this story entirely – they loathe being in the bar, are confused by everything, and really just want to take a nap. This troubles the image of the sexually desperate aging gay man who lingers at the corners of the bar, sad and horny. However, it is not that Stuart or Freddie is sexually neutered or produced as asexual grandfather figures, as they (as well as Violet) are constantly flirting with Ash, who is seemingly clueless about the constant attention thrown at him.

Vicious opens up several temporal possibilities that work to trouble the history of gay aging discourses on television. On the most surface of levels, a sustained and recurring focus on older gay men, in itself, is groundbreaking. In addition, the show directly engages ageist and youthist discourses in gay culture (often flung at one another), in a way that laughs at the myths, stereotypes, and cautionary tales. These men are old, and while their aged dog Balthazar may or may not be dead and decomposing on their kitchen floor, they still have sexual drive, a sense of humor, love, and acerbic wit. They lived a full life together, long before the cultural recognition or televised normalization welcomed them as a new form of modern family. In this point, then, they speak to how queer family and queer relations can exist on differing temporal maps than the one's prescribed by mainstream television. Their queerness is centralized, and their disconnect and removal from the gay normalization happening all around them celebrates alternative times and lives beyond the *Glee* (2009-present) teens, the Will Truman 30s, and the homonormative suburbia of the new *Modern Family*. They are not slick, modern or colorful, lacking the pastel consumerist image of gay culture, or the thumping strobe lights of *Queer as Folk's* Club Babylon. Their queerness is timeless, placed out of tidy gay rights timelines, which marks each step toward normalization and gay and lesbian equality as an untroubled leap toward progress. Their life is not about before (or after) kids, before (or after) marriage, or hinged to biological or heteronormative family systems. They are older, but playfully resisting proper performances of maturity, restraint, or decorum in their space-off.

Conclusion: Deviations and Innovations Beyond Straight Time

Hollywood representation of gay male aging, and specifically the gay male relationship to future, has historically reproduced mythologies of pain, loss, punishment and failure. These were not stories of hope, but cautionary tales of pity, fear, or mockery. Gay males, historically in mainstream media, have had tortuous relationships with time. Even when they appear, the story being told was rarely their own, but in the service of normative characters and audiences – as well as mainstreamed comforts, assumptions, and perspectives. The emergence of increased gay representation through the television series provided an opportunity for gay characters to not merely be present within a story but to age and evolve within an extended narrative arc. Slowly pushing past the confines of 'being' a gay character, television afforded a space for gay characters to continue on being, and thus grow and develop in and over time. This chapter works to demonstrate how these limited discourses are disrupted through the extended format of the television series. Although these 90s models rarely deviated from the gay representational dichotomy of aging failure or good gay citizen, these texts established a relationship with aging gay men and future that more recent television shows are complicating, troubling and extending. The contemporary television series offers greater opportunities to challenge conventional logics, assumptions, and stories of the aging gay male. By pushing beyond the mere presence of gay bodies to the temporal process of *being with* gay representations, in time and through time, the television series continues to provide a unique intervention into tacit normative assumptions that dictate the limits of what a gay male future is and might be. Even as Brian cannot imagine going on, and Dom is unsure how he should or ought to move on, they return in the next episode. Their narrative, even if stalled or unclear, is faced with choices and possibilities. Hopefully, those possibilities push deviation and innovation, and continually nudge the camera to inch toward those spaces, aging bodies, and aging processes not yet seen.

WORKS CITED

Battles, Kathleen, and Wendy Hilton-Morrow. "Gay Characters in Conventional Spaces: *Will & Grace* and the Conventional Comedy Genre." *Critical Studies in Media Communication*.19 (2002): 87-105. Print.
Becker, Ron. *Gay TV and Straight America*. New Brunswick: Rutgers UP, 2006. Print.
Berger, Raymond M. *Gay and Gray: The Older Homosexual Man*. Urbana: U of Illinois P, 1982. Print.
Berger, Raymond M. "Realities of Gay and Lesbian Aging." *Social Work* 29 (1984): 57-82. Print.
Berger, Raymond M., and James J. Kelly. "What Are Older Gay Men Like: An Impossible Question." *Midlife and Aging in Gay America*. Eds. Douglas C. Kimmel and Dawn Lundy Martin. NY: Harrington Park Press, 2001. 55-64. Print.
Boellstorff, Tom. "When Marriage Falls: Queer Coincidences in Straight Time." *GLQ: A Journal of Lesbian and Gay Studies* 13.2-3 (2007): 227-48. Print.
Brookey, Robert Alan. "A Community Like *Philadelphia*." *Western Journal of Communication* 60.1 (1996): 40-56. Print.
Brown, Lester B., et al. "'Gay Men: Aging Well!'" *Midlife and Aging in Gay America*. Eds. Douglas C. Kimmel and Dawn Lundy Martin. NY: Harrington Park Press, 2001. 41-54. Print.
De Lauretis, Teresa. "The Technology of Gender." *Technologies of Gender: Essays on Theory, Film and Fiction*. Bloomington: Indiana UP, 1987. 1-30. Print.
De Vries, Brian, and John A. Blando. "The Study of Gay and Lesbian Aging: Lessons for Social Gerontology." *Gay and Lesbian Aging*. Eds. Gilbert Herdt and Brian de Vries. NY: Springer Publishing, 2004. 3-28. Print.
Dorfman, Rachel, et al. "Old, Sad, and Alone: The Myth of the Aging Homosexual." *Journal of Gerontological Social Work* 24 (1995): 29-45. Print.
Dow, Bonnie J. "Ellen, Television, and the Politics of Gay and Lesbian Visibility." *Critical Studies in Media Communication* 18 (2001): 123-40. Print.

Duggan, Lisa. "The New Homonormativity: The Sexual Politics of Neoliberalism." *Materializing Democracy: Towards a Revitalized Cultural Politics.* Eds. Russ Castronovo and Dana D. Nelson. Durham: Duke UP, 2002. 175-94. Print.
Dyer, Richard. *The Matter of Images: Essays on Representation.* London: Routledge, 2002. Print.
Edelman, Lee. *No Future: Queer Theory and the Death Drive.* Durham: Duke UP, 2004. Print.
Ellis, Alan L. *Gay Men at Midlife.* NY: Harrington Park Press, 2001.Print.
Fejes, Fred, and Kevin Petrich. "Invisibility, Homophobia, and Heterosexism: Lesbians, Gays and the Media." *Critical Studies in Media Communication.*10 (1993): 395-422. Print.
Friend, R. A. "Gayging: Adjustment and the Older Gay Male." *Alternative Lifestyles* 3 (1980): 231-48. Print.
Goltz, Dustin B. *Queer Temporalities in Gay Male Representation: Tragedy, Normativity, and Futurity.* New York: Routledge, 2010. Print.
Goltz, Dustin B. "Investigating Queer Future Meanings: Destructive Perceptions of 'the Harder Path.'" *Qualitative Inquiry* 15, 3. (2009): 561-86. Print.
Goltz, Dustin B. "It's Been Getting Better; Now Someone Tell Hollywood: Debunking the American Horror Story of Gay and Lesbian Aging." *In These Times.* In These Times and The Institute of Public Affairs. 16 March 2013. Web. 3 Jan. 2014.
Gross, Larry. *Up from Invisibility: Lesbians, Gay Men, and the Media in America.* NY: Columbia UP, 2002. Print.
Halberstam, Judith. *In a Queer Time and Place: Transgender Bodies, Subcultural Lives.* NY: New York UP, 2005. Print.
Hart, Kylo Patrick R. "Representing Gay Men on American Television." *Gender, Race, and Class in the Media.* 2nd ed .Eds. Gail Dines and Jean M. Humez. Thousand Oaks: Sage 2000. 597-607. Print.
Herdt, Gilbert H., and Brian de Vries. *Gay and Lesbian Aging: Research and Future Directions.* NY: Springer Pub. Co., 2004. Print.
Hostetler, Andrew J. "Old, Gay, and Alone? The Ecology of Well-Being Among Middle-Aged and Older Single Gay Men." *Gay and Lesbian Aging.* Eds. Gilbert Herdt and Brian de Vries. NY: Springer Publishing, 2004. 143-76. Print.

Kertzner, Robert, Ilan Meyer, and Curtis Dolezal. "Psychological Well-Being in Midlife and Older Gay Men." *Gay and Lesbian Aging*. Eds. Gilbert Herdt and Brian de Vries. NY: Springer Publishing, 2004. 97-116. Print.

Kooden, Harold, and Charles Flowers. *Golden Men: The Power of Gay Midlife*. NY: Avon Books, 2000. Print.

Muñoz, José Esteban. "Cruising the Toilet: Leroi Jones/Amiri Baraka, Radical Black Traditions, and Queer Futurity." *GLQ: A Journal of Lesbian and Gay Studies* 13.2-3 (2007): 353-67. Print.

Muñoz, José Esteban. "Stages: Punks, Queers, and the Utopian Performance." *The Sage Handbook of Performance Studies*. Eds. D. Soyini Madison and Judith Hamera. Thousand Oaks: Sage, 2006. 9-20. Print.

Russo, Vito. *The Celluloid Closet: Homosexuality in the Movies*. Rev. ed. NY: Harper & Row, 1987. Print.

Seidman, Steven. *Beyond the Closet: The Transformation of Gay and Lesbian Life*. NY: Routledge, 2002. Print.

Shugart, Helene A. "Reinventing Privilege: The New (Gay) Man in Contemporary Popular Media." *Critical Studies in Media Communication* 20 (2003): 67-91. Print.

Tropiano, Stephen. *The Primetime Closet: A History of Gays and Lesbians on Television*. NY: Applause Theater and Cinema Books, 2002. Print.

Walters, Suzanna Danuta. *All the Rage: The Story of Gay Visibility in America*. Chicago: U of Chicago P, 2001. Print.

Yep, Gust A. "The Violence of Heteronormativity in Communication Studies: Notes on Injury, Healing and Queer World-Making." *Queer Theory and Communication: From Disciplining Queers to Queering the Discipline(s)*. Eds. Gust A. Yep, Karen E. Lovaas and John P. Elia. NY: Harrington Park Press, 2003. 11-60. Print.

Yoakam, John R. "Gods or Monsters? A Critique of Representations in Film and Literature of Relationships Between Older Gay Men and Younger Men." *Midlife and Aging in Gay America*. Eds. Douglas C. Kimmel and Dawn Lundy Martin. NY: Harrington Park Press, 2001. 65-80. Print.

TELEVISION

Alice. Creator Robert Getchell, CBS (1976-1985).
All in the Family. Creator Norman Lear, CBS (1971-1979).
Barney Miller. Creators Danny Arnold and Theodore J. Flicker, ABC (1974-1982).
Boyhood. Director Richard Linklater (2014).
Beverly Hills 90210. Creator Darren Star, Fox (1990-2000).
Brothers. Creators David Lloyd and Greg Antonacci, Showtime (1984-1989).
Brothers & Sisters. Creator Jon Robin Baitz, ABC (2006-2011).
Days of Our Lives. Creators Ted Corday and Betty Corday, NBC (19650–present).
Dawson's Creek. Creator Kevin Williamson, The WB (1998-2003)
Degrassi: The Next Generation. Creators Kit Hood, Yan Moore, Linda Schuyler, CTV (2001-2010), MuchMusic (2010-2013), MTV Canada (2013-present).
Desperate Housewives. Creator Marc Cherry, ABC (2004-2012).
Dynasty. Creators Richard Shapiro and Esther Shapiro, ABC. (1981-1989).
Frasier. Created by David Angell, Peter Casey and David Lee, NBC (1993-2004).
Glee. Creators Ian Brennan, Brad Falchuck and Ryan Murphy, Fox (2009–present).
How I Met Your Mother. Creators Carter Bays and Craig Thomas, CBS (2005-2014).
Modern Family. Creators Steven Levitan and Christopher Lloyd, ABC (2009–present).
Looking. Creator Michael Lannan, HBO (2014–present).
Noah's Arc. Creator Patrik-Ian Polk, Logo (2005-2006).
Queer as Folk. Creators Ron Cowen and Daniel Lipman, Showtime (2000-2005).
Rosanne. Creator Matt Williams, ABC (1988-1997).
Sex and the City. Creator Darren Star, HBO (1998-2004).
Six Feet Under. Creator Alan Ball, HBO (2001-2005).
Spin City: Michael J. Fox's All-Time Favorites. Creators Gary David Goldberg and Bill Lawrence, ABC (1996-2002).
Soap. Creator Susan Harris, ABC (1977-1981).

The Mary Tyler Moore Show. Creators James L. Brooks and Allan Burns, CBS (1970-1977).
The Nancy Walker Show. ABC (1976).
Vicious. Creators Mark Ravenhill and Gary Janetti, ITV (2013–present).
Will & Grace. Creator James Burrows, NBC (1998-2006).

"You've Got Time"
Ageing and Queer Temporality
in *Orange is the New Black*

EVA KRAINITZKI

> Remember all their faces
> Remember all their voices
> Everything is different
> The second time around
> And you've got time...
> REGINA SPEKTOR – "YOU'VE GOT TIME"

Introduction

Orange is the New Black (*Orange*) is Netflix's successful new series (2013–present), loosely based on Piper Kerman's memoir *Orange is the New Black: My Year in a Women's Prison* and created by Jenji Kohan. Protagonist Piper Chapman (Taylor Schilling) is a privileged, white New Yorker, in her early thirties who is sentenced to 15 months in a minimum security prison for a crime she committed 10 years ago, when transporting drug money for her lesbian lover Alex Vause (Laura Prepon). Her boyfriend, Larry Bloom (Jason Biggs), is surprised by her criminal and bisexual past but appears tolerant and supportive. *Orange* introduces life in prison through Piper's eyes before moving on to the plethora of fellow prisoners at Litchfield Penitentiary with incursions into their more distant or recent past through flashback scenes.

Much like other television series set in a women's prison, *Orange* provides a wide range of female gender representations, including depictions of more mature female identities. Although its protagonist is a younger, white, upper-middle-class woman, *Orange* portrays complex and multi-layered black and Hispanic characters, including a transsexual black woman.[1] In terms of lesbian, gay and trans-visibility, *Orange* distinguishes itself from other prison dramas by its purposeful inclusion and centring on queer characters and has been warmly received by *AfterEllen*, the lesbian/bi pop culture website (Bendix), and has received GLAAD[2] approval through several nominations for its cast members. Creator Jenji Kohan admits the show consists of an innate queerness, which is about human connectivity through sexuality, rather than lesbianism in itself (Bendix).

This article focuses on representations of non-normative female ageing in *Orange* using the concept of queer temporality (Freeman, Halberstam). It suggests that *Orange*'s delivery platform (on-demand streaming), its format (serial), and its non-linear narrative structure (flashback sequences) both enable and enhance non-normative representations of ageing. *Orange*'s non-linear narrative structure, combined with the freedoms associated to online media streaming, multiplies the possibilities of transgressing "chrono-normative" structures, described by Elizabeth Freeman as "the use of time to organize individual human bodies toward maximum productivity" (3). Foregrounding prison's queer spacio-temporality, *Orange*'s flashback scenes result in non-linear narratives that can be interpreted as instances of queer temporality and which open up new understandings of ageing.

This article explores instances where stereotypical images of older women are challenged, allowing for more complex or alternative representations to emerge. Conceptualising disruptions to age-appropriate behaviour through the concept of queer temporality provides the opportunity to understand how normative temporalities of ageing are closely intertwined with heteronormative constructions of gender and sexual identity. Turning to a group of characters known as the "golden girls," this article examines how the stereotype of the vulnerable, little 'old lady' is easily subverted within a

---

1   Exploring race and ethnicity is out of the remit of this article, yet research about race and identity in *Orange* is emerging (Belcher, Charlton).
2   Gay & Lesbian Alliance Against Defamation.

prison setting with its imminent threat of violence. It then analyses the character of Miss Rosa Cisneros (Barbara Rosenblat) and the disavowal of the narrative of decline through one character's prison break narrative.

Representing Age(ing)

As scholars in ageing studies posit, there is a need to analyse visibility and interpret invisibility; we need "to reflect on what we see and what we don't" (Woodward, "Performing Age" 162) and to pay attention "to the specific forms visibility might take" (Wearing 298). Against the backdrop of television portrayals that seek to promote the notion of "successful ageing" (Bülow and Söderqvist) as the norm, interventions from ageing studies seek to challenge this binary between decline and success (Gullette) and to deconstruct the predominant discourse of age, which "pivots on the blunt binary of young and old, as if there were only two states of age" (Woodward, "Introduction" xvii). To explore how *Orange* brings visibility to the ageing woman I employ the notion of queer temporality, which proves fruitful in deconstructing binaries of old age and youth, linear understandings of temporality, and consequently, paradigms of decline and success (Moglen, Port, Segal).

Amir Cohen-Shalev notes that

cinema is best suited for the task of faithfully serving the case for capturing the plight of old age. The vehicles of representation at the disposal of the filmmaker simply cry out for a mindful, intelligent and profound picture of aging: the free manipulation of time and space, and back and forth movement of flashback and flash-forward, mapping vast territories of the mind (9).

Orange makes use of this "free manipulation of time and space" Cohen-Shalev refers to through its flashback sequences. Combined with the longevity and continuity offered by a serialised format, *Orange* enables the representation of a wide range of characters, through in-depth and multi-layered portrayals rather than snapshots of familiar stereotypes. A diverse ensemble cast can be seen as particularly valuable in terms of representing women. *Orange* relies on seriality and a large, multi-racial, and age-diverse ensemble cast as a strategy to offer multiple narrative perspectives. As Vicky Ball concurs, television shows featuring a female ensemble cast present the opportunity to engage "with subaltern feminine identities that have been marginalized on television and in history more generally" (246). Indeed, *Orange*'s prison setting gives "space and expression to these matriarchal communities" (246), centring on "women's relationships with other women outside of their familial roles as wives and mothers" (246).

Orange's ensemble cast enables the portrayal of intergenerational relationships, as well as a wider range of female gender roles, sexual and ethnic identities, as is announced from the outset by its distinctive title sequence (analysed later in this article). Not only does *Orange* bring visibility to different identity categories, it depicts intersectional aspects of identity such as age, race and sexuality in one and the same character, which allows for more complex constructs to emerge.

Set mostly within the confinements of prison, *Orange* continues the popular female prison genre, alongside series like British-Australian co-production *Tenko* (1981–1984), UK's *Bad Girls* (1999–2006), or the Australian cult series *Prisoner: Cell Block H* (1979–1986) and its recent remake *Wentworth Prison* (2013–present). Unlike these shows, *Orange* does not merely maintain the enduring presence of lesbian characters in the women-in-prison genre (Ciasullo), but moves beyond "the occasion for a safe but titillating exploration of female homosexuality" (196) by purposefully representing a vast range of lesbian, bisexual and other queer identities. While the prison setting "creates a space where a range of differences is represented, however briefly" as Mayne argues (119), in *Orange* the representation of difference is the norm rather than an interlude, and sexual, like other identities, are represented as fluid and queer. Characters include self-identified lesbians, straight women who engage in same-sex relationships and those who do not assume any sexual identity; queer characters can be located at the centre as well as at the margins of *Orange*'s narrative. Although it creates a rupture with the "lesbian chic" image that is representative of the 1990s and early 2000s television landscape (Hamer and Budge) through more diverse representations, *Orange* replicates what I previously described as the "hypervisibility paradox" (Krainitzki), when a growing number of young/er lesbian and bisexual characters give the impression that "lesbians are everywhere" (T. Jenkins), thus concealing the absence of images of lesbian ageing.

The limits of lesbian representability, even within the context of a post-network, online subscription service series, are revealed by Carrie 'Big

Boo' Black (played by comedienne Lea DeLaria, in her mid-fifties), the *one* self-identified and visible lesbian character who appears to be over the age of 50. At least up until *Orange*'s second season, this character was not portrayed in any flashback scenes, remaining a comedic supporting role, who is visible as a butch lesbian but less so as an old/er lesbian. Although this seems to suggest that a visibly lesbian identity is incompatible with old age, this article seeks out other non-normative representations that can be explored through queer temporality.

The inclusion of multiple middle-aged and old/er female characters in *Orange* allows for interesting plot developments, subversion of stereotypes of age and a critique of the inadequacies of prison health care for an ageing prison population, as explored later in this chapter through my analysis of the "golden girls." If temporal displacement is one reason that allows non-stereotypical representations of ageing, "that contrast sharply with the conventional Hollywood template" (Tincknell 770), alternative spaces similarly provide this opportunity. *Orange*'s prison setting places all characters within a spacio-temporality removed from hetero- and chrono-temporality; they inhabit an alternative spacility, a heterotopia (Foucault) removed from quotidian reality, as well as queer temporality.

(Queer)Temporality and Ageing

Temporality, which is central to ageing studies (Baars; Segal) has recently been explored through the notion of 'queer' in an attempt to deconstruct binaries of old age and youth, or the paradigms of decline and success (Moglen; Port; Segal). *Orange* can be seen to challenge normative temporality in different ways, via its distribution and release model, its non-linear narrative structure, and old/er characters who do not comply with chrono-normative images of ageing. The type of emergent post-network, online television viewing practices encouraged by Netflix, and *Orange*'s non-linear narrative offer interesting instances of temporal transgressions. Combined with a multi-generational cast, *Orange* opens up alternative modes of representing ageing.

"Temporal Tease"

Television watching practices have changed considerably in the last decades, as acknowledged and addressed by recent research within television studies (Lotz; Spigel and Olsson). Online streaming services such as Netflix have enabled multi-screen viewing and further promote media convergence (Kackman; H. Jenkins). Some might argue that *Orange* should not even be denominated 'television' (Seitz). Whether Netflix's claims to quality television are upheld remains to be seen but it has already revolutionised television practices with their production and distribution model (Barker). Catering to contemporary viewers' habits – as opposed to linear scheduling, broadcasting one weekly episode at a scheduled time – Netflix releases whole seasons, all episodes at once, allowing viewers to watch the show at their own pace, or to 'binge watch' an entire season.

Netflix thus promotes a specific mode of time-shifting (Sodano), allowing viewers to indulge in whole season marathons as soon as they are released. This specific release model removes any time constraints a scheduled broadcast show involves, leading to an *a priory* shift in temporal structures for the viewer. This disruption of television's chrono-normativity is mirrored in the series' non-linear narrative structure, which relies heavily on flashback sequences. If *Orange*'s narrative structure provides the "temporal tease" Ames identifies as the crucial characteristic of contemporary television – shows that "play with time", "disrupting the chronological flow itself" (9) – Netflix's innovative distribution method allows the viewer a level of control over television's flow. The possibility of watching any number of episodes, of pausing and rewinding allows greater control. An open-ended episode can simply be followed by another episode; episodes merge into one another, without clear boundaries.

Orange includes lengthy and frequent flashback sequences, which like other prison-shows (*Block H, Prison Break, Wentworth Prison*) reveal a character's pre-prison-life, depict the actual moment when the crime is being committed or provide further levels of characterisation. Inherent to the flashback device "is a certain assumption of temporality and order" (Turim 13), although a flashback "always implies a departure from the continuity assumed by narration" (189). Each flashback sequence interrupts not only narrative linearity, it also generally disrupts prison temporality – structured, scheduled, institutionalised. As recent sociological research explores (Matthews; Wahidin; Wahidin and Tate), temporality is central to prison experience. Wahidin and Tate argue that in prison "the trajectory of 'time as never ending' is systematically welded into forms of punishment" (74). With temporality at the centre of prison experience, the idea of 'doing' or 'getting' time is of concern for all of its characters, no matter their chronological age, as Regina Spektor's original theme tune, "You've got time" (analysed next), effectively conveys.

"You've Got Time"

The theme of temporality is central to the show as illustrated by *Orange*'s title sequence. Title sequences are of added relevance for a TV show and tend to reflect a series' aesthetic and/or thematic dimension (Michlin), they represent the continuity, the cohesion, the brand carried through each episode and season. When binge-watching a series, this tune would be played repeatedly, the only marker signalling the start of a new episode, thus making a lasting impression.

Spektor's title theme song fixates on the idea of 'doing time' as its chorus repeats the lines "you've got time" to exhaustion. It implies that in prison time is all there is, as Steinberg describes in the following: "[t]ime to dwell on the past, time to rethink choices and mistakes, and time to figure out just what the future may provide" (2). The accompanying opening sequence consists of a photo-montage of previously incarcerated women (Dunne) in a fast-paced succession of close-ups, of women's faces, or of their nose, mouth, chin, or eyes – in what appears a parody of the 'mug shot'. The song's slower and faster paced rhythm determines the speed by which photos flash by, adding a temporal dynamic to the sequence, which is bookmarked by the sound of a prison cell-door clanging shut, followed by the sound of a bolt locking. The title sequence encapsulates (one of) the aims of the show, namely, to tell a variety of women's stories, women of different skin colours and ages, who lead a less than glamorous prison-existence – with close-ups of wrinkles, moles, under-eye bags, lip hair, ungroomed eyebrows, tattoos, and piercings, rarely seen on our screens. These details usually signify grotesque and abject femininity, in opposition to the idealised, glamorous version of femininity generally represented on screen; yet in this context they are normalised.

Intersected with these 'real' images of former inmates, are images of Litchfield's fictional setting, cast members' names superimposed over images of handcuffed hands, orange prison uniforms, a sign announcing "Weekend visiting hours" attached to a wired prison fence; a row of telephones in one of the prison corridors, the prison kitchen, or an exterior shot of the prison guard watch tour. This establishes *Orange*'s mise-en-scène, the prison space where these women's lives are 'doing' their time.

Transgressing Chrono-Temporality

The spacio-temporality of prison can be perceived in terms of Foucault's concept of heterotopia, a place "outside of all places" (24). Foucault did indeed define prison (as well as retirement homes) as one of these heterotopias of crisis, where "individuals whose behaviour is deviant in relation to the required mean or norm are placed" (25) and where "a sort of absolute break with their traditional time" (26) occurs. Halberstam establishes a link between space, time and sexuality, describing queer uses of time and space in opposition to "heteronormative time/space constructs" (*Queer Time* 10). If understood beyond the realms of sexuality, as Halberstam also proposes, queer as a concept has the "potential to open up new life narratives and alternative relations to time and space" (2). Queer temporality allows an alternative understanding of ageing, as opposed to the heteronormative constructs, which are regulated by notions of "reproductive time" (10); queer time is "unscripted by the conventions of family, inheritance, and child rearing" (2).

The particularities of prison existence make this the ultimate queer, space-time heterotopia – women living together, governed by alternative temporalities, 'freed' from temporal structures of heteronormativity, establishing sub-cultural 'families' through ties of queer kinship (Halberstam, "Smell"). Applying Halberstam's concept to reverse chronological narratives, Cynthia Port argues that queer temporalities provide "potentially asynchronous modes of time [which can] open up the interpretive possibilities for recognizing alternative temporal experiences of old age" (5). Queer theory's refusal of fixed identity categories (Jagose) can thus be explored to unsettle other identity categories understood as biologically determined. The disruption of chrono-normativity challenges a linear understanding of temporality, the institutionalised organisation of time (Freeman), and the staged progression from young to old, towards decline in old age.

Helene Moglen, for instance, proposes thinking of ageing "in terms of 'transageing' – emphasizing the constant, erratic movement that takes place in consciousness across, between, and among the endlessly overlapping states of being and stages of life" (306). And the idea of being old and young at the same time has been further theorised by Lynne Segal, who argues that several age identities can be contained within us simultaneously: "As we age, changing year on year, we also retain, in one manifestation or another, traces of all the selves we have been, creating a type of temporal vertigo and rendering us psychically, in one sense, all ages and no age" (4). Another dynamic concept of temporality and ageing as change or becoming has been proposed by Pamela Gravagne. The notion of Deleuzian time, Gravange suggests, "can free us to live, continually opening up possibilities for becoming by giving us chance after chance to combine our past with our present in all sorts of new and unexpected ways" (57). Jan Baars similarly draws on the notion of ageing as becoming suggesting that "the past will remain important in shaping the future" (151), that the "past is never complete or transparent, but changes as time or life go on" (151).

Orange's non-linear narrative, with its multiple and non-chronological flashback sequences, combines past and present, and allows the viewer to glimpse into each characters' multifaceted past, as it informs the present, shapes their future, as well as re-shapes their past. Described by Ames as "temporal tease" (8), this type of temporal upheaval could also be understood as "temporal vertigo" (Segal 4), where viewers engage with characters who are "all ages and none" (4) and whose past is combined with their present in "all sorts of new and unexpected ways" (Gravagne 57). In short, the series may encourage viewers to be more receptive to "alternative temporal experiences of old age" (Port 5).

As the protagonist of *Orange*, Piper has more flashback scenes than other characters, detailing, in non-linear fashion, how both of her main relationships (with Alex and with Larry) started and eventually broke-off, and everything in between. The opening scene of *Orange*'s first episode ("I Wasn't Ready", 1.01) in particular establishes the type of ruptures to narrative linearity that result in a queering of sexual identity and announce one of the show's characteristics, its constant flow through non-linear time, capturing inmates' different 'pasts' as these continuously shape their present and future(s). As glimpses into Piper's past are revealed, "traces of all her selves" (Segal 4) collide, rendering her both young/er and old/er, depicting her as bisexual or queer, rather than heterosexual or lesbian. Whereas Piper's non-linear characterisation *queers* the notion of a stable heteronormative or homonormative identity, other ruptures of linear temporality can open up our understanding of ageing through "potentially asynchronous modes of time" (Port 5).

As far as *Orange*'s old/er characters are concerned, these narrative transgressions are less about sexuality but can be read as queering chrononormative age-identities. San Filippo enumerates the following instances of queer spacio-temporality (Halberstam) provided by *Orange*'s fictional prison narrative: "its single-sex population; [...] in the past's anti-nostalgic intrusion ('temporal drag') on the present, visualized through recurring flashbacks and characterizations composed non-chronologically; [...] and in OITNB's imaginings of queer futures" (2). In a prison-setting, these characters are removed from (hetero)normative time/space constructs (Halberstam *Queer Time*), and inhabit a queer heterotopia. It is in this context that the concept of queer temporality and Segal's idea of being all ages and none, or of being old and young at the same time, can be particularly useful in deconstructing stereotypes and binaries of age. If a "stubborn lingering of pastness" can be read as "a hallmark of queer affect" (Freeman 8), *Orange*'s anachronistic rendering of its characters' pasts through extensive, non-linear flashback scenes certainly evokes these queer temporalities.

One character in particular illustrates the notion of queer temporality in terms of asynchronous and alternative experiences of old age, as will be explored later in this article. Rosa Cisneros' storyline resists the clichés associated to the pathological model of ageing and illustrates the possibilities of queer temporality. Other challenges to traditional age-narratives and ageist stereotypes are made possible through the characters referred to as "golden girls."

Orange's "golden girls"

Orange's prison setting allows for non-normative versions of youthful- and ageing femininities to be represented on screen, in itself a welcome break from the narrow range of media images generally available. As with other identity categories, such as sexuality and race, *Orange* acknowledges the ageist stereotypes, exaggerating them for comic effect and eventually subverting them or presenting more nuanced and complex images instead. The "golden girls" are first mentioned in "WAC Pack" (1.06), on occasion of the women's prisoner council campaign. Lorna (Yael Stone) and Nicky (Natasha Lyonne) explain an incredulous Piper that each "tribe" selects a representative from their "own" group – "it's tribal, not racist", as Lorna assures Piper on her arrival ("I wasn't ready", 1.01). The groups comprise "the whites, blacks, Hispanics, golden girls, and others" (1.06). As the camera pans past the table where each group sits, it becomes clear that the "golden girls" are the elderly prisoners who all sit together. The representation of a group of characters mockingly denominated as the "golden girls" appears to align with paradigmatic representations of ageing such as the model of decline, or the 'ageing other,' with characters being presented as a homogeneous group of not-young women. This suggests that their age identity overshadows other identity categories, a homogenous category positioned as 'the ageing other', and the binary opposite to the youthful, relatively healthy and active prisoner. The "golden girls'" age emerges as the "overdetermined signifier, signalling physical and economic incapacity, social marginality, and impending death" (Dittmar 70). Explorations of ageing and abjection (Kaplan; Gilleard and Higgs) have demonstrated how old age is seen as abject in our youth-oriented culture, where visible signifiers of ageing (body fat, grey hair, wrinkled skin) or older women themselves have to be eliminated or hidden. In season 2 however, *Orange* returns to the "golden girls" and develops them into complex and individualised characters.

"Who Are You Calling Old?"

In Red's (Kate Mulgrew) first encounter with the "golden girls" – Jimmy (Patricia Squire), Frieda (Dale Soules), Taslitz (Judith Roberts), and Irma (Yvette Freeman) – in "Looks Blue, Tastes Red" (2.02), she sees them as the abject other, as the old women who "we have to push away from both the social body and even the individual body in order for that body to remain clean, whole, pure" (Kaplan 188). In this instance it is Red who best illustrates how identities can be negotiated (Hurd; Slevin) and that both age and femininity require constant work and performance. Red's flashback sequences portray her evolution from a self-conscious and insecure housewife and cook to her involvement with the Russian mafia ("Tit Punch", 1.02, and "Moscow Mule", 1.08). In prison she becomes the head chef who runs a successful smuggling operation from the stronghold of her kitchen. The end of season one illustrates her demise, as she is decommissioned from her kitchen post and loses the prestige, power and the trust of her group of friends ("Can't Fix Crazy", 1.13).

In season 2, Red is portrayed as having 'let herself go', which is visually conveyed by her make-up free face and greying roots on her fading red hair. The encounter between Red and the "golden girls," who perceive her as one of them, illustrates Red's reluctance in identifying as old (2.02). Frieda, Taslitz, Irma and Jimmy join Red at the canteen table where she sits on her own. Frieda is aware that Red has been rejected by her friends and suggests they sit together, "Nobody notices us. We're old and invisible, so why not be old together?", to which Red replies indignantly, "Who are you calling old?" (2.02). This distancing process has been explored in Hurd's analysis of women's negotiations of ageing and oldness, where a youthful status must be maintained in order to keep the distance from the category 'old'. Being called "old" suddenly makes Red aware of her "snow-white roots" and she touches her hair, stating "Oh, s**t. I gotta deal with that, huh?". Frieda suggests, "Or just let it go. F**k it. Who we trying to impress?" (2.02). For Red, however, power and respectability are conveyed by her appearance. While she is in control, she undertakes the 'works of femininity' or beauty work (Clarke and Griffin), and is portrayed shaving her legs, plucking chin hair, covering up greying hair. In the end, it is not her encounter with the "golden girls" that make her realise that she has 'let herself go'. It is the arrival of her long-time opponent, Vee (Lorraine Toussain), who is back in prison. "I need to look fierce", she tells hairdresser Sophia (Laverne Cox) and starts wearing her black eye-liner and red lipstick again (2.02). Red performs youthful femininity as a shield, her make-up resembling war-paint, the perfect mask (Biggs) – while simultaneously identifying as old when inclusion in this group benefits her. Banned from her kitchen, Red sets up a gardening-club for the retired prison population as a front for her illegal smuggling activities assisted by her newly recruited gang, the "golden girls."

Maierhofer argues that just as with sex and gender, we should distinguish "between chronological age and the cultural stereotypes associated with old people" in order to escape "the confining binary opposition of young and old" ("Anocritical" 27). The concept of performance has productively been applied to age-identity, challenging the idea that old age is a natural and fixed category, with pre-determined characteristics (Brooks, Woodward, "Performing"). In season 2 of *Orange*, as the "golden girls" feature more prominently, their portrayal subverts ageist cultural stereotypes and challenges the old/young binary. More than that, they also dismiss the type of benevolent ageism expressed by Piper in "Appropriately Sized Pots" (2.08). Piper, Frieda and Taslitz discuss the roots of age discrimination and the meanings attached to old age, and Frieda states, "No one gives a s**t about old ladies. We remind everyone that they're gonna die". When Piper assures them that she doesn't "feel that way. I find it comforting to be around old people," they dismiss her cliché reply in a condescending tone, "Glad we could be of service" (2.08).

Rather than denying illness and decline in old age, the inclusion of the "golden girls" allows *Orange* to draw attention to the inadequacies of the prison health-care services to cater for an increasingly aged female prison population, something which has been explored in a growing body of sociological and gerontological research (Aday and Krabill, Wahidin, Wahidin and Tate). When Jimmy, whose mental health is deteriorating, with signs of dementia or Alzheimer's disease, wanders off and suffers an accident, she is released from prison under the "compassionate release" scheme ("Comic Sans", 2.07). Sister Ingalls (Beth Fowler), a former political activist and nun, confronts one of the wardens and accuses him of negligence. She demands to know: "What are you going to do about the quality of senior care in this prison?" ("Take a Break from your Values", 2.11). The inclusion of an image of 'ageing as decline' is thus introduced alongside a variety of other representations and with the specific aim of social critique.

The awareness that these characters are prisoners, some of them with a violent past, allows *Orange* to portray older prisoners as 'salty old women' (Maierhofer *Salty*) rather than 'sweet' or 'little old ladies.' It thus presents a complex characterisation of the "golden girls," rather than taking their chronological age as the determining identity category. It is the capacity for violence and the revelation of a violent past that challenges one of culture's most pervasive ageist stereotypes – that of vulnerable old age. One scene in particular depicts how three of the "golden girls" fight back against an ageist slur (quite literally in this instance) and disrupt cultural expectations of vulnerable old age ("Oz of Furlough", 2.09). Frieda, Taslitz, and Irma, now part of Red's gang, walk into Mendonza's kitchen in order to collect a payment and are received by a storm of ageist insults. Marisol (Jackie Cruz) and Maritza (Diane Guerrero) mock them in a belittling baby-voice, implying that 'old people' get easily lost and confused, are always in a foul mood and have a tendency to volunteer "morality lessons" (2.09). The stereotype of the 'sweet' old lady is readily subverted as the younger women are confronted with three armed inmates. Frieda threatens Marisol with a makeshift knife while describing what she was convicted for – mutilating her husband's genitals with a butcher's knife. Her action punishes the type of patronising ageist discourse that constructs old age as mental and physical decline and frailty. Having collected what they came for, they walk away, Irma complaining that "It is so disappointing being underestimated as you age" (2.09), which ends a threatening scene on a (dark) comedy note.

Orange's seriality allows the portrayal of ageing to be multi-layered, moving from familiar stereotypes to comedic transgression of ageing. Much like the characters in the hidden camera show *Benidorm Bastards* Aagje Swinnen refers to, Irma, Frieda, and Taslitz are "age bending" (8), transgressing expected age-appropriate roles. They are acting anachronistically (Russo), challenging normative, age-appropriate behaviour as constructed by the kitchen staff's ageist discourse. Unlike the "superficial reversal of age roles" (Swinnen 8) employed for comedic effect, it is Irma's deadpan complaint of being "underestimated as [they] age" ("Oz of Furlough", 2.9) that invites comic laughter. *Orange* suggests that all characters, no matter what chronological age, and whether or not they are serving a prison sentences due to violent crime, are capable of violence, as the viewer finds out when mere threat turns into actual violence in "Take a Break from your Values" (2.11), when Taslitz is seen stabbing another prisoner.

Frieda's confrontation with Marisol is not only anachronistic and thus transgressive of chrono-normative representations of older women; it further transgresses heteronormative gender-roles. In addition to abject old age, Frieda embodies the monstrous-feminine, the castrating (grand) mother, the aged-psychopath (Creed). Links between 'deviant' sexuality, violence and criminality have been previously explored (Creed, Hart), and Hart in particular traces the intersections of the figure of the lesbian with that of the aggressive woman (x-xii). Frieda's threat is, in this instance, directed at the heterosexually identified, and normatively beautiful Marisol;

and thus transgresses age-appropriate behaviour as well as heteronormativity. If the violent woman is "not-woman" (xii), the violent older woman is 'not old' in addition to 'not woman.'. This interpretation is not intended as age denial but as an attempt to open up understandings of ageing femininities outside rigid hetero- and chrono-normative modes of representation. In this instance, the "golden girls'" age-*in*appropriate behaviour disturbs a linear understanding of temporality. Frieda's violence can be seen as a trace of "all the selves [she has] been" (Segal, *Out* 4), creating a sensation of a 'temporal vertigo' for characters (and viewers) who expect chrono-normative, age-appropriate behaviour in the representation of the "golden girls."

"Go fast": Escaping the Narrative of Decline

In this section, I explore Rosa Cisneros' story arch, from marginal supporting character in season 1, to the character whose storyline dominates the season 2 finale. Rosa is one of the first inmates Piper meets at her arrival at Litchfield, when Rosa explains how she keeps to herself, without getting involved in any power games ever since she was diagnosed with cancer. She is blunt and pragmatic about her illness, and recognises its advantages within a prison setting: "Thank god I have cancer, No one f***s with cancer!" ("Tit Punch", 1.02). The character's introduction resists the clichés associated to the pathological model of ageing, without the denial of pain and decline involved in her illness. Rosa illustrates the possibilities of queer temporality in terms of an asynchronous and alternative experience of old age. One particular scene, which corresponds to the season 2 finale ("We Have Manners. We're Polite", 2.13), depicts Rosa as simultaneously old and young.

As the terminally-ill cancer patient, Rosa's story first develops according to a familiar script for older female characters, in accordance to one stereotype of age, equating late life with illness (Cruikshank 152). Rosa evokes the prospect of dying in prison as opposed to living and growing old in prison, and her fears of dying behind bars are confirmed when she finds out that chemotherapy is not working, and she has three to six weeks to live ("We Have Manners. We're Polite", 2.13). This diagnosis is in line with the typical narrative of decline; Rosa's ageing, diseased body appears, only to be written off, "first we see it, then we don't," as Woodward described the older female body on screen ("Performing" 163).

Rosa's confession to fellow prisoner Anita (Lin Tucci) reveals how much she struggles with being confined within the prison walls, especially when facing what is in effect a death sentence (the prison system allows chemotherapy but not the operation her doctor recommends): "I always pictured myself going out in a blaze of glory. Hail of gunfire, screech of tires. But this kind of death, this slow, invisible, disappearing into nothing... It's terrifying" (2.08). Rosa expresses the same feeling to Lorna – she is not afraid of death but of dying in prison. This anxiety of dying in prison is one of the issues that sociological research explores in relation to the older female prison population (Aday and Krabill), as is skilfully fictionalised in *Orange*.

"A Whole Other Whole" (2.04) portrays the beginning of an intergenerational friendship between Rosa and Yusef (Ben Konigsberg), a teenage boy who is receiving his chemotherapy in the chair next to hers. More interested in his iPhone than talking to "some old bald lady", his curiosity grows once he figures out Rosa is a prisoner, and that that her outfit, which Yusef assumed where "comfy old lady chemo clothes" (2.04), is actually a prison uniform. Yusef is gripped and wants to know what she was convicted for. Rosa tells him she robbed banks. More detail is provided later in the season, in "Appropriately Sized Pots" (2.08), an episode which depicts a younger Rosa (Stephanie Andujar) when she joins her boyfriend and his gang on her first bank robbery. Rosa becomes addicted to the adrenaline rush and further flashbacks depict her successive robberies and the tragic death of all her lovers, first Marco, then Andy, which leads Rosa to believe she is cursed. Eventually Rosa becomes the leader but grows reckless and is finally arrested when she tries to rob a bank on her own without appropriate planning. One final flashback portrays her behind bars, telling her lover Don, the last remaining member of her gang, how she misses the "smell" of money, "the excitement, the performance, the rush" (2.08).

Back in hospital, Yusef challenges Rosa to plan "one last heist", and together they steal money out of a nurse's purse. As she counts the dollar bills, Rosa snickers and admits "I never thought I'd get so excited over $63". Later that day, back in her bunk, Rosa holds on to her share of notes and breathes in deeply (2.08). This gesture mirrors an earlier flashback scene, Rosa smelling the cash from their latest robbery. The peculiar odour of money brings back the memory of her past. In line with Segal's description, Rosa's experiences

unfold and collapse back, like concertinas, into narratives that are rarely reducible to age itself, but reveal multiple threads that can remain visible from the struggles, choices, contingencies of the younger life once lived, their psychic traces enduring to the end (Out 62).

Rather than portraying the paradigmatic death-bed scene which ends most narratives 'of decline,' Orange finishes season 2 with a prison escape scene (2.13). Upon returning from the chemo, Lorna, Rosa and one of the correctional officers find Litchfield in a state of commotion (one of the inmates, Vee, is nowhere to be found). While the officer is momentarily distracted, Lorna urges Rosa to use the opportunity, "Don't die in here, Miss Rosa. Go do it your own way". Lorna suggests "Go fast!" as she leaves the prison van behind, keys dangling in the ignition. After a brief moment of indecision, Rosa 'goes fast' and her confidence grows as she blasts through barriers and out onto the road. Orange's moment of 'poetic justice' arrives when Rosa spots Vee on the roadside having just escaped through the woods – Rosa swerves to the right, hitting Vee violently with her van. Rosa had not been one of Vee's main victims but obviously never forgave her for inciting her gang to bully her. It is Rosa's casual remark, in dark comedy fashion, "Always so rude, that one", that eases the viewer's shock as Vee's body is seen lying lifeless on the side of the road (2.13).

Rosa drives on, enjoying her first minutes of freedom; winds down the window and switches on the radio – on cue, Blue Öyster Cult song "Don't Fear the Reaper" (1976) blasts out of the speakers. It is clear that Rosa does not fear the Reaper now that she is out on the road. Rosa laughs, and suddenly her image morphs into her younger self, complete with make-up, hair and rings (again portrayed by Stephanie Andujar as in the earlier flashback scenes), 1970s police car sirens in the background (2.13). If music has the capacity to form "an emotional bridge to a nostalgic mode of being, allowing access to memories and feelings connected with the past" (Jennings 45), this interconnectedness of Rosa's pasts and present is established through the thrill of a fast getaway and an appropriately themed soundtrack. To a certain extent, this visual representation of 'temporal vertigo' is more effective than a flashback in evoking a past self onto the present self. Rather than longing for her youthful body or her lost youth, Rosa's transformation signals her lifelong longing for adventure and freedom, the rush of an escape renders her both old and young at the same time (Segal). The open-ended narrative gives us a glimpse of Rosa at the point where her wish "to go out in a blaze of glory" (2.08) is a possibility.

Not unlike the show's depiction of the "golden girls," *Orange* introduces Rosa early on and establishes an elaborate characterisation throughout the series. Rosa is part of a mosaic of ageing femininities that is made possible through *Orange*'s intergenerational cast and its seriality, allowing for a complex and layered portrayal of an older woman, who is diagnosed with cancer, who establishes friendships, with Lorna and Yusef, and who takes up the role of the avenger in relation to the season's main villain. The simultaneous rupture of chrono-normativity and the narrative of decline provides an example of the free manipulation of time and space available for the representation of non-paradigmatic narratives of ageing. As different traces of Rosa's past selves intersect with the present, she herself can be seen as embodying queer temporality. If Moglen's notion of 'transageing' where to be represented on screen, Rosa transformation could be seen as a possible illustration, her present and past merging, portraying the "constant, erratic movement that takes place in consciousness across, between, and among the endlessly overlapping states of being and stages of life" (Moglen 306).

Conclusion

The fact that *Orange* portrays more fluid sexualities, even if reserved to its young/er characters, and that it represents some of its old/er characters' age identities as in flux, allowing them to be old and young at the same time, indicates the potential for further non-normative images to emerge. The images of non-normative ageing featured in this article have been explored as transgressive of chrono-normativity. Frieda's, Taslitz', Irma's, and Rosa's experiences of ageing illustrate an ultimate queer, space-time heterotopia of prison, their lives unscripted by the rhythms of heteronormativity. Their layered portrayals, combining glimpses of their past, as flashbacks intersect with their diegetic present, disrupt linear narrative as well as the assumption of a chronological progression from young to old. Netflix's platform, as well as the serialised format combined with *Orange*'s multi-generational ensemble cast are essential conditions for these innovative representations.

Orange subverts stereotypical images of older women and allows complex representations of non-age-appropriate femininities to emerge. Within a prison setting, the potential for violence is presented as shared characterisation, from Piper to the "golden girls" and emerges as transgressive of normative images of ageing. If violent behaviour is considered 'un-lady like,' violent ageing femininities may contain the power to disrupt representational hetero- and chrono-normativity. Whether exploring the mark of aggression (Hart) or the queer transgression of chrono-normativity of Rosa's portrayal, the concept of queer temporality can be a useful theoretical tool even outside of the realms of sexuality. Now that *Orange* has been renewed for a third season, it can be expected that this series will further engage in complex ageing subjectivities within a non-normative context.

WORKS CITED

Aday, Ronald H. and Jennifer J. Krabill. *Women Aging in Prison: A Neglected Population in the Correctional System*. Boulder: Lynne Rienner Publishers, 2011. Print.

Ames, Melissa, ed. *Time in Television Narrative: Exploring Temporality in Twenty-First-Century Programming*. Jackson: UP of Mississippi, 2012. Print.

Baars, Jan. "Critical Turns of Aging, Narrative and Time." *International Journal of Ageing and Later Life* 7.2 (2012): 143-65. Print.

Ball, Vicky. "Forgotten sisters: the British female ensemble drama". *Screen*, 54.2. (2013): 244-248. Print.

Barker, Cory. "Does Netflix Know What It s Doing?" *TV.com*. CBS Interactive Inc., 13 Jun. 2013. Web. 15 Oct. 2014.

Belcher, Christina. "This Ain't The Help? OITNB's White Savior Industrial Complex." *Flow* 20.03 (2014). Web. 15 Nov. 2014.

Bendix, Trish. "*Orange is the New Black* is Netflix's best yet." *AfterEllen*. TOTALLYher Media, 2013. Web. 8 July 2013.

Biggs, Simon. "Choosing Not to Be Old? Masks, Bodies and Identity Management in Later Life." *Ageing and Society* 17, (1997): 553-70. Print.

Brooks, Jodi. "Performing Aging/ Performing Crisis (for Norma Desmond, Baby Jane, Margo Channing, Sister George - and Myrtle)." *Figuring Age. Women, Bodies, Generations.* Ed. Kathleen Woodward. Bloomington: Indiana UP, 1999. 232-47. Print.

Bülow, Morten Hillgaard, and Thomas Söderqvist. "Successful Ageing: A Historical Overview and Critical Analysis of a Successful Concept." *Journal of Aging Studies* 31.0 (2014): 139-49. Print.

Charlton, T.F. "*Orange Is the New Black*, and How We Talk About Race and Identity." *RH Reality Check.* RH Reality Check, 3 Sep. 2013. Web. 15 Nov 2014.

Ciasullo, Ann. "Containing "Deviant" Desire: Lesbianism, Heterosexuality, and the Women-in-Prison Narrative." *Journal of Popular Culture* 41.2 (2008): 195-223. Print.

Clarke, Laura Hurd and Meridith Griffin. "Visible and Invisible Ageing: Beauty Work as a Response to Ageism." *Ageing and Society* 28.05 (2008): 653-74. Print.

Cohen-Shalev, Amir. *Visions of Aging: Images of the Elderly in Film.* Eastbourne: Sussex Academic P, 2011. Print.

Creed, Barbara. *The Monstrous-Feminine. Film, Feminism, Psychoanalysis.* London: Routledge, 1993. Print.

Cruikshank, Margaret. *Learning to Be Old. Gender, Culture, and Aging.* 2nd ed. Lanham: Rowman & Littlefield Publishers, 2009. Print.

Dittmar, Linda. "Of Hags and Crones: Reclaiming Lesbian Desire for the Trouble Zone of Aging." *Between the Sheets, in the Streets. Queer, Lesbian, Gay Documentary.* Eds. Chris Holmlund and Cynthia Fuchs. Minneapolis: U of Minnesota P, 1997. 71-90. Print.

Dunne, Carey. "Move Over, Dove. *Orange is the New Black* Celebrates Real Women." *FastCompany.* Fast Company, 20 Aug. 2013. Web. 6 Mar. 2015.

Edelman, Lee. *No Future: Queer Theory and the Death Drive.* Durham: Duke UP, 2004. Print.

Foucault, Michel. "Of Other Spaces." Trans. Jay Miskowiec. *diacritics* (1986): 22-27. Print.

Freeman, Elizabeth. *Time Binds: Queer Temporalities, Queer Histories.* Durham: Duke UP, 2010. Print.

Gilleard, Chris and Paul Higgs. "Ageing Abjection and Embodiment in the Fourth Age." *Journal of Aging Studies.* 25.(2) (2010): 135-42. Print.

Gravagne, Pamela H. "The Magic of Cinema: Time as Becoming in *Strangers in Good Company*." *International Journal of Ageing and Later Life*. 8.(1) (2013): 41-63. Print.

Gullette, Margaret Morganroth. *Aged by Culture*. Chicago: The U of Chicago P, 2004. Print.

Halberstam, Judith. *In a Queer Time and Place: Transgender Bodies, Subcultural Lives*. New York: New York UP, 2005. Print.

Halberstam, Judith. "What's That Smell? Queer Temporalities and Subcultural Lives." *International Journal of Cultural Studies* 6.(3) (2003): 313–33. Print.

Hamer, Diane and Belinda Budge, eds. *The Good, the Bad and the Gorgeous: Popular Culture's Romance with Lesbianism*. London: Pandora, 1994. Print.

Hart, Lynda. *Fatal Women: Lesbian Sexuality and the Mark of Aggression*. New Jersey: Princeton UP, 1994. Print.

Hurd, Laura C. "'We're Not Old!': Older Women's Negotiation of Aging and Oldness." *Journal of Aging Studies*. 13.4 (1999): 419-39. Print.

Jagose, Annamarie. *Queer Theory. An Introduction*. New York: New York UP, 1996. Print.

Jenkins, Henry. *Convergence Culture: Where Old and New Media Collide*. New York: New York UP, 2006. Print.

Jenkins, Tricia. "'Potential Lesbians at Two O'clock': The Heterosexualization of Lesbianism in the Recent Teen Film." *The Journal of Popular Culture*. 38.3 (2005): 491-504. Print.

Jennings, Ros. "It's All Just a Little Bit of History Repeating: Pop-Stars, Audiences, Performance and Ageing - Exploring the Performance Strategies of Shirley Bassey and Petula Clark." *"Rock On": Women, Ageing and Popular Music*. Eds. Ros Jennings and Abigail Gardner. Farnham: Ashgate, 2012. 35-51. Print.

Kackman, Michael, ed. *Flow TV : Television in the Age of Media Convergence*. New York: Routledge, 2011. Print.

Kaplan, E. Ann. "Trauma and Aging. Marlene Dietrich, Melanie Klein, and Marguerite Duras." *Figuring Age. Women, Bodies, Generations*. Ed. Kathleen Woodward. Bloomington: Indiana UP, 1999. 171-94. Print.

Kerman, Piper. *Orange Is the New Black: My Year in a Women's Prison*. London: Abacus, 2010. Kindle file.

Krainitzki, Eva. *Exploring the Hypervisibility Paradox: Older Lesbians in Contemporary Mainstream Cinema (1995-2009)*. Unpublished PhD thesis, U of Gloucestershire, UK, 2012. Print.

Lotz, Amanda D. *The Television Will Be Revolutionized*. New York: New York UP, 2007. Print.

Maierhofer, Roberta. *Salty Old Women: Eine Anokritische Untersuchung zu Frauen, Altern und Identität in der Amerikanischen Literatur*. Essen: Die Blaue Eule, 2003. Print.

Maierhofer, Roberta. "An Anocritical Reading of American Culture: The Old Woman as the New American Hero." *Journal of Aging, Humanities and the Arts*. 1.1/2 (2007): 23-33. Web. 30 June 2013.

Matthews, Roger. *Doing Time: An Introduction to the Sociology of Imprisonment*. London: Palgrave Macmillan, 1999. Print.

Mayne, Judith. *Framed: Lesbians, Feminists, and Media Culture*. Minneapolis: U of Minnesota P, 2000. Print.

Michlin, Monica. "More, More, More: Contemporary American TV Series and the Attractions and Challenges of Serialization as Ongoing Narrative." *Mise au point*. 3 (2011). Web. 28 Mar. 2015.

Moglen, Helene. "Ageing and Transageing: Transgenerational Hauntings of the Self." *Studies in Gender and Sexuality* 9 (2008): 297-311. Print.

Port, Cynthia. "No Future? Aging, Temporality, History, and Reverse Chronologies." *Occasion: Interdisciplinary Studies in the Humanities*. 4 (2012). Web. 13 June 2013.

Russo, Mary. "Aging and the Scandal of Anachronism." *Figuring Age. Women, Bodies, Generations*. Ed. K. Woodward. Bloomington: Indiana UP, 1999. 20-33. Print.

San Filippo, Maria. "Doing Time: Queer Temporalities and *Orange is the New Black*." *Media Commons*. 10 Mar. 2014. Web. 15 Apr. 2014.

Segal, Lynne. *Out of Time: The Pleasures and Perils of Ageing*. London: Verso, 2013. Print.

Seitz, Matt Zoller "Should Netflix Shows Be Considered 'Television'?" 6 June 2013. Web. 15 Sep. 2014.

Slevin, Kathleen F. "The Embodied Experiences of Old Lesbians." *Age Matters. Realigning Feminist Thinking*. Eds. T. M. Calasanti and K. F Slevin. New York: Routledge, 2006. 247-68. Print.

Sodano, Todd M. "Television's Paradigm (Time) Shift." *Time in Television Narrative: Exploring Temporality in Twenty-First-Century Program-*

ming. Ed. Melissa Ames. Jackson: Univ. Press of Mississippi, 2012. 27-42. Print.

Spigel, Lynn and Jan Olsson. *Television after TV: Essays on a Medium in Transition.* Durham: Duke UP, 2004. Print.

Steinberg, Lisa. "You've Got Time." *Huffington Post.* AOL-HuffPost TV Group, 16 Jul. 2014. Web. 20 Aug. 2014.

Swinnen, Aagje. "Introduction: *Benidorm Bastards*, or the Do's and Don'ts of Aging." *Aging, Performance, and Stardom: Doing Age on the Stage of Consumerist Culture.* Eds. Aagje Swinnen and John Stotesbury. Münster: LIT Verlag, 2012. 7-14. Print.

Tincknell, Estella. "Dowagers, Debs, Nuns and Babies: The Politics of Nostalgia and the Older Woman in the British Sunday Night Television Serial." *Journal of British Cinema and Television* 10.4 (2013): 769-84. Print.

Turim, Maureen. *Flashback in Film: Memory & History.* New York: Routledge, 1989. Print.

Wahidin, Azrini. "Time and the Prison Experience." *Sociological Research Online* 11.1 (2006): n.pag. Web. 15 Sep. 2013.

Wahidin, Azrini and Shirley Tate. "Prison (E)Scapes and Body Tropes: Older Women in the Prison Time Machine." *Body & Society* 11.2 (2005): 59-79. Print.

Wearing, Sadie. "Subjects of Rejuvenation. Aging in Postfeminist Culture." *Interrogating Postfeminism. Gender and the Politics of Popular Culture.* Eds. Yvonne Tasker and Diane Negra. Durham: Duke UP, 2007. 277-310. Print.

Woodward, Kathleen. "Introduction." *Figuring Age. Women, Bodies, Generations.* Ed. K. Woodward. Bloomington: Indiana UP, 1999. ix-xxix. Print.

Woodward, Kathleen. "Performing Age, Performing Gender." *NWSA Journal* 18.1 (2006): 162-89. Print.

TELEVISION

Bad Girls. Creator Maureen Chadwick, Ann McManus and Eileen Gallagher, ITV, DVD (1999–2006).

Orange is the New Black. Creator Jenji Kohan, Netflix, Web (2013–present).
Prison Break. Creator Paul Scheuring, Fox, Broadcast (2005–2009).
Prisoner: Cell Block H. Creator Elspeth Ballantyne, Betty Bobbitt and Sheila Florance, Network Ten, Broadcast (1979–1986).
Tenko. Creator Lavinia Warner, BBC & ABC, Broadcast (1981–1984).
Wentworth Prison. Creator Reg Watson, SohoTV/ Channel 5, Broadcast (2013–present).

"I'm Too Old to Pretend Anymore"
Desire, Ageing and *Last Tango in Halifax*

KRISTYN GORTON

The UK's Skillset's *Creative Media Workforce Survey* (2010) found that in television "71% of men compared with 56% of women are 35 years or older," which reminds us that ageing continues to be a gendered issue in British television. Against this trend, Sally Wainwright's *Last Tango in Halifax* (2012-present) explores desire that emerges later in the lives of three 'older' women. In so doing, her drama positions older woman's desire in the forefront of the narrative, as opposed to the margins. This chapter will focus on the construction of desire in the series and the role age plays in the narrativisation of desire through a close examination of story and mise en scene.

The series, which won a Bafta for best drama and best writer, centres on the renewed love affair between Alan Buttershaw (Derek Jacobi) and Celia Dawson (Anne Reid). The two, now widowed and in their late seventies, first fell for each other as teenagers, but fate kept them from acting on their feelings. Then, after the death of their partners and through the help of social media, they meet up and re-kindle their romance. The series focuses on their desire for each other, and their respective daughters', Gillian (Nicola Walker) and Caroline (Sarah Lancashire), love lives. Caroline, in her late forties, has recently separated from her husband following his affair and soon realizes that she desires a female colleague in the school where she is headmistress. The series explores Caroline's struggles and uncertainty in accepting her emergent lesbian identity. Gillian, also in her late forties, must face her past in order to make way for her true desire, but in so doing, puts her future at risk.

Throughout the narratives, the fact that the characters are older adds a new dimension to the sexuality explored and a new meaning to the title which references *Last Tango in Paris* (dir. Bertolucci, 1972). Instead of being seen as negative thing, age is constructed as a positive and empowering force that can make way for new expressions of desire. In other words, it is *because* they are older, rather than *in spite* of being older, that the desire is seen as deeper and more sustainable. The last tango, as it were, gives them a chance to get things right and express their true feelings. In this respect, Wainwright offers narratives of love and older age that come across as authentic. And perhaps most importantly, we have older female characters as romantic leads, in a way that makes older women on screen more visible and acceptable. Too often older women (often categorised as '35 or older') are featured in mother roles where their desire is often subsumed by their responsibility to nurture and foster their childrens' aspirations (Gorton 2008).

Ageing on Television

In their work on ageing and television, Healey and Ross point towards an emerging paradox in our global television landscape:

On the one hand, globalization, media conglomerization and the ICT explosion gives us (or at least those of us in the developed world who enjoy cheaper and accessible media services) unparalleled access to a rich diversity of programmes and genres. But, at the same time, the actual content, as least of mainstream, prime-time TV, appears to reflect an identikit world of young/ish people, mostly white, mostly heterosexual, mostly obeying conventional social norms. (106)

As they suggest, despite the proliferation of programmes, there is nowhere near the same amount of diversity and difference in the content of the programmes that we have access to. This is a significant problem when it comes to older audiences who rarely see plot lines, let alone romantic storylines, linked to older couples. This is part of what makes Wainwright's series so unique and inventive, and yet, at the same time, it is in the format of a cosy, predictable and well-known British drama format. So she offers

British audiences something they understand and yet with content that is new and refreshing. Audiences are not expecting the two oldest cast members to be the central romantic leads. The melodramatic nature of the series draws its viewers in emotionally and encourages them to follow the long story arc of two older people falling in love and yet to also enjoy the short beats where the plot twists and turns to reveal sub-stories and new characters. The serial structure allows the audience to 'get to know' the characters slowly, which is significant as it creates the potential for the audience to eventually accept these older desiring characters more fully than they would in watching a two hour movie.

It is also worth noting the ways in which regulation governs viewers' taste and acceptance of differing kinds of sexuality. In her work on television and sexuality, Jane Arthurs explains that:

[t]he processes of regulation set limits to ensure that mainstream drama conforms to normative assumptions about sexual behavior. If broadcast before the 9.00 p.m. watershed, it must be deemed suitable for family viewing. For drama this has meant an almost exclusive focus on heterosexual relationships [...]. (117)

Perhaps part of the reason *Last Tango* is post-watershed is that it contains a lesbian relationship as a centre story plot, but, it could be argued, it is also because the romantic leads are in their late seventies. Although the relationship is heterosexual, it is not mainstream to focus on the love and desire of people in that age range.

Indeed, in her work on "reading the 'sexy oldie'" Vares points out that "the absence of portrayals of later life sexuality was notable in television, advertising and film" until the 1990s (503).[1] She sees the 1990s and the popular use of Viagra (amongst other cultural shifts) as marking the moment in which the 'sexy oldie' enters into popular culture. However, she also notes a double-standard of ageing, in which older women are represented less often than older men and where the older man/younger woman combination is more prevalent than the opposite situation (505). There is also a distinct lack of older couples actually having sex. As Bildtgard argues, "none of these films *actually shows* an elderly couple having sex, it is

---

1   Vares does not mention *The Golden Girls* (NBC, 1985-1992), which I think would make an interesting exception to her argument.

only hinted at" (Bildtgard qtd. in Vares 505; author's italics). Two notable exceptions are noted by Vares, *Something's Gotta Give* (dir. Meyers, 2004) and *The Mother* (dir. Michell, 2003). The second film forms the basis of Vares's ethnographic research in which she interviews focus groups with older women and older men (divided by gender).

Vares' research reveals an interesting contradiction to the logic espoused by theorists such as Margaret Cruikshank who argues that "[t]he *shame* of ageing is perpetuated when old bodies are *hidden* from view" (520; emphasis in the original, cited in Vares). Indeed Vares' participants suggest that "*to be seen* 'is the ultimate devaluation'" (520; emphasis in the original).

As mentioned earlier, *Last Tango* is in the format of a comfortable, even somewhat predictable television series, and so there are no naked bodies or uncomfortable sexual suggestions. The only actual romantic activity between any of the three couples is suggested at rather than depicted. The series is not designed to push the boundaries of what we, as a society, *see* in terms of older bodies; however, it does manage to challenge what we *think* about ageing couples and their desire. The serial format incorporates a slow but sustained recognition of an 'othered' sexuality which allows for a more gradual acceptance.

It also contributes to questions that are raised concerning the role of television, as a medium that bridges 'the public and the private spheres,' such as Arthurs posits in her notion of the 'sexual citizen: "For instance, what cultural rights do minority sexual cultures have to be represented, to have a voice in the factual and fictional outputs of television?" (26). However, as Arthurs goes on to argue, insisting on such representation can lead to issues regarding 'political correctness' and to exposure for groups of people who may prefer their invisibility.

Narratives of Desire

The concept of desire maintains a strong influence in the narratives we watch on television. One of the most potent metaphors of desire used within film and television is desire as an awakening, as a force or movement that propels the subject from her position and transforms her life. I have written elsewhere (2009) about the construction of desire in popular American television series such as *Six Feet Under* and *Brothers and Sisters*. In both series the mother figure is central to the "emotional fabric of the text" (137). She is often in the kitchen dispensing advice, tissues and glasses of wine to her older children. Despite the fact that they are older, and have mostly left home, both mother figures are often punished if they pursue desirous relationships. Indeed, when each woman attempts to find desire with another man she ends up with someone who wants her to take care of him or someone who is more interested in his own desires. Likewise, these moments of sexual freedom are often punished when one of her children calls her to be there for them.

In both series daughters emphasise the differences between the generations, the choices that feminism has created and the mistakes that are inherited despite best intentions. The mother figure is portrayed as the caretaker above all else but also the person everyone comes to with their emotional needs and revelations. In so doing, she provides the series with a character that not only unites the cast but also privileges and fosters intimate and emotional moments.

The same cannot be said of the mother figure central to Sally Wainwright's *Last Tango*. Although Celia is seen as important to her daughter's life, indeed, she lives in a flat attached to her home; as a character, she is not simply there to facilitate the other characters' emotional needs. Pairing her with Alan, the two are more often seen as the 'parents' of the two daughters, rather than putting the mother figure at the centre of 'caring' for the daughters' emotional needs. In order to consider how desire functions within the series, and more specifically, how Wainwright presents new narratives of older women's desire, I want to focus on each character in turn and to draw on mise en scene to examine the ways in which Wainwright constructs desire in older women.

In contrast to other television series discussed earlier, such as *Brothers and Sisters* and *Six Feet Under*, Celia is not the maternal figure conflicted between her role as carer and her desire. Instead she is often seen as uninterested in getting involved in the drama of her daughter's life. For instance, her son-in-law John tries to draw her into the problems between her daughter and himself, to which she replies by asking him whether he has heard the news of her engagement. This is a somewhat insignificant moment on the one hand, and yet on the other, it constructs a character who is not in the role of carer, but rather as someone who is free to desire. This is not to suggest that she is uninterested in her daughter's emotional feelings, but that she is clear with herself and her family that she is free to pursue her own desires.

To complicate this, Wainwright shows both daughters as uncomfortable, and often unhappy, with their parents' ability to put their desire before their role as parent, which suggests that although they are able to do this, they have previously been seen primarily in the role of carer. As Celia and Alan cement their plans for their wedding, both daughters' lives fall apart and they each blame their parents, at different moments, for not helping enough.

The opening montage of the series features a moving family tree which references the way in which the two families become related through the love affair between Alan and Celia. Wainwright wastes no time in setting up the central relationship between the two 70-somethings and by the end of the first episode, they are engaged to be married. The first episode is a clever introduction to the central characters and to the focus on family, love and desire throughout the series. But the fact that the two oldest characters take centre stage puts older women's *passion* central to the text, which is very uncommon for a mainstream television programme. That the *desire* is led by Celia further underlines the importance of older women's *sexuality* and audiences are invited to see her character as someone who is still very much capable of sexual desire and a 'new chance' in life.

The episode begins with the two older characters communicating over social media (facebook). They are seen as comfortable and experienced with this form of communication, even though it is more often associated with younger users. Alan invites Celia to meet her in Skipton, a market town near Halifax, for coffee. Celia tells her daughter that he has invited her, but says that she is not going to go. However, she changes her mind and tells him that she would be "delighted" to meet him. We later learn that this change of heart has a lot to do with her daughter's ongoing problems with her unfaithful husband. His infidelity reminds Celia of her own disappointing marriage and furthers her interest in rekindling her feelings for Alan. In anticipation of their meeting, Alan tells his daughter Gillian that he and her mother were "pals" whereas Celia was "a bit of heaven on earth," so we are first introduced to his desire for her. Here 'pals' and 'heaven on earth' signify the difference between a long, solid partnership and the chance at desire, even if later in life.

The two meet in a cosy café, filled with other older couples enjoying their tea and coffee. Alan returns to his car to put some more money in the parking machine only to realize that it has been stolen. The two go to the police station to report the incident, then on their ride home spot the car and enter into a high speed chase which results in Celia crashing into the back of Alan's (stolen) car. The two end up back in the police station where Celia ends up confessing her love for Alan. The episode reflects the way in which Wainwright subverts our expectations of a 'boring' old couple and suggests that their reunion not only sparks desire, but adventure.

"I'm Too Old to Pretend Anymore"

In an interview, Anne Reid, who plays Celia, remarks about the series, "It's so un-ageist, [...] I get scripts all the time that say: 'This old lady comes in on a zimmer frame.' And I think: 'Oh hello, that's my part, is it?' No, thank you. Lots of people in their 60s and 70s are not doddery old idiots, and [they] are having interesting lives" (qtd. in Rees). Far from 'doddering,' one of the first things that the new couple ventures into together is the purchase of a very expensive convertible. Their rationale is that instead of spending the money on an engagement ring, they will treat themselves to a luxurious car that they can both travel in.

As the couple stand in the car dealership, Celia notices that the car salesman is ignoring them. She tells Alan that he probably think they are "time wasters." When it comes to negotiating a price, Celia surprises the car dealer not only by being able to calculate the sums quickly but also by negotiating a deal on when the car is delivered and she insists on a lower price. Here Celia proves that she is not a 'doddering old idiot' but faster and more able than the man selling the car. When the car arrives during their engagement party, Caroline treats her like a child and says: "So you bought a car that you're probably going to need a hip replacement to get in and out of," thus underscoring her age and implying that she has been silly to make such a decadent and unpractical choice. Celia just dismisses her with a look. This decision causes some conflict with Alan's daughter as well who finds the expense unnecessary and indulgent and worries that Celia is leading Alan in the wrong direction. The car becomes symbolic of the notion that they 'don't care anymore' and that they are taking out a new lease on life. Their decision, although one both daughters initially reject, becomes part of the energy that later forces change in both the daughters' lives, which I will discuss later.

As noted already, there is a distinct lack of older women and ageing, more generally, represented within mainstream television. One of the issues raised regards the lack of visibility, especially in terms of bodies. *Last Tango* does not advance this issue insofar as showing more graphic sex scenes between the older couple, but then it also does not do this in terms of the 'younger' couples. All the sexual desire is kept as subtle and suggestive. There is an implicit suggestion that they are having sex, but we never see them actually doing it. For instance, when they arrive home after their elopement, the following dialogue is suggestive that they will have sex, but we never see them having it:

Celia: 'So...
Alan: 'wedding night'
Celia: 'hmmm....60 years later than anticipated' maybe but...'
Alan: 'Well worth the wait'
Celia: 'We'll find out won't we...' (giggles) (S02, E02)

In one respect this is a result of the format itself. *Last Tango* is post-watershed BBC programme and therefore has the latitude to take more risks, particularly in terms of sex, but the tone of the series is one of comfort and predictability. *Last Tango* has an appeal to a wide demographic and can be watched by 'all the family'. There is nothing offensive or objectionable within the series. *Happy Valley*, Wainwright's other television success within this period was not as 'cosy' and received numerous complaints from audiences regarding the violence in one episode. As a writer, Wainwright is clearly able to push boundaries and to offend. But, as discussed, this is not the remit for *Last Tango*. And yet, within the cosy atmosphere of the programme, Wainwright is pushing character boundaries which deserves recognition and praise, particularly in light of the way in which she constructs characters that are free to desire and allowed to pursue their desires, despite their older age and role as parents. Drawing on a long story arc and using short beats, the series follows a similar format to other serial television melodramas (Williams) to focus the audience's attention on the desire between the characters as they develop and face challenges in life.

So it is not a matter of shying away from 'saggy' bodies, but rather that the series uses light, suggestion and plot to elicit desire instead of relying on gratuitous sex scenes. As Anne Reid who plays Celia has said about sex scenes: "It would ruin it," she says. "People can see that we're physical and I like to think that we have a pretty good sex life but I certainly wouldn't want the public to watch it" (qtd. in Ward). Reid's comments chimes with Vares' research that there is often a preference *not* to see.

Mise en Scene and Melodrama in *Last Tango*

Although, as the series' title suggests, Halifax is the central locale – the series divides itself between Halifax, Harrogate and an unspecified rural location outside of Halifax. Both series draw heavily on the landscape around all three locations, often including long takes of the windmills set in the vast countryside; narrow, winding cobblestone streets; and the elegance of the spa town of Harrogate. As well as evoking the mood and atmosphere of the locations, Wainwright, to a great extent, is matching location with character to draw on specific aspects regarding their personalities.

In *Television Drama: Realism, Modernism and British Culture*, John Caughie explores the difference in the histories between cinema and broadcasting noting that the visual dominated film (as there was no sound for 30 years) and the word dominated broadcasting (there was no image). It leads him to argue that: "Cinema narrative deploys its visual rhetoric to seduce us into a fantasmatic relationship to its narrative space; television drama uses the word to tell us about the world. Film allows us to dream; television drama invites us to be responsible." Although Caughie goes on to say that this distinction is too simplified, he feels that it underlines a difference between film criticism and television theory. "The mise en scene of cinema holds secrets – even from its creators – which criticism can uncover. More than that it creates desire: it is, as Laura Mulvey says, 'an illusion cut to the measure of desire'" (18). I would argue that aesthetics and production values within the televisual landscape have changed significantly enough from 2000 when Caughie wrote his book, particularly in terms of 'quality' television drama, to argue that television is just as capable of both allowing audiences 'to dream' and to create desire on screen. It is also worth arguing for the ability of the television theorist to use television's mise en scene as a way of reading the desire in the series. John Gibbs identifies the following as fundamental elements of mise en scene: "lighting, costume, colour, props, décor, action and performance, space, the position of the camera, framing, and the interaction of elements" (6-26). I want to focus on lighting, décor, action and performance in particular to think through some of the ways in which Wainwright constructs desire within the series.

Throughout the first two series, diffused sunlight is used as a metaphor for love and desire. For example, in the second episode of the first series, Alan is in his living room thinking about Celia and looking at an old picture of her while sun streams in through the window. He is bathed in light and, by extension, we see him as full of desire: he has a dreamy expression on his face. The doorbell rings, and there is Celia, standing at the door showered in sunlight. She stands there as the object of his desire and affection. Following their ordeal trapped in a manor house, Celia lies asleep on the couch while sunlight covers her. Alan gazes at her with a look of love and desire. Anyone familiar with Halifax and North Yorkshire will know that sunlight is not very common and so Wainwright uses this deliberately as means of softening and enlightening the space and actors. In so doing, the suggestion is one of joy, transformation and movement. Sunlight or diffused light is also used in the scenes between Caroline and Kate, particularly in the moments where Caroline recognizes her feelings for Kate. Light is used as a subtle and yet very powerful expression of desire and is seen as enlightening force upon the characters, thus underlining desire's powerful influence in terms of personal transformation.

Décor is used throughout the series to distinguish between the two families both in terms of class and cultural background. Celia lives in a small apartment which has been built behind the substantial brick home in which her daughter Caroline, her partner and two sons live. The house and its surrounds make it clear that they live a very middle class lifestyle. Much of the shots take place in the well designed and tasteful kitchen in Caroline's house. This setting plays into the later arguments regarding class that are raised as an early conflict to the relationship between Alan and Celia. She is characterized as someone who reads the right wing paper *The Daily Mail*, who votes for the Tory party and who shops at Marks & Spencers.

Gillian, Alan's daughter, is, in many respects, the counterpoint to Caroline. In their initial meeting with each other Caroline refers to her as 'trash,' looking down her nose at the way she is dressed and the car she drives. Living and working a farm in rural Yorkhire, Gillian has little care for her appearance and is often seen with her hair tied back and looking very dishevelled. In stark contrast to Caroline and Celia, Gillian is not a woman that spends a great deal of time tending to her physical appearance. And yet, she is introduced as someone who enjoys sex and has sex with much younger men without intimacy or a great deal of relationship. The décor in her house reflects a working farm and a woman who does not see herself as someone interested in housework or 'making an effort'. At the same time, the hearth that is the focal point of the main room is warm and inviting, and when there are moments of revelation or confrontation – such as when Gillian tells Caroline that she killed her ex-husband or when Robby, her ex-husband's brother, punches John, the fire is lit and the glow works to warm the scene and reflects the desire shared between the characters.

Jeremy G. Butler argues that "[t]heories of film and television have traditionally neglected the significance of performance and the many functions of the screen the star's image" (7) in the introduction to his collection on *Star Texts: Image and Performance in Film and Television*. While this was true in the early 90s, the last two decades have given rise to a developing interest in television and film performance as a serious area for criticism (Cantrell and Hogg 2016). The performances that Anne Reid and Derek Jacobi bring to the series are exemplary of the reasons why performance has become such an important area of study in television theory. Both actors are well known and well respected on the British film, television and stage. Sir Derek Jacobi won a British Academy Television award for Best Actor in the BBC series *I, Claudius* and has won numerous other accolades as a film, stage and television actor. Reid was nominated for the 2013 British Academy Television Award for Best Actress (Sheridan Smith won). Her first major acting role was as Valerie Tatlock on ITV's long-running soap opera *Coronation Street*. She starred in the Victoria Wood's comedy series *Dinnerladies* along with numerous appearances in British television dramas such as *Marchlands* and *Shameless*. Interestingly, she was also nominated for the British Academy Film Award for Best Actress in a Leading Role for her performance as an ageing mother who sleeps with her daughter's boyfriend in *The Mother* in 2003. In *The Mother*, Anne Reid goes from looking like a very dowdy and frumpy older woman to a colourful, much younger and much happier woman as a result of her affair with her daughter's boyfriend (played by Daniel Craig). In both *The Mother* and *Last Tango in Halifax*, Reid is vibrant on screen. She is not only an attractive older woman but she exudes sexual confidence and this is partly due to her performance. Throughout the series we see her dancing, winking, addressing the camera directly with a strong gaze – a repertoire of movements and expressions that is more in common with a romantic lead much younger than Reid.

Last Tango can be seen as a melodrama and as Laura Mulvey argues, melodrama can be understood as "the genre of mise en scene, site of emotions that cannot be expressed in so many words" (29). Offering a 'basic model' for melodramas, Mercer and Shingler argue that melodramas "chiefly concerns the conflicts and tensions of a middle-class family, more often than not, this conflict is between the generations" (12). *Last Tango* adheres to this basic model and reflects the transformations and emotional journeys the women in the text go on – but Celia is not the tortured widow of Douglas Sirk's *All That Heaven Allows* (1955) and Alan is an equal to her, not a domineering other. However, Celia often refers to the joyless marriage she had with Kenneth and the sadness that filled her, which not only adds to the joy at finding Alan, but suggests that she was the woman of the melodrama before meeting him. In other words, rekindling her relationship with Alan saves her from becoming the tragic heroine of melodrama and allows her to realize her desire.

Everlasting Love

The love between Alan and Celia is characterized as a lost love, a love that had it happened might have changed the lives of all those around them – and as it does come together, helps to sort out their daughters' lives. Wainwright has been quoted as saying that she enjoyed writing Celia, who is loosely based on her mother. She writes: "The older people get, the more personality they've got, the more experience they've got, the less inhibited they are …the things about old people is they dare" (qtd. in Frost). This 'daring' nature characterizes the experiences Alan and Celia have as they are first reunited. In the first episode they go on a car chase to try and catch the people who stole Alan's car and later they are trapped in an old, haunted manor house all night. Celia tells Alan: "We keep having adventures […] I didn't have much in the way of adventures until I met you" (1.5). This sense of adventure draws out their youthful nature and places them in the centre of the text. It is if their desire informs and aids their daughters' lives. The story of the relationship between Celia and Alan runs parallel to the problems both daughters confront in terms of their own desire.

Wainwright constructs a back and forth movement of desire between the older and younger generations – particularly between mother and daughter and father and daughter. One generation is seen as teaching the other about desire and taking a risk on love. In the first instance, we see that the love between Celia and Alan causes Caroline and Gillian to re-think their romantic lives. When Celia and Alan are trapped overnight, Caroline realizes for the first time how tragic it would be if her mother would die having only just found her true love. This realization forces her to both end her relationship with her cheating husband and to embrace the feelings she has for her work colleague, Kate.

However, when she confronts her mother about her feelings and bourgeoning identity as a lesbian, she is met with disgust and disavowal. In an attempt to get her mother to know Kate better she invites Celia and Alan to dinner, which erupts into an argument between mother and daughter. Celia's rejection of Caroline and her feeling that the desire she has is 'wrong' in turn upsets Alan, who sees her reaction as "bigoted and small-minded." He ends up splitting up with Celia because he is disappointed at the way she has handled her daughter's feelings. In the final episode of the first series, Celia confronts Kate about her concerns and not only apologises but reunites Caroline and Kate. It is at this moment however that she learns that Alan has had a heart attack and is in critical condition in the hospital. Celia tells him: "I'm not bigoted and small-minded ... it turns out I was blaming myself for her being the other way inclined... but they're back together, so I'm hoping, I'm assuming that you and I are back on vis-à-vis the wedding" (1.6).

There is a clear correlation in Celia's mind between the desire she has found and the desire her daughter has that she has learned to accept. The two are not only interrelated in terms of the plot and story arc but also in terms of our perceptions about the desire between a much older couple and a lesbian couple. Both are relatively invisible, especially on screen and are represented less often than heterosexual romance. As Arthurs points out: "[T]he main problem with gay and lesbian representation in television drama hasn't been a plethora of negative stereotypes but their invisibility" (117). As discussed earlier, it is not simply a matter of ageing women being seen as undesirable, it is more a problem of them being unseen. However, in the fictional world that Wainwright constructs, these desires, however forbidden or unrecognized, are given full exploration and value.

In the second series the focus shifts to the relationship between Alan and his daughter, Gillian. We discover that he has been disappointed with Gillian's choice in men and the way she sleeps around. In the first series we learn that she has been sleeping with a much younger man and ends up sleeping with John, Caroline's ex-husband. It is slowly revealed, through the second series, that Gillian killed her ex-husband after years of domestic violence. She faces her demons and tells Caroline the truth about Eddie's death. This is aided in large part by the way in which her father stops treating her like a child and expects her to act like an adult. It is also underscored by the birth of her granddaughter. The second series also deals with Kate's desire to have a baby. Kate and Caroline arrange to spend a romantic weekend at a country hotel to meet a man that Kate thinks could father their baby. However, Caroline books them separate rooms which leads Kate to leave Caroline suggesting that "nothing ever really got started" between them.

Series 3 sees Caroline and Kate get married, however, what is interesting, especially in terms of earlier discussions about a mother's role to care, is that Celia decides not to go to the wedding. Despite Caroline's pleas and her attempt to make Celia feel guilty for past mistakes, Celia is firm in her decision not to be there. She puts her own feelings before her daughter's and we see little remorse in her decision. When Kate is tragically killed in a car accident, Celia cares for Caroline and helps her with Flora, Kate's child. Caroline never makes Celia feel guilty for her decision not to go to the wedding and instead embraces her mother's love. Kate's death also brings Caroline and Gillian closer together which culminates in the final episode where we see Caroline literally getting her hands dirty to make sure Gillian's wedding is a success.

Happy Endings?

Like a good Austen novel, series 2 ends with a wedding which acts as a chance to bring all the story threads together and reunite Caroline and Kate. In fact, the ending cleverly shows each couple either sleeping or just waking up in bed: first Celia and Alan, then Caroline and Kate, and finally Gillian and Robby. The final shot is of Gillian awake and clearly concerned with her decision to sleep with Robby, her ex-husband's brother. Not only does the final episode tie up the romantic threads, but it also suggests that there is room for more drama, and indeed the third series also ends with a wedding, but this time Gillian is at the altar. The third series deals more explicitly with Alan's long lost son, Gary (Rupert Graves) and their reconciliation. In many respects, the third series drags out the storylines explored in the first two series which is partly why this article has focussed so heavily on the first two. It also extends the feeling of comfort and predictability that is becoming more prevalent in modern serials. We are encouraged to care for and become attached to the characters.

Last Tango has been commissioned for a fourth series and the rights to the programme have been bought by Diane Keaton for a potential remake on HBO, so here is hoping that we see more older ageing on television in the future (Eames).

WORKS CITED

Arthurs, Jane. *Television and Sexuality: Regulation and the Politics of Taste*. Berkshire: Open University Press, 2004. Print.

Brunsdon, Charlotte, Julie D'Acci, Lynn Spigel, eds. *Feminist Television Criticism: A Reader*. Oxford: Oxford University Press, 1997. Print.

Butler, Jeremy G. "Introduction." *Star Texts: Image and Performance in Film and Television*. Detroit: Wayne State University Press, 1991. Print.

Cantrell, Tom and Chris Hogg. *Acting in British Television*. Basingstoke: Palgrave Macmillan, forthcoming, 2016. Print.

Caughie, John. *Television Drama: Realism, Modernism and British Culture*. Oxford: Oxford University Press, 2000. Print.

Cruikshank, Margaret. *Learning to be Old: Gender, Culture and Aging*. Lanham, MD: Rowman and Littlefield Publishing, 2003. Print.

Eames, Tom. "Last Tango in Halifax to Return for Fourth Series." *Digital Spy*. Hearst Magazines UK. 2 Feb. 2015. Web. 16 March 2015.

Frost, Vicky. "'Sally Wainwirght: "I like Writing Women, They're Heroic."'" *Guardian Online*. Guardian News and Media Ltd. 6 Jun. 2014. Web. 10 Nov. 2014.

Gibbs, John. *Mise-en-Scene: Film Style and Interpretation*. London: Wallflower Press, 2002. Print.

Gorton, Kristyn. *Theorising Desire: From Freud to Film to Feminism*. Houndsmills: Palgrave Macmillan, 2008. Print.

Gorton, Kristyn. *Media Audiences: Television, Meaning and Emotion*. Edinburgh: University of Edinburgh Press, 2009. Print.

Healey, Tim and Karen Ross. "Growing old invisibly: older viewers talk television." *Media Culture Society*. 24.1 (2002):106-120. Print.

Hodgetts, Darrin, Kerry Chamberlain, and Graeme Bassett. "Between Television and the Audience: Negotiating Representations of Ageing." *Health*. 7. 4 (2003): 417-438. Print.

Martin, Liam. "Last Tango in Halifax begins filming series 3." *Digital Spy*. Hearst Magazines UK. 28 July 2014. Web. 10 Nov. 2015.

Mercer, John and Martin Shingler. *Melodrama: Genre, Style and Sensibility*, London: Wallflower Press, 2004. Print.

Mulvey, Laura. *Fetishism and Curiousity*, London: BFI, 1996.

Rees, Caroline. "Sally Wainwright: not the same old." *Guardian Online*. Guardian News and Media Ltd. 3 Nov 2013. Web. 10 Nov., 2014

Shilling, Jane. "*Last Tango in Halifax*: A Triumph Against TV's Ageism." *The Telegraph*. Telegraph Media Group Ltd. 11 Dec. 2012. Web. 16 March 2015.

Vares, Tiina. "Reading the 'Sexy Oldie': Gender, Age (ing) and Embodiment." *Sexualities*, 12. 4 (2009): 503-524. Print.

Ward, Rachel. "*Last Tango in Halifax*: Anne Reid Interview." *The Telegraph* (online). Telegraph Media Group Ltd. 19. Nov. 2013. Web. 16 March 2015.

Williams, Linda. *On The Wire*. Durham: Duke University Press, 2014 Print.

TELEVISION

All That Heaven Allows. Director Douglas Sirk (1955).
Brothers and Sisters. Creator Jon Robin Baltz, ABC (2006-2011)
Coronation Street. Creator Tony Warren, ITV (1960-present).
Dinnerladies. Creator Victoria Wood, BBC (1998-2000).
Last Tango in Halifax. Writer Sally Wainwright, BBC (2012-present).

Last Tango in Paris (Ultimo tango a Parigi). Director Bernardo Bertolucci (1972).
Marchlands. Wirter Stephen Greenhorn and David Schulner, ITV (2011).
Shameless. UK version. Writer Paul Abbott, C4 (2004-2013).
Six Feet Under. Creator Alan Ball, HBO (2001-2005).
Something's Gotta Give. Director Nancy Meyers (2003).
The Golden Girls. Creator Susan Harris, NBC (1985-1992).
The Mother. Director Roger Michell (2003).

"Blanche and the Younger Man"
Age Mimicry and the Ambivalence of Laughter
in *The Golden Girls*

THOMAS KÜPPER

The situation comedy *The Golden Girls* (1985-1992) has been the subject of controversial discussion ever since it first went to air on NBC on 14 September 1985.[1] On the one hand, the TV series is acclaimed for its portrayal of older women living together in a house and their zest for life, including not least sexual desire. In the 1980s it was considered innovative to focus attention on such figures. Setting the scene for the broadcast of the first episodes, the *New York Times* published an article entitled *NBC's 'Golden Girls' Gambles on Grown-Ups*, commenting: "When it comes to women, television has always had an obsessive love affair with youth. Creamy skin and firm thighs are a prerequisite for leading roles" (Harmetz). It is precisely these conventions which Brandon Tartikoff, president of NBC Entertainment, wished to dispense with as he planned the show. He had told the television producers Paul Witt and Tony Thomas: "Take some women around 60. Society has written them off, has said they're over the hill. We want them to be feisty as hell and having a great time." Witt was sceptical at first: "You won't put it on the air", he claimed, only to be "giv-

---

1   The present essay is a reworked version of a paper given in October 2011 at the conference *Theorizing Age: Challenging the Disciplines* in Maastricht, The Netherlands. For the financial assistance required to take part in the conference I would like to thank the German Academic Exchange Service (Deutscher Akademischer Austauschdienst, DAAD).

en a commitment for 13 episodes before a single word was written." The sense of still "having a great time" anchored in this founding narration of the series is echoed in interviews with viewers for whom "the hopeful message of 'there's life after 50'" is decisive: "As one 53-year-old married woman put it, '[...] I think the basic premise holds up: There are a lot of golden girls out there, full of life and mischief, not ready to roll over and play dead. They have sexual desires, too, destroying the myth that they're nonentities just because they're growing older!'" (Cassata and Irwin).

On the other hand, it is often critically asked if "a comedy series centering around the issues of aging" does really enhance "the identity of older people, especially older women", or if, on the contrary, they are not demeaned (Cassata and Irwin). This suspicion was remarked on in the *New York Times* the very day the series was launched: "A little too much of the humor is directed at ridiculing certain signs of aging, from having hair in one's ears to incontinence" (O'Connor). Such doubts are meanwhile fuelled by research: In their analysis of *The Golden Girls* Jake Harwood and Howard Giles show that "humor and age marking often coincide, and that quite frequently humor is derived explicitly from age markers" (428). From this perspective, it cannot be ruled out "that the show might be sustaining, and contributing to, an ageist culture" (405). Ultimately, as Anne K. Kaler has noted, it must be considered if not calling the main characters "girls" alone implies that they are unable "to function as adult women" (52). Are the characters made to look ridiculous in this way?

In the following article, I would like to argue that the laughter provoked by *The Golden Girls* is ambivalent. As Miriam Haller has explained, the concept of ambivalence in the context of post-structuralist approaches is linked to a "logic of dynamic dual valency": the relationship between two poles is not dissolved into a bivalence, i.e. not in the two-valued logic of an either-or decision for one of the two poles; instead, "ambivalence serves to continuously defer the decision between the two poles" ("Dekonstruktion" 361).[2] Drawing on this concept enables a reading of the laughter in *The Golden Girls* that goes beyond the usual binary schemata like a 'positive' or 'negative image of old age', an 'esteeming' or 'disdaining' of the elderly. A dynamic comes into view that cannot be captured with such either-or models. The ambivalent comicality oscillates – undetermined – between the

---

2   All translations from the German texts are mine.

two poles. The result, however, is not merely some additive "a little bit of both;" what emerges is something completely different that calls into question the binarity of valuations itself – hierarchical categorisations of age brackets are subverted.

I would like to trace this ambivalence in the episode "Blanche and the Younger Man" (1.9) from 1985. In this episode Blanche (Rue McClanahan), one of the four starring characters, behaves – when viewed from a traditional perspective – inappropriately for her age: she flirts with the 'younger man' featuring in the title, a fitness instructor called Dirk (Charles Hill), and even begins to work out to enhance her attractiveness. Here one could presume that all the effort she puts in to make herself desirable for the markedly 'younger man' makes Blanche seem ridiculous – the laughter triggered would 'punish' Blanche's violation of the traditional rules that it is not suitable for a woman to flirt with a 'younger man' and that age boundaries are to be respected when it comes to physical exercise. Moreover, would it not be reasonable to assume that youth and midlife are more highly valued than older age in *The Golden Girls* when Blanche tries to match the 'younger man' and do all she can to make herself young again, just to appeal to him? This would give the impression that the series hierarchises age and ranks older age lower.

These possible hierarchies of age soon begin to unravel however: Ultimately unsuccessful, Blanche's attempts to match the 'younger man' seem like a mockery of him and his fitness. The ambivalence emerging with respect to judging age can best be elaborated, in my view, by transferring Homi K. Bhabha's concept of colonial mimicry to the category of age, allowing one to work with a notion of 'age mimicry'.

Beforehand, it has to be asked to what extent the elderly characters featured in *The Golden Girls* and their comedic impact are determined by the basic structures of TV series in general and the genre of the sitcom in particular. How do these figures fit into these structures and by which means do they provoke laughter? Not least the genre of the sitcom furnishes conditions congenial for theatrics. In the case of *The Golden Girls* this theatric is so pronounced that the series can be described as 'campy', a point to be elaborated in a later section. What transpires is that, due to the theatric exaggeration, distinctions like 'old'/'young', 'true age'/'pretended age' precipitate their own collapse.

Structures of the Series *The Golden Girls*

Episodic structures underlie *The Golden Girls* – 'episodic' in the Aristotelian sense that there is neither probability nor necessity (*oút' eikòs oút' anágke*) in the sequence of episodes (Aristotle 38-39 [1451b]). The episodes are only loosely connected with one another as the plot strands are usually brought to a conclusion in each individual episode; new plot strands begin with the new episode. Usually narrative patterns recur in a series running from episode to episode: "Put into the most general terms, in every episode a disturbance is introduced into the starting situation; frequently from an external source, it escalates over the course of the episode and is dealt with in such a way that at the end the initial state of calm is restored" (Ruchatz 81).

The episode "Blanche and the Younger Man" perfectly illustrates this principle: the initial state of calm is the four women living together in a house in Florida. This intact community is disturbed by an outside influence, with Blanche, a member of this community, flirting with Dirk, who is suddenly standing one day at the door of the house. Were Blanche to enter into a steady relationship, the house community would cease to exist in the same way. The escalation of this disturbance, a date between Blanche and Dirk, ends however when Blanche feels disappointed and retreats back as it were to the community. With the threat averted, the initial state of calm is restored.

This state of calm can then be threatened by new disturbances in the following episodes; here the protagonists need not remember what had gone on in the episode "Blanche and the Younger Man." Protagonists of such sitcoms do not usually remember what took place in the individual episodes, whereas the viewer endowed with a memory is able to compare episodes and notice the recurring patterns (Ruchatz 84, Eco 85-87).

From this perspective, the predominant[3] temporal structure of the series is cyclical (Berzsenyi). The cyclical resides not only in the recurring plot schemata but also – and in particular – in the repeating of the opening title credits from episode to episode and the same weekly time slot. A single episode itself is cyclically framed: the theme song *Thank You for Being a*

---

3 While there are plot strands which embrace more than one episode, these strands are clearly subordinated to the cyclical structure.

Friend, to be heard during the opening credits, returns at the conclusion of an episode in an instrumental version. Thus, it is also made clear musically that the state of calm, the harmonious order of the house community, is re-attained; the circle is completed.

With this cyclical structure the series deviates starkly from linear time as it is represented in the mass media, in particular by the news. Whereas the news focuses almost exclusively on upheavals and changes, conveying mostly to viewers the idea of an open, insecure future (Luhmann 141), a series like *The Golden Girls* offers familiarity and security, firmly anchored in the dependable return of elements which have already featured. The impression given to the viewer – that he/she is not at the mercy of a volatile world – is reinforced by the primary setting, the house in which the quartet lives, is often associated with a place of providing comfort and safety. At the same time however, the series is not a mirror held up to the audience sitting at home in front of the television, reflecting their own lives. They are presented rather with an idealised image: The city of Miami itself appears in the opening sequence in soft golden light. As John Bell has noted: "The women in *The Golden Girls* seem to live totally in a world of their own making in their communal home, the creators of an idyllic Miami" (308). Frequently confronting viewers with unexpected news and creating an impression of insecurity, television also offers a counter principle, a delight in repetition and a feeling of being safe and sound after all. While current pressing issues and problems featuring in the news are discussed in *The Golden Girls*, for example the spread of AIDS (Gahrmann 110-113), the references to such uncertainties are set in the framework of the cyclical structure of the series and its idyllic location, absorbing and offsetting a world fraught with uncertainty.

To what extent do elderly women in particular fit into these basic structures as main characters? First of all, assigning elderly women to the cyclical course of events in a house is of course nothing unusual; the figures are consistent with a few traditional, clichéd notions of age and femininity. Femininity is associated with domesticity in an influential tradition and not immediately with actions which change the world in linear elapsing time; rather, femininity is seen as tied to cyclical activities beyond historical time. It is also often assumed that the elderly gradually withdraw from the dynamic of current world events and take up a quieter and more sedate lifestyle (the expectations of active involvement manifest in designations like 'the young-old' will be taken up below). As mentioned, the main characters of *The Golden Girls* are very much aware of the specific problems of contemporary life and by no means dwell beyond historical time. But because they are confronted with such problems in the framework of cyclical structures – and time and again eat cheesecake together in the kitchen to restore harmony in the home –, their interest and participation in current-day happenings in linear time is mantled and reshaped by a principle that is connected with traditional notions of age and femininity.

The principle of the cyclical, the recurring, contributes to the situation comedy of the series as well: each of the four elderly protagonists is characterised by an oddity they display over and over again so that the continual repetition elicits laughter. It is characteristic for Sophia (Estelle Getty), the eldest of the four, to state her opinion on every occasion in an outspoken manner, completely disregarding what etiquette may demand. Sophia's way of communicating thus recalls the stereotype that old age goes hand in hand with excessive directness, if not with downright rudeness (Harwood and Giles 418, 424). Allegedly, Sophia's behaviour is due to a stroke that damaged the part of her brain steering social discretion, while the ability to stir up trouble has remained intact (Colucci 25). A character of this ilk is particularly suited for the sitcom genre, her wit often propelling her beyond the limits of polite conversation and decorum. Crucially, given the back story of the stroke, Sophia's behaviour is predictable. The audience thus harbours expectations and these are repeatedly confirmed. Sophia generally prefaces her remarks with the phrase "picture it," and this predictability transforms the phrase into a running gag. That what is expected does in fact occur offers the audience the joy of recovering something familiar, generating amusement through its constant repetition. The elderly woman thus turns into a guarantor of situation comedy.[4]

This begs the question if older age is not actually stereotyped and ridiculed in *The Golden Girls*: "Debates over stereotyping in sitcom consistently argue that comedy is a political form because it relies on lampooning particular social groups via assumptions about their 'inherent' characteristics" (Mills 79). Is this discernible in *The Golden Girls* in terms of age? In

---

4   It is not by chance that a number of other elderly characters have become established figures in sitcoms: amongst others Grandma Yetta in *The Nanny* (1993-1999) and Father Arthur in *The King of Queens* (1998-2007).

general, stereotyping "reduces people to a few simple, essential characteristics, which are represented as fixed by nature" (Hall 257). Is age in the series essentialised in this way?

Such a view of the series would be too one-sided. It would mean ignoring that the elderly women in part defy established and rigid expectations of how people of such an age are to behave, without however being set up as mere objects of ridicule through these deviations from such expectations. Many of the punchlines in this sitcom are based on showing up the expectations foisted upon the elderly and not the elderly themselves. In the episode "Blanche and the Younger Man" for example, Rose (Betty White), another of the quartet, is confronted with how her own mother Alma (Jeanette Nolan) fails to conform to the behaviour expected of someone her age. Alma refuses to being coddled and treated indulgently by Rose, answering to the appellation "Mother!" with the punning demand: "Stop mothering me!" Rose and her housemate Dorothy (Beatrice Arthur) speak unusually loud when introducing Alma to the other housemates – the 'girls' obviously assume that Alma must be hard of hearing due to her age. Alma takes part in this 'shouted conversation' until she surprisingly asks, just which of the housemates has such poor hearing that they all have to speak so loud.

Whereas in such sequences age is de-essentialised through the elderly rejecting or defying expectations that are taken for granted, in other situations the de-essentialising is achieved through expectations being overfulfilled in an exaggerated, theatrical way. This second kind of de-essentialising will be considered in closer detail – as I hope to show, it is precisely the theatricality of *The Golden Girls* that subverts the socially widespread stereotyping of age.

'Camp' and Theatricality

The series *The Golden Girls* already has a theatrical appearance or 'feel' thanks to the simple fact that it is recorded in front of a live studio audience. As Heike Klippel remarks: "All rooms open up in the same direction and all camera movements are arranged in a semi-circle along the axis of the missing wall. Similar to other theatrical forms, the persons onstage always assort themselves in groups that are open towards the audience / towards the camera" (93).

This theatricality is reinforced foremost by the exuberant gestures of the figures: from the very outset, in the standard title sequence presenting the four starring characters, they are seen wildly gesticulating. Moreover, the outfit of the women recalls costuming and masquerade, confirming the impression that they are on a stage. Sabine Kampmann has noticed that with their rouged faces and pastel-coloured, high-necked garments, these characters seem to affirm expectations about the look of 'elderly women'; at first glance, it would seem that age stereotypes are being reinforced. Kampmann goes on to query this however, asking if exaggeration is not in fact part of the overly perfect, bright and rhinestone-covered feminine outfits (55). Here exaggeration destabilises the expectations concerning age, unravelling the seemingly tightknit associations: age is so strongly signalled that it becomes patently obvious that this signalling is part of a theatrical presentation. Once this signalling is noticed, age no longer seems to be a given but appears as something that is artifice, stylised and aestheticised.

Sophia, for example, is specifically 'made old,' fitted out with certain 'typical' attributes matching common assumptions about age. Not only does she wear orthopaedic lace-up shoes, but she also carries a box-shaped handbag made of straw – an accessory that seemingly never leaves her side, even when donned in her dressing grown (Colucci 28-29, Klippel 98). Especially such repetitively appearing props, always the same and confirming expectations in an exaggerated way, indicate the extent to which age is being staged here – it is a 'product of art' and not the realistic portrayal of a 'natural' condition.

The accentuation on theatricality is particularly prominent in queer contexts. Bea Arthur is cited in *The Q Guide to The Golden Girls* as follows: "Yes, I think that gay people like *The Golden Girls* because it's a nontraditional family – that's part of it. But I think it's also the outrageousness of it. It's like a friend of mine once said, 'Why do gay people love opera? Because it's so much bigger than life'" (Colucci 83). As Jan Gahrmann has suggested, given this operatic or theatrical disposition of *The Golden Girls*, it seems cogent to consider the series from the perspective of 'camp', which is especially popular among homosexuals (86-87, 94-95). In her *Notes on "Camp"*, Susan Sontag explains this term by highlighting a theatrical element: "To perceive Camp in objects and persons is to understand Being-as-Playing-a-Role. It is the farthest extension, in sensibility, of the metaphor of life as theater" (280). According to Sontag, "Camp sees everything in quotation marks [...] not a woman, but a 'woman'" (280).

Due to its affinity to theatricality and 'unnaturalness,' 'camp' opens up the possibility of questioning the common gender order: gender identity no longer appears to be given by nature (Meyer). Exaggerated gestures in connection to 'camp' clarify that one 'is' not inevitably 'essentially' a man or a woman when one behaves as a man or a woman.[5] The show *The Golden Girls* demonstrates that, like gender identity, age identity is not something unquestionably given but specifically staged.

This is in particular illustrated by the character of Blanche: On the one hand, she seems to affirm the stereotype of the 'lusty widow' and 'lusty old woman' by acting man-hungry and telling many stories of sexual encounters; on the other hand, her lustiness and her stories appear to be exaggerated. Her behaviour has a staged look about it, especially the body language of her desire is hyperbolic. Moreover, her presence as an artificial character is bolstered by how she – quote-like – recalls certain prototypes drawn from literature and film: from Bianca in Shakespeare's *The Taming of the Shrew* through to Blanche Dubois in Tennessee Williams' *A Streetcar Named Desire* and Scarlett O'Hara in Margaret Mitchell's *Gone With the Wind* (Gahrmann 38-40, Kaler 54). Not least, Blanche can be seen sitting at her

---

5   At this point connections to approaches in age studies informed by theories of performativity emerge. For instance, Anne Davis Basting discusses the subversive potential of theatricality and exaggeration by drawing theoretically on Judith Butler, among others; according to Butler "theatrical acts of gender parody reveal the performative quality of gender in everyday life" (Basting 8; see also Biggs, "Age" 49, Haller, "'Unwürdige Greisinnen'" 53-54, Swinnen). Butler explains: "As the effects of a subtle and politically enforced performativity, gender is an 'act,' as it were, that is open to splittings, self-parody, self-criticism, and those hyperbolic exhibitions of 'the natural' that, in their very exaggeration, reveal its fundamentally phantasmatic status" (146-147). The performativity of age is considered in a similar way to the performativity of gender (see also Lipscomb and Marshall 2). By taking up Butler's theory of performativity, it is feasible to see the theatricality of *The Golden Girls* as disclosing the phantasmatic status of the so-called 'true age;' such naturalisations of age are disrupted by the hyperbolic display of age attributes.

makeup table, dolling herself up for the role of the attractive woman. Of course, makeup is an attribute of the traditional stock character of the 'lusty old woman' (Henderson 118) and is often ontologically devalued by drawing a distinction between 'pretended' and 'true age.' In her essay *The Double Standard of Aging*, Sontag expresses the opinion that women who grow older should not try to look younger by applying makeup: "Women should allow their faces to show the lives they have lived. Women should tell the truth" (38). In this way Sontag uses a construction of 'true age' and asserts that makeup is a kind of deception; she problematises the meaning of being a woman as being an actress:

> To be a woman is to be an actress. Being feminine is a kind of theater, with its appropriate costumes, *décor*, lighting, and stylized gestures. [...] Women have been accustomed so long to the protection of their masks, their smiles, their endearing lies. [...] But in protecting themselves as women, they betray themselves as adults (34, 38).

However, from a 'camp' point of view, such constructions of 'truth' may be questioned, although Sontag does not consider this point of view in her essay *The Double Standard of Aging* (Haller, "Ambivalente Subjektivationen" 32f.). Referring to 'camp,' Fabio Cleto explains:

> Depth-anchored subjectivity is dissolved and replaced by the mask as paradoxical essence, or depthless foundation of subjectivity as actor [...] on the world as stage. And as an object of a camp decoding, the actor exists only through its in(de)finite performing roles, the ideal sum of which correspond to his own performative 'identity,' personality being equal to a co-existence of personae on the stage of Being (25).

Precisely because *The Golden Girls* is compatible with the 'camp' sensibility, it becomes clear how age is de-essentialised in the series. The "depthless foundation of subjectivity" and "in(de)finite performing roles" identified by Cleto make it undecidable as to what can be considered as 'real' and 'true age' (25).

Age Mimicry in *The Golden Girls*

In another respect, however, it could seem that age is essentialised after all in *The Golden Girls*, namely insofar as Blanche comes up against age barriers in her attempts to rejuvenate herself. In a conversation with Dorothy for instance, Blanche claims that the age difference between herself and Dirk is only slight: she concedes that she might be five years older than Dirk. Dorothy asks back however if these five years are not in fact to be measured in terms of how dogs age, in other words, amounting to a much longer time in human life.

Blanche's efforts to reduce the age gap between herself and Dirk can be ascribed to two rules in particular which were still widely kept in the 1980s: firstly, it was not becoming for a woman to flirt with much younger men – such behaviour, as noted in the introduction, was considered 'age-inappropriate' –; and secondly, women were supposed to try to look as youthful as possible and come as close as they could to the prevailing norm of female attractiveness (Matlin 460; for the notions of attractiveness in the series, see especially Grant and Hundley 115-120). When Blanche behaves according to these rules, does this mean that elderly women are disparaged vis-à-vis their younger counterparts in *The Golden Girls* after all? And does Blanche make herself look ridiculous by trying to once again overturn the age barrier and become younger?

To discuss these questions it is necessary to precisely contextualise Blanche's efforts to make herself young again in the respective episode and the accompanying laughter. In order to match the fitness instructor Dirk, she works her body extremely hard, adopting the motto: 'no pain, no gain.' She does her workout exercises in close-fitting sportswear and takes protein pills. Around the 1980s, as the aerobics boom took off, such exercises became associated with sex appeal (Stern and Stern 1). Jane Fonda, whose *Workout Book* published in 1982 became a bestseller, was "making fortunes as the dominant name in female body toning" by the late 1980s. As the Sterns remark: "Her role as health and fitness queen was especially satisfying to many aging baby boomers because she was over fifty years old and still looked great in leotards" (183-184). This was part of a redefinition of age: Fitness and seductiveness as attributes of a woman over fifty became important for the identity construction of the young-old. Blanche's fitness training in *The Golden Girls* corresponds to these tendencies. At the same time however, such training is not simply taken for granted or seen as normal in the series, but is indeed commented on ironically. Observing one of Blanche's workout positions, Dorothy remarks: "The only time I get in that position is when I give birth." The laughter of the audience marks this sentence as a gag. But who or what is being mocked in this situation?

At first glance, it may seem as if Blanche is the target of mockery here. If we assume that it is the function of laughter to punish behaviour deviating from the norm (Bergson), then it would seem that Blanche is being mocked – after all, by following a new fitness trend and seeking to match the younger fitness instructor she is not behaving in a manner traditional notions would condone as age-appropriate. The assumption that Blanche is being laughed at could also be based on how all her effort is ultimately futile: Despite her workout exercises, a satisfying relationship with Dirk does not eventuate. As she meets Dirk for dinner, she finds out that he is only interested in her because of her resemblance to his mother. Here, it would seem that age boundaries are indeed drawn and the assumption confirmed that Blanche's efforts to begin a relationship with Dirk conforming to her ideas is being laughed at as age-inappropriate.

At the same time however, the episode "Blanche and the Younger Man" cannot be reduced to such mocking of older age. In particular the category of age-inappropriate is relativised in the episode. In contrast to Blanche's unsuccessful flirt, Alma for example tells a story about a felicitous love affair she once had with a 'younger man.' Taking this story into account, an 'older woman's' flirt with a 'younger man' as such does not appear to be age-inappropriate or ludicrous.

But what about Blanche's futile efforts to look younger and match Dirk's fitness through a strict training regimen? It is not – as I wish to show in the following – Blanche who makes herself ridiculous in the first instance with her desire to realise an ideal of youthfulness and sportiness, an ideal that she actually cannot achieve. Rather, in this context laughter once again proves to be ambivalent: the younger Dirk and his fitness routine are not safe from mockery. In this way, any possible hierarchy between 'fit' and 'unfit' as well as 'younger' and 'older age' is called into question.

This ambivalence of laughter in *The Golden Girls* comes into sharp relief when Homi Bhabha's notion of mimicry, articulated in Postcolonial Studies, is transferred to age studies and applied to this episode. Bhabha uses a concept of colonial mimicry to describe the effects when colonised people are expected to try and assimilate to the ways of their colonial rulers, confirming the alleged superiority of the latter, while at the same time being told that they are not supposed to imitate them flawlessly: "colonial mimicry is the desire for a reformed, recognizable Other, as a subject of difference that is almost the same, but not quite" (Bhabha 86). The colonised are to be capable of assimilating the colonisers, but not completely: a difference between the colonisers and colonised is essentialised and asserted to be indelible. "Almost the same but not white: the visibility of mimicry is always produced at the site of interdiction" (89). At the same time though, the pretences and values of the colonisers are not unequivocally confirmed through mimicry. Rather, the outcome of mimicry is more of "a 'blurred copy' of the colonizer that can be quite threatening. This is because mimicry is never very far from mockery, since it can appear to parody whatever it mimics" (Ashcroft, Griffith, and Triffin 105-106). Bhabha describes mimicry as ambivalent: He focuses on

a discursive process by which the excess or slippage produced by the *ambivalence* of mimicry (almost the same, *but not quite*) does not merely 'rupture' the discourse, but becomes transformed into an uncertainty which fixes the colonial subject as a 'partial' presence. [...] It is as if the very emergence of the 'colonial' is dependent for its representation upon some strategic limitation or prohibition within the authoritative discourse itself. The success of colonial appropriation depends on proliferation of inappropriate objects that ensure its strategic failure, so that mimicry is at once resemblance and menace" (86; emphasis in the original).

The image of the superiority of the colonisers over the colonised is dented when the latter transform into a distorted picture of the former.

On an abstract level, comparable structures can be found in the relationship age groups have to one another (Küpper). For instance, the young-old are expected to orient themselves on midlife norms in particular, i.e. being active, fit and productive (Biggs, "New Ageism" 103-104), yet only to a certain degree and only when respecting the allegedly natural differences between the ages of life. The differences between such age groups and their appointed position in life's stages are essentialised and deemed unshakeable. Thus, the young-old are seen as 'almost the same' as the middle-aged, but 'not quite': efforts to imitate midlife turn into mockery, irrespective of whether the young-old intended such subversive effects or not. The indiscernibility between mimicry and mockery results in ambivalence: the midlife norms are at once affirmed and undermined (van Dyk, "The Appraisal of Difference" 101).

Such mechanisms are at work in the episode "Blanche and the Younger Man:" With her derided training Blanche not only affirms the norms of youthfulness and fitness, but also weakens them at the same time. When Dorothy says that she only takes such positions to give birth, then it is not only Blanche who is targeted: The workout routine as such and the values associated with it are not excluded from the barb. 'Fitness' is parodied also in how Dirk goes 'over the top' in his efforts to stay in shape and demonstrate his prowess: During dinner with Blanche he lifts up the table to show off his strength. Because such a display seems inappropriate and exaggerated, Dirk's fit body oscillates between an ideal and a caricature.[6]

In the end, Blanche renounces the fitness ideal: Directly after her hopes are dashed by Dirk in the restaurant, she reorders. Instead of a low-calorie watercress salad, which she had picked out to fit in with Dirk's eating habits and dietary regimen, she now craves something a little less disciplined and more substantial, ordering a double whiskey and an orange duck. With this opulent dish Blanche confronts the fitness norm with something that is literally weightier. Blanche's deviation from this norm does not come across solely as a failure, but it also signals a gain: By not keeping the diet Blanche may be retreating from her aspiration to become as fit as Dirk, but at the same time she is laying claim to something else, namely enjoyment and pleasure. The failed flirt can be seen as coming to a successful conclusion in another respect as well: As described above, had a stable romantic relationship between Blanche and Dirk eventuated, then the house community – and indeed the very structure of the series itself – would have been endangered. For this reason, the position of the 'younger man,' functioning as a kind of temporary disturbance, is already defused by the structural principles of the series.

---

6   Similarly ambivalent is the 'hard body' evident in the action cinema of the 1980s, where the norm of muscle-bound masculinity is confirmed and at the same time overfulfilled to such a degree that it is reduced to an absurdity and called into question (Morsch).

Conclusion

As the example of the episode "Blanche and the Younger Man" shows, the sitcom *The Golden Girls* undermines widespread stereotyped judgements about older age and youthfulness. And it is precisely fitness – which had gained greatly in relevance for the identity of the young-old in the 1980s thanks to the popularity of Jane Fonda – that is presented as ambivalent: Blanche's efforts to match – as best she can – the 'younger man' and his fitness can be described as an age mimicry that is inseparable from mockery. Considering this example, a desideratum emerges – the need to precisely examine the dynamic through which values like youthfulness or fitness are appropriated by the young-old (van Dyk and Lessenich, "Die 'jungen Alten'"). Potentially, it seems that such values are dropped the very same moment they are held up.

Works Cited

Aristotle. *Poetics*. Ed. S[amuel] H[enry] Butcher with critical notes and a translation. 4th ed. London: Macmillan, 1922. Print.

Basting, Anne Davis. *The Stages of Age. Performing Age in Contemporary American Culture*. Ann Arbor: The University of Michigan Press, 1998. Print.

Bell, John. "In Search of a Discourse on Aging: The Elderly on Television." *The Gerontologist* 32.3 (1992): 305-311. Web. 10 Oct. 2014.

Bergson, Henri. *Le rire. Essai sur la signification du comique*. Paris: Presses Universitaires de France, 1969. Print.

Berzsenyi, Christyne A. "The Golden Girls Share Signature Stories: Narratives of Aging, Identity, and Communal Desire." *Americana: The Journal of American Popular Culture* 9.2 (2010). Web. 10 Oct. 2014.

Bhabha, Homi. "Of Mimicry and Man: The Ambivalence of Colonial Discourse." *The Location of Culture*. London: Routledge, 1994: 85-92. Print.

Biggs, Simon. "Age, Gender, Narratives, and Masquerades." *Journal of Aging Studies* 18 (2004): 45-58. Web. 10 Oct. 2014.

Biggs, Simon. "New ageism: Age Imperialism, Personal Experience and Ageing Policy." *Ageing and Diversity. Multiple Pathways and Cultural Migrations*. Ed. Svein Olav Daatland and Simon Biggs. Bristol: The Policy Press, University of Bristol, 2006. 95-106. Print.

Butler, Judith. "Performative Acts and Gender Constitution: An Essay in Phenomenology and Feminist Theory." *Theatre Journal* 40.4 (1988): 519-531. Print.

Cassata, Mary, and Barbara Irwin. "Going for the Gold: The Golden Girls are a Hit!" *Media&Values* 45 (1989). Web. 24 Sept. 2014.

Cleto, Fabio. "Introduction: Queering the Camp." *Camp: Queer Aesthetics and the Performing Subject*. Ed. Fabio Cleto. Ann Arbor: The University of Michigan Press, 1999. 1-42. Print.

Colucci, Jim. *The Q Guide to The Golden Girls*. New York: Alyson, 2006. Print.

Dyk, Silke van. "The Appraisal of Difference: Critical Gerontology and the Active-Ageing-Paradigm." *Journal of Aging Studies* 31 (2014): 93-103. Web. 10. Oct. 2014.

Dyk, Silke van, and Stephan Lessenich. "Die 'jungen Alten' zwischen Aktivität und Widerstand." *Die jungen Alten. Analysen zu einer neuen Sozialfigur*. Ed. Silke van Dyk and Stephan Lessenich. Frankfurt am Main: Campus, 2009. 405-408. Print.

Eco, Umberto. *The Limits of Interpretation*. Bloomington and Indianapolis: Indiana University Press, 1990. Print.

Fonda, Jane. *Jane Fonda's Workout Book*. London: Allen Lane, 1982.

Gahrmann, Jan. *"The Girls and the City." Relevanz und Variation als innovative Aspekte der Populärkultur*. Master's thesis at the Institute for Theater, Film, and Media Studies, Goethe University Frankfurt, 2009. Unpublished.

Grant, Jo Anna, and Heather L. Hundley: "Myths of Sex, Love, and Romance of Older Women in *Golden Girls*." *Critical Thinking about Sex, Love, and Romance in the Mass Media*. Ed. Mary-Lou Galician and Debra L. Merskin. Mahwah, New Jersey: Lawrence Erlbaum Associates, 2007. 106-121. Print.

Hall, Stuart. "The Spectacle of the 'Other'." *Representation: Cultural Representations and Signifying Practices*. London: Sage, 2003. 223-290. Print.

Haller, Miriam. "'Unwürdige Greisinnen'. 'Ageing trouble' im literarischen Text." *Alter und Geschlecht. Repräsentationen, Geschichten und Theorien des Alter(n)s*. Ed. Heike Hartung. Bielefeld: transcript, 2005. 45-63. Print.

Haller, Miriam. "Dekonstruktion der 'Ambivalenz'. Poststrukturalistische Neueinschreibungen des Konzepts der Ambivalenz aus bildungstheoretischer Perspektive." *Forum der Psychoanalyse* 27.4 (2011): 359-371. Web. 10 Oct. 2014.

Haller, Miriam. "Ambivalente Subjektivationen. Performativitätstheoretische Perspektiven auf die Transformation von Alters- und Geschlechternormen im geronto-feministischen Diskurs." *Alterswelt und institutionelle Strukturen*. Kölner Beiträge zur Alternsforschung. Ed. Miriam Haller, Hartmut Meyer-Wolters, and Frank Schulz-Nieswandt. Würzburg: Königshausen und Neumann, 2013. 19-36. Print.

Harmetz, Aljean. "NBC's 'Golden Girls' Gambles on Grown-Ups." *New York Times*, 22 Sept. 1985. Web. 24 Sept. 2014.

Harwood, Jake, and Howard Giles. "'Don't Make Me Laugh': Age Representations in a Humorous Context." *Discourse & Society* 3 (1992): 403-436. Web. 24 Sept. 2014.

Henderson, Jeffrey. "Older Women in Attic Old Comedy." *Transactions of the American Philological Association (TAPA)* 117 (1987): 105-129. Print.

Kaler, Anne K. "Golden Girls: Feminine Archetypal Patterns of the Complete Woman." *Journal of Popular Culture* 24.3 (1990): 49-60. Web. 10 Oct. 2014.

Kampmann, Sabine. "Looping mit dem Treppenlift. Visuelle Alterskultur im 21. Jahrhundert." *Die Kunst des Alterns*. Exhibition catalogue. Ed. Neue Gesellschaft für Bildende Kunst (NGBK) and Kunsthaus Dresden. Berlin, 2008. 50-57. Print.

Klippel, Heike. "Orgie in Pastell. Zur Fernsehserie *Golden Girls*." *Frauen und Film* 50/51 (1991): 92-106. Print.

Küpper, Thomas. "Of Mimicry and Age. Fashion Ambivalences of the Young-Old." *"The Ages of Life": Living and Aging in Conflict?* Ed. Ulla Kriebernegg and Roberta Maierhofer. Bielefeld: transcript, 2013. 133-143. Print.

Lipscomb, Valerie Barnes, and Leni Marshall. "Introduction." *Staging Age: The Performance of Age in Theatre, Dance, and Film*. Ed. Valerie

Barnes Lipscomb and Leni Marshall. New York: Palgrave Macmillan, 2010. 1-10. Print.

Luhmann, Niklas. *Die Realität der Massenmedien*. 2nd ed. Opladen: Westdeutscher Verlag, 1996. Print.

Matlin, Margaret W. *The Psychology of Women*. 7th ed. Belmont, CA: Wadsworth, Cengage Learning, 2012. Print.

Meyer, Moe. "Introduction: Reclaiming the Discourse of Camp." *The Politics and Poetics of Camp*. Ed. Moe Meyer. London: Routledge, 1994. 1–22. Print.

Mills, Brett. *TV Genres: Sitcom*. Edinburgh: Edinburgh University Press, 2009. Print.

Morsch, Thomas. "Muskelspiele. Männlichkeitsbilder im Actionkino." *Männer, Machos, Memmen. Männlichkeit im Kino*. Ed. Christian Hißnauer and Thomas Klein. Mainz: Bender, 2002. 49-74. Print.

O'Connor, John J. "From NBC, Two New Saturday Nights Sitcoms." *New York Times*, 14 Sept. 1985. Web. 24 Sept. 2014.

Ruchatz, Jens. "Sisyphos sieht fern oder Was waren Episodenserien?" *Zeitschrift für Medienwissenschaft* 7 (2013): 80-89. Print.

Sontag, Susan. "The Double Standard of Aging." *The Saturday Review*. 23 Sept. 1972: 29-38. Print.

Sontag, Susan. "Notes on 'Camp'". *Against Interpretation*. New York: Farrar Straus Giroux, 1986. 275-292. Print.

Swinnen, Aagje. "Introduction: Benidorm Bastards, or the Do's and Don'ts of Aging." *Aging, Performance, and Stardom: Doing Age on the Stage of Consumerist Culture*. Ed. Aagje Swinnen and John A. Stotesbury. Berlin: LIT, 2012. 7-14. Print.

TELEVISION

The Golden Girls. Creator Susan Harris, NBC (1985-1992).

Epilog:
The Social and Cultural Relevance of Studying Age in Television

Aging beyond the Rhetoric of Aging

MITA BANERJEE AND NORBERT W. PAUL[1]

From media discussion and academic discourses to biopolitical, bioethical and biomedical frameworks we are constantly confronted by the rhetorics of aging. In this rhetoric it is as consoling as it is politically correct that experiences of aging are increasingly being differentiated and, above all, are discussed against the background of the notion of "empowerment". Yet, in this context it is often overlooked that even these discourses are ultimately deeply rooted in an understanding of old age and aging as a challenge or slight, and thus as a deficient period of life. In this manner the various rhetorics of aging at the intersection between individual, society, and the medical sphere are currently characterized by three specific topics. First, what is at issue are questions about old age and the newly emergent category of the "oldest old", as well as the ways in which an appropriate social and medical care can be provided against the background of the often precarious balance between autonomy and support. At present, accounts proliferate, as bestsellers and widely acclaimed forms of life-writing on book tables about living with relatives in need of constant care (cf. Kunow 2009), about coping with one's own experiences of aging and the ensuing loss of capabilities, the profound change of corporeality and finally the changing perception of temporality up to the finiteness of human life, which is experienced as the ultimate offence. Second, and related to the questions of autonomy versus support, what is at stake is the possibility of social partic-

---

1 This interdisciplinary dialog is informed by the research training group „Life Sciences – Life Writing," supported by the German Research Foundation (DFG), under the grant 2015/1.

ipation and care in one's old age especially given the aspect of the allocation of resources and concept of inter- and trans-generational justice. Old age and poverty, old age and loneliness, old age and special-care homes, old age and (inevitable) illness confront us as part of the ubiquitous rhetorics of aging. These rhetorics remind us, on the one hand, of the imperfection of our species and, on the other hand, of the relative comfort of our present condition which involves the potential use of tools for controlling the contingencies of age in our post-industrial societies. Third, an alternative rhetoric of a full life (*gelingendes Leben*) has been brought about by life-writing narratives of individuals living with challenges on the levels of ability, corporeality, and temporality (Westerhof 2009; Kunow 2009). All in all this includes availing oneself of medical options for the compensation of age-induced impairments as well as for the extension of the time-span of life. As a utopian vision this implies our mastery over the temporality and very materiality of our lives including the maintaining of possibly all our human capabilities. The topics involved here are sexuality and aging, the aesthetics of the aging body (also invoked by the fashion and life-style industry; cf. Willems and Kautt 2002, Swinnen 2009; Hearn 1995; Lauzen/Dozier 2005, Swinnen 2009, Maierhofer 2003, Woodward 1999) up to the compensation of biopsychocognitive impairments. The replacement of dysfunctional tissue and organs as well as questions of enhancement, e.g. the improvement of faculties and functions without prior deficiencies, are also part of this agenda.

These levels of rhetoric have in common a culturally co-constructed understanding of age as challenge or even threat. But what if the discourse of aging, as the present volume implies, were understood as an anthropological inventory? What if an "appreciation of difference" were also applied here, if a liberal concept of age and ageing were cultivated in which we would focus above all on the possibilities and options of a full life in our extended present, as described by Hans-Ulrich Gumbrecht? Such an approach has already been sketched out by the field of disability studies, which argues that disability does not in itself constitute an illness but merely involves the physical and psychological manifestation of lived reality in different manifestations embedded in culturally co-constructed connotations of the self. If one transcends even this level and radically thinks through the notion of "empowerment" as proposed by disability studies, we need to find a new language in which to speak about age.

An unrestricted concept of a full life in all stages of life enriched by an appreciation of difference would inevitably lead to profound changes on an individual, institutional and societal level. On an individual level this would encourage a radically open concept of aging, a highly individualized attitude towards ability, corporeality, and temporality. On the level of ability such a concept would welcome the acceptance or compensation of impairments in an equal manner. On the level of corporeality the molding of the body – also in biomedical terms – would be discussed regardless of age, ranging from pharmacological aid to enhancement, from corporeal modification to an alternative body aesthetics unencumbered by quotations of youthful beauty. Finally, on the level of temporality an open-ended discussion about the self-directed constitution of one's own temporality up to the autonomous framing of the finiteness of our lives (even through forms of aid in dying and self-termination) would have to be facilitated.

In order to overcome the established rhetorics of aging, we are in need of "wake-up calls." In our aging societies (itself an expression taken from the rhetorics we seek to overcome) the medical community has so far avoided addressing this phenomenon in more constructive and productive terms. Clinical trials involving the "oldest old," basic research in gerontology with regard to an age-related physiology and pathophysiology, questions of biopsychocognitive enhancement in old age have – if anything – not been implemented as highly relevant and prestigious research fields, but linger in niches of academic marginality. The curative and preventive medicine of the 21st century is neither well-prepared nor especially willing to speak of age in terms other than those of deficiency. To the extent that the humanities succeed in understanding age not as a romantically tinted playing-field for explanation and empowerment but take into account the "real" and inexorable aspects of this topic – up to the material decay and destruction of individuals – a fertile ground would be provided for an interdisciplinary dialog between medicine and applied humanities, a ground on which a liberal discourse about the significance and possibilities of aging could unfold, freed from an obsolete and only seemingly time-honored rhetoric. For such a new age of age studies it is high time to overcome the boundaries between medicine and the humanities, between life sciences and life writing to promote life itself."

WORKS CITED

Gumbrecht, Hans-Ulrich. *Unsere breite Gegenwart*. Frankfurt: Suhrkamp, 2010. Print.

Hearn, Jeff. "Imagining the Ageing of Men." *Images of Aging: Cultural Representations of Later Life*. Eds. Mike Featherstone and Andrew Wernick. London: Rotuledge, 1995. 97-115. Print.

Kunow, Rüdiger. "Narrative as Intercultural Drama: Life-Writing by Aged Migrants." *Narratives of Life: Mediating Age*. Eds. Roberta Maierhofer and Heike Hartung. Münster: LIT, 2009. Print.

Lauzen, Martha, and David Dozier. "Maintaining the Double Standard: Portrayals of Age and Gender in Popular Films." *Sex Roles* 52.7/8 (2005): 437-46. Print.

Maierhofer, Roberta. *Salty Old Women: Eine anokritische Untersuchung zu Frauen, Altern und Identität in der amerikanischen Literatur*. Essen: Blaue Eule, 2003. Print.

Swinnen, Aagje. "'One Nice Thing about Getting Old is that Nothing Frightens You': From Page to Screen: Rethinking Women's Old Age in How's Moving Castle." *Narratives of Life: Mediating Age*. Eds. Roberta Maierhofer and Heike Hartung. Münster: LIT, 2009. Print.

Westerhof, Gerben. "Identity Construction in the Third Age: The Role of Self-Narratives." *Narratives of Life: Mediating Age*. Eds. Roberta Maierhofer and Heike Hartung. Münster: LIT, 2009. Print.

Willems, Herbert, and York Kautt. "Theatralität des Alters. Theoretische und empirisch-analytische Überlegungen zur sozialen Konstruktion des Alters in der Werbung." *Theoretische Beiträge zur Alternssoziologie*. Eds. Ursula Dallinger and Klaus Schroeter. Opladen: Leske und Budrich, 2002. Print.

Woodward, Kathleen. *Figuring Age: Women, Bodies, Generations*. Bloomington: Indiana UP, 1999. Print.

Contributors

MITA BANERJEE is Professor of American Studies at Johannes Gutenberg University Mainz. Among her recent publications are *Ethnic Ventriloquism: Literary Minstrelsy in Nineteenth-Century American Literature* (Heidelberg: Winter, 2008) and *Color Me White: Naturalism/Naturalization in American Literature* (Heidelberg: Winter, 2013). Her main areas of research are the American Renaissance, Naturalism, ethnic American literature, Life Writing, Critical Race Theory, Whiteness Studies, South Asian Diasporic Film and Bollywood Cinema. Together with Norbert W. Paul, she is the speaker of the DFG graduate program "Life Sciences – Life Writing."

SALLY CHIVERS is Professor of English Literature at Trent University. Author of *From Old Woman to Older Women: Contemporary Culture and Women's Narratives* and *The Silvering Screen: Old Age and Disability in Cinema*, and co-editor of *The Problem Body: Projecting Disability on Film*, she is currently researching the interplay between aging and disability in the public sphere, with a focus on care narratives in the context of austerity.

CECILIA COLLOSEUS is a PhD student in the Graduate School "Life Sciences – Life Writing" at Johannes Gutenberg University Mainz. She is a cultural anthropologist and her research interests are pregnancy, childbirth, gender and online life writing.

DUSTIN GOLTZ is Associate Professor of Performance Studies and Rhetoric at DePaul University (Chicago, USA). He is the author of *Queer Temporalities in Gay Male Representation: Tragedy, Normativity, and Futuri-*

ty published by Routledge in 2010, and the co-editor of *Communicating Identity: Critical Approaches* published by Cognella. His research examines and explores issues of queer temporalities and futurity, queer popular culture, the performance of personal narrative, the rhetoric of gay male aging, and performative research methods.

KRISTYN GORTON is Senior Lecturer in the Department of Theatre, Film and Television at the University of York (U.K.). She is the author of *Theorising Desire: From Freud to Feminism to Film* (Palgrave, 2008) and *Media Audiences: Television, Meaning and Emotion* (Edinburgh, 2009) and has published in a wide range of journals such as *The Journal of British Cinema and Television, Feminist Review, Studies in European Cinema, Critical Studies in Television* and *Feminism and Psychology*.

C. LEE HARRINGTON is Professor of Sociology/Social Justice Studies and Collaborating Faculty with the Comparative Media Studies Program at Miami University (Ohio, USA). Her work on audiences, fans, and television studies has been published in such journals as *International Journal of Cultural Studies, Feminist Media Studies, Media, Culture & Society*, and *Television & New Media*. Current research interests include aging, death, and media.

ROS JENNINGS is Head of Postgraduate Research, Director of the Centre for Women, Ageing and Media (WAM) and Reader in Cultural Studies. She is Deputy Executive Director and founder member of the European Network in Aging Studies (ENAS) and a founder member of the ENAS InHeritage research group. Her published work has been concerned with popular culture and questions of gender, sexuality and identity but since 2007, when Ros was Principal Investigator for the successful Arts and Humanities Research Council (AHRC) networking project Women, Ageing and Media, her work has focussed on women, ageing and popular culture.

NEAL KING is Professor of Sociology and an affiliate of the Center for Gerontology at Virginia Tech. His research on film genres, media violence, aging, and inequality includes the books *Heroes in Hard Times: Cop action films in the U.S.* (Temple University Press, 1999), *Reel Knockouts: Violent Women in the movies* (University of Texas Press, 2001), and *The Passion of*

Christ (Palgrave Controversies series, 2011); and articles in such journals as *Gender & Society, The New Review of Film and Television, Men and Masculinities, Sociology Compass*, and the *Journal of Aging Studies*. He earned a PhD at the University of California at Santa Barbara.

EVA KRAINITZKI is a postdoctoral researcher at the Centre for Women, Ageing and Media (WAM) at the University of Gloucestershire, where she researches in the areas of Age/ing Studies, Gender and Sexuality. Her most recent publications include: "Abject Ageing Bodies and Transgressive Desire in *Notes on a Scandal*" in Joel Gwynne's edited volume *Transgression in Anglo-American Cinema* (2016) and, with Ros Jennings, "'Call the Celebrity': Voicing the Experience of Women and Ageing through the Distinctive Vocal Presence of Vanessa Redgrave" in Deborah Jermyn and Su Holmes' edited volume *Women, Celebrity and Cultures of Ageing* (2015).

THOMAS KÜPPER works as a lecturer in German literature at the University of Düsseldorf. Previously, he was guest professor for media studies at the University of Frankfurt am Main and visiting professor for cultural studies at the Braunschweig University of Art. His latest publications include: "Of Mimicry and Age. Fashion Ambivalences of the Young-Old" in Ulla Kriebernegg and Roberta Maierhofer (eds.) *The Ages of Life* (2013).

MARTA MIQUEL-BALDELLOU is a researcher of the Dedal-Lit research group at the English Department of the University of Lleida, and she is also a member of the European Network in Aging Studies. Within the framework of the research project *Aging and Gender in Contemporary Literary Creation in English* (FFI2012-37050) – which the Spanish Ministry of Economy and Competitiveness awarded the Dedal-Lit group with in the year 2012 – she is currently looking into ageing in the late short fiction of the writer Daphne du Maurier. The results of her research have been recently published in journals such as *Age, Culture, Humanities*, and books such as *The Trace of Age and Memory in Contemporary Narrative* (Bielefeld: Transcript, forthcoming), and *Literary Creativity and the Older Woman Writer: A Collection of Critical Essays* (Bern: Peter Lang, forthcoming).

MARICEL ORÓ-PIQUERAS is assistant professor at the Department of English and Linguistics, Univerity of Lleida (Spain). She is also a member of research group Dedal-lit since it started to work on the representation of fictional images of ageing and old age in 2002. In 2007, she defended her PhD thesis entitled "Ageing Corporealities in Contemporary English Fiction: Redefining Stereotypes", which was published in book format by Lap Lambert in 2011. She is currently conducting research on British contemporary writer Penelope Lively's fiction and in the portrayal of ageing and old age in TV series.

NORBERT W. PAUL is Professor and Director of the Institute for the History, Philosophy and Ethics of Medicine at the Johannes Gutenberg University Medical Center, Mainz. He was a visiting scholar and professor at Georgetown University in Washington DC, Stanford University, California and the Max-Delbruck-Center for Molecular Medicine in Berlin, Germany. He has published widely on the topics of ethics, organ transplantation, molecular medicine, genetics and medical history. Together with Mita Banerjee, he is the speaker of the DFG graduate program "Life Sciences – Life Writing."

JULIA REICHENPFADER is a PhD student in the Graduate School "Life Sciences – Life Writing" at Johannes Gutenberg University Mainz. Her academic background is in German studies and Gender Studies. She is currently working on a dissertation topic on female bodies and body modifications.

ANITA WOHLMANN is a postdoctoral researcher at Johannes Gutenberg University Mainz, Germany. She graduated in American studies and film studies in 2009 and completed her doctorate in age studies and American cultural studies in 2012. Her interdisciplinary dissertation, *Aged Young Adults: Age Readings of Contemporary American Novels and Films* (2014), applies theories from cultural and literary gerontology as well as life course research to characters who are in their twenties and thirties. She published on age and aging in films and blogs, among others, in the *Journal of Aging Studies* and *Age, Culture, Humanities*.